PERSPECTIVES ON
ORGANIZATIONAL COMMUNICATION

The Guilford Communication Series

Editors

Theodore L. Glasser, *Stanford University*

Marshall Scott Poole, *Texas A & M University*

Recent Volumes

Perspectives on Organizational Communication: Finding Common Ground, *Steven R. Corman and Marshall Scott Poole, Editors*

The Idea of Public Journalism, *Theodore L. Glasser, Editor*

Communicating Across Cultures, *Stella Ting-Toomey*

Communications Policy and the Public Interest: The Telecommunications Act of 1996, *Patricia Aufderheide*

The Business of Children's Entertainment, *Norma Odom Pecora*

Case Studies in Organizational Communication 2: Perspectives on Contemporary Work Life, *Beverly Davenport Sypher, Editor*

Regulating Media: The Licensing and Supervision of Broadcasting in Six Countries, *Wolfgang Hoffman-Riem*

Communication Theory: Epistemological Foundations, *James A. Anderson*

Television and the Remote Control: Grazing on a Vast Wasteland, *Robert V. Bellamy, Jr., and James R. Walker*

Relating: Dialogues and Dialectics, *Leslie A. Baxter and Barbara M. Montgomery*

Doing Public Journalism, *Arthur Charity*

Social Approaches to Communication, *Wendy Leeds-Hurwitz, Editor*

Public Opinion and the Communication of Consent, *Theodore L. Glasser and Charles T. Salmon, Editors*

Communication Research Measures: A Sourcebook, *Rebecca B. Rubin, Philip Palmgreen, and Howard E. Sypher, Editors*

Persuasive Communication, *James B. Stiff*

Perspectives on Organizational Communication

Finding Common Ground

Steven R. Corman
Marshall Scott Poole

Editors

𝔤𝔭

THE GUILFORD PRESS
New York   London

Library of Congress Cataloging-in-Publication Data

Perspectives on organizational communication : finding common
  ground / edited by Steven R. Corman and Marshall Scott Poole.
     p.   cm. — (The Guilford communication series)
  Includes bibliographical references and index.
  ISBN 1-57230-602-5 (pbk.)
     1. Communication in organizations.   2. Telecommunication.
  3. Communication.   I. Corman, Steven R.   II. Poole, Marshall Scott.
  III. Series.
HD30.3P46 2000
302.2—dc21   00-061695

Contents

IV. AFTERWORD

PART I

INTRODUCTION

CHAPTER 1

The Need for Common Ground

Steven R. Corman

There is a very real danger of conflict, because you become a prisoner of your own rhetoric and you begin a spiral of action and reaction and you end up doing things you didn't plan to do.

—RIFFAT HUSSEIN, Qaid-e-Azam University, Pakistan, commenting on the state of tension between his country and India.[1]

I organized a conference panel[2] that led to this volume because of my growing concern about the tone of scholarly disagreement about metatheory. There is reason to worry, I think, that we have indeed become imprisoned in our own rhetoric(s), and that debating and defending our paradigmatic containers has become more important than working together to discover things about organizational communication.

The debate over metatheoretical commitments is not new. More than a decade ago Rosengren (1989) was already writing that the debate had been around for a "decade or two." Since then the field of organization studies in general has become "more and more fragmented" (Scherer, 1998, p. 148). Increasingly, scholars seem encamped in particular metatheoretical positions: we have humanists, scientists, realists, relativists, modernists, postmodernists, functionalists, interpretivists, and so on.

How did we get here? As a group, organizational communication scholars have spent the last twenty years diversifying their portfolio of theories and methods. This has not been a painless process, as it has involved the critique and countercritique of beliefs and values that people hold dear and take very seriously. Gergen (1991) explains the danger in a situation like this: "No one value in itself recognizes the importance of any alternative value. And so it is with the chorus of social ghosts. Each voice of value stands to discredit all that does not meet its standard" (p. 77). Without some shared point of reference, parties to a value disagreement become imprisoned in their positions, confined to discrediting and debunking their opponents.

There must be some kind of effort to avoid this. After twenty years of differentiating, it is time for our discipline to devote its attention to constructing some kind of common ground. Let me be clear that I am not proposing an elimination of disagreement, debate, or even conflict. Rather, I hope to persuade readers to give more attention to what different perspectives have in common, and less attention to what divides them.

That, in a nutshell, is the motivation for this book, and the main idea I hope to defend in this introduction. I begin by offering evidence for my claim that metatheoretical debate is becoming increasingly strident, and then examine the danger this creates. Next I argue that the *incommensurability thesis* is a likely source of the discord and that it has lost the warrant it once might have had. Then I appeal for a rejection of the incommensurability thesis in the interests of an orientation toward the common ground. Finally, I describe the structure of the book and preview its essays.

INCREASING STRIDENCY

You need not look far in the literature to find examples of strident debate about metatheoretical commitments. In a recent issue of *Communication Monographs* we find spirited rowing involving Kramer and Miller (1999) (and Miller & Kramer [1999] in the rejoinder), on the one hand, and Bullis (1999), Clair (1999), and Turner (1999), on the other. Each side seems to be appalled by what the other is saying, and everyone claims to be misunderstood and misrepresented.

In a volume on postmodernism and social theory, Collins (1992) argues against embracing "dangerous" critical ideology in social research. Seidman (1992), in the same volume, claims the scientific enterprise is devoid of morality.[3] Alvesson and Deetz (1996) tell us that "critical theorists see the modernist project as sick . . . postmodernists pronounce its death" (p. 195). Meanwhile, Barnett (1997) argues that critical theory leaves us in a vacuum where little can be explained. If all of these arguments are correct, the intrepid scholar of organizational communication is faced with a grim choice between the dangerous, the amoral, the sick, the dead, and the vacuous!

Occasionally, paradigmatic disagreements take on a harsher character. For some reason, the allied field of management studies seems to be especially likely to carry such disagreements into print. Calás and Smircich

(1991) described "male" leadership as little but an expression of "homo-social *domination* and *servitude*" (original emphasis, p. 594). Two years later Schwartz (1993) mocked them in a piece entitled "deconstructing my car at the Detroit airport." He told a tale of returning from a conference where everyone had just read the Smircich & Calás article. *Faux*-enlightened about the power of feminist deconstruction, he analyzed the penetration involved in getting into the car, the inherent domination of the steering system, and so on.

In a well-known exchange, Pfeffer (1993) argued that the management field is in need of some metatheoretical weed pulling, lest it be spread too thin. He was not explicit about which perspectives were to be considered noxious, but Van Maanen (1995b) clearly viewed himself as a potential victim of herbicide. He decried the idea of a "Stalinist purge" (p. 133) of the field in order to create a "Pfefferdigm" (p. 133). He denounced the " 'I'm-a-Pfeffer, you're-a-Pfeffer, wouldn't-you-like-to-be-a-Pfeffer too?' view of the world" (p. 134).

Now it is important that we guard against alarmism over cases like these. Strong disagreement has its place in constructive scholarly discourse. Czarniawski (1998) chides those of us who spout "doomsday rhetoric" and asks what danger we really face: "All those self-absorbed organization scholars, mumbling to themselves, while the [more] totalitarian sciences gobble up all the Nobel Prizes?" (p. 273).

Even ignoring the possible loss of Nobel Prizes, I find it worrisome that we may be headed in the direction of a system of destructive conflict, if we are not over that threshold already. Destructive conflict interaction is characterized by "protracted, uncontrolled escalation cycles or prolonged attempts to avoid the issue" (Folger & Poole, 1984, p. 6). A good example of destructive conflict is a war (though not all examples are so extreme or dramatic). Especially when the combatants are well matched, there can be a seemingly endless series of offensives and counteroffensives, with no corresponding movement toward resolution of the root disagreement.

More and more, scholars are using war metaphors to describe conflict over metatheoretical perspectives. Ellis (1996), in a special issue of *Communication Theory*, laments the " 'science wars,' a battle between a conservative search for the truth and the science bashers" (p. 329). Martin and Frost (1996) discuss the "organizational culture war games." They see a continuing struggle for intellectual dominance that is comparable to the children's game "King of the Hill." In the adult academic version, one perspective makes its way to the high ground only to be knocked off shortly thereafter by another perspective. The skirmishing is not limited to studies of organizational culture, either. McKelvey (1997) supposes that "even a hermit in the bleakest Antarctica must be aware of the organizational science paradigm war by now" (p. 352). There have even been acts of infiltration and sabotage: Sokal (1996a) had a "Trojan Horse" article published in the journal *Social Text*, which he promptly revealed as a hoax (Sokal, 1996b). Subsequent exchanges between Sokal and the journal editors have sounded more like war rhetoric than a debate between scholars engaged in a cooperative search for truth.[4]

"APARTHEID FOR PARADIGMS"

If scholarship is degenerating into war, then we should ask: What is the cause of the fighting? I submit that it is the *incommensurability thesis*. Formally, according to Scherer (1998), incommensurability has three requirements:

> First, there have to be at least two (radically) different systems of orientation. Second, the systems of orientation must be competing with each other concerning a way of acting or using language, e.g., the definition or solution of a concrete problem, so that coexistence of the different perspectives is not possible. Third, an accepted system of reference to objectively evaluate the competing perspectives must be lacking. (p. 150)

The thesis that these conditions exist with respect to organizational theory was popularized by Burrell and Morgan (1979). They argued that their four paradigms were inherently incommensurable and that no synthesis or reconciliation between them was possible or even desirable. Others have also pursued this line of argument (see, e.g., Jackson & Carter, 1991, 1993).

Scherer (1998) believes that a clear warrant for the incommensurability thesis has never been established, and that it found acceptance mainly because it helped legitimize alternative perspectives on organizations. Others (Deetz, 1996; Weaver & Gioia, 1994) argue in a similar vein that Burrell and Morgan's book helped make the intellectual world safe for critical theorists and others with alternative perspectives. Such a rationale for accepting the idea of incommensurability "may have been appropriate at a time when scholars were attempting to overcome the hegemony of the functionalist paradigm in the social sciences" (Scherer, 1998, p. 153).

However, functionalism no longer dominates the theoretical landscape. On the contrary, I have heard it referred to as the "F word," not to be used in proper intellectual company. It is fair to say that untraditional approaches are now accepted by most, and are welcomed or even favored by many, scholars in our field. Thus the political rationale for maintaining the incommensurability thesis no longer seems so compelling. In its wake we work under an institutionalized intellectual policy that Donaldson (1988) has aptly described as "apartheid for paradigms" (p. 31).

COMMON GROUND

Rather than maintaining warring encampments fortified by the incommensurability thesis, we should abandon the "paradigms mentality" (Wilmot, 1993) in favor of a search for common ground. There are compelling reasons for us to do this, some pragmatic and others aesthetic. With regard to the former, the incommensurability thesis forces us to conceptualize our field—as an organization—in outdated terms that few of us would apply to the organizations we study in our research. For example, the different systems of orientation are *closed* systems, and are incommensurable precisely because they are closed. Scholars working within paradigms are *contained* by them, intellectually speaking. Well known are the limitations of closed systems thinking (Scott, 1992) and container metaphors for conceptualizing organizations (Smith & Turner, 1995). Why should these outdated ideas guide thinking about our field?

Worse, the dualistic thinking encouraged by the incommensurability thesis is hegemonic. Incommensurability assumptions invite reification of perspectives (Deetz, 1996), casting them as either/or choices. According to Wilmot (1993), "A tendency in our theories to gravitate to one or the other of [the] poles is cast into a metaphysical principle, thereby promoting a new form of closure because the coherence of all attempts to resist this tendency is denied" (p. 682). We are forced into a system of "growing fragmentation and disorientation that makes it very difficult for academics and practitioners to use theoretical advice" (Scherer, 1998, p. 148).

There are also good aesthetic reasons for choosing to abandon the incommensurability thesis. War is ugly. The examples in the first section above show how tense the interaction can become, and this is only a small sample of what goes on "above the surface." Most paradigmatic squabbling takes place in conference panels and during the article review process where it is largely hidden from view. I have personally been accused by an anonymous reviewer of foolishly chasing a "nomothetic dream."[5] Colleagues with different paradigmatic lifestyle choices have complained to me of similar disrespect from antagonistic reviewers.

No one would argue that we should be free of disagreement, but chronic conflict is tiresome and unpleasant. It degrades the quality of our work lives:

> In the argument culture, war metaphors pervade our talk and shape our thinking. Nearly everything is framed as a battle or game in which winning or losing is the main concern. These all have their uses and places . . . but the scale is off balance, with conflict and opposition overweighted. (Tannen, 1998, p. 4)

Practically everyone these days would agree that scholarly fields are socially constructed, and that the choices made by individual scholars make a difference in the emergent character of the whole. So why not simply choose to abandon the incommensurability thesis in favor of (at least a limited) search for the common ground? Rather than spending energy defending our metatheoretical fortifications, we should construct some common system of reference that could allow explanations from different points of view to be compared or integrated.

Of course this is easier said than done. There is considerable moral support (Deetz, 1996; McKelvey, 1997; Scherer, 1998; Weaver & Gioia, 1994; Wilmot, 1993). However, few multiparadigm projects have even been attempted (Hassard, 1991, and Schultz & Hatch, 1996, are exceptions). The important details of how we can bridge the very real differences between metatheoretical perspectives remain elusive, but the goal is nonetheless worth pursuing.

THE ESSAYS

As a step toward bridge building, we have invited three distinguished scholars to write essays on the subject from the interpretive, post-positivist, and critical perspectives. Before previewing their essays, let me emphasize that none of the authors intends or wants to be viewed as Mr. Interpretive, Ms. Post-Positivist, or Mr. Critical, as the case may be. On the contrary, they support the idea of reducing categorization of scholars and scholarship with labels such as these. However, the goal of the volume is to promote dialogue about how people from different perspectives can work together. Toward this end, the authors have agreed to sketch the common ground from a particular and idealized metatheoretical point of view.[6]

In the first essay, George Cheney argues for applying principles of interpretation to the interpretive perspective, and for earnest self-reflexivity on the part of all perspectives. For him, common ground lies in recognizing a multiplicity of meanings, including multiple ideas of what it means to be "in" any of the three perspectives.

In the case of the interpretive perspective, multiplicity has a number of positive outcomes, like a focus on language, symbolism, intersubjectivity, and empathic observation. It also has some negative outcomes, like promoting the idea among some practitioners that interpretive research is purely an experiential exercise without requirements of rigor and systematic communication of results. On balance, the interpretive perspective has moved the field in many important ways, detailed in the essay.

In situating intepretivism in the context of multiple perspectives, Cheney applies the concept of *heteroglossia*. Spotlighting a particular perspective foregrounds its concerns. Some illumination spills over to nearby perspectives, but others are left in the dark. The key, then, is to keep in mind the selectivity of any perspective, being especially cognizant of what it keeps hidden. Toward that end, Cheney details the main failings of each perspective from the viewpoint of its counterparts: the distanced reductionism of post-positivism, the parochial tendencies of interpretivism, and the arrogance of critical perspectives.

Cheney's solutions center on Burke's notion of perspective by incongruity, and he suggests three concrete practices that can help achieve this. First, perspectives must really speak to one another, something too rare in his judgment. Second, perspectives can appropriate one another or one another's problems, sidestepping theoretical incommensurability without abandoning their commitments. Third, perspectives can "become" one another through a process of revisiting and reinterpreting research results. He concludes the chapter with a set of issues for furthering dialogue about bringing interpretation to bear on itself and other perspectives.

The second essay by Kathy Miller urges us to let go of the bogeyman of positivism. She argues that perspective labels, such those attached to Burrell and Morgan's (1979) famous cells, have become caricatures that perpetuate false ideas about what scholars do. This is especially true of the perspective called "functionalism" or "positivism" or the "normative science" approach. Scholars using this perspective are tarred with critiques applicable to old-fashioned positivism, yet it is difficult (if not impossible) to locate any actual person who practices classical or logical positivist orthodoxy in organizational communication.

Miller argues that we should abandon "straw person" arguments in favor of a more accurate view of what scientifically oriented scholars *actually do*. That is best described as *post-positivism*. This perspective retains something of the scientific spirit of positivism, while abandoning assumptions that have so obviously succumbed to years of critique. Consequently, it resists solitary confinement in Burrell and Morgan's *functionalist* cell by sharing interests in social construction and politics that are characteristic of the interpretive and critical approaches.

While it retains the belief in an objective reality, post-positivism draws a distinction between reality and beliefs about reality. The latter are subject to processes of social construction, and these processes make direct apprehension of objective reality problematic. While it retains the assumption that knowledge is best pursued through a focus on regularities and causal relationships, it abandons the idea that the search for these can be value-free. Thus while in theory we cannot attain objective knowledge, we can (and should) treat objectivity as a "regulatory ideal."

Miller sees two distinct possibilities for achieving common ground with scholars who emphasize the other perspectives. One is a dialogic approach focusing on suspending judgment in order to understand one another's frames of reference. A second is to focus on some theory or approach that transcends the different perspectives. The search can be best conducted by focusing on the "border" areas between perspectives. Miller argues that Giddens's structuration theory may be a good candidate for opening up bridges across these.

The third essay, by Dennis Mumby, invites us to interrogate binary oppositions. He warns that while the idea of a common ground or shared disciplinary language seems inviting, it can easily become a disciplinary "club" in both the social and material senses of the metaphor. Mumby says we could avoid this danger—yet still address the problems a common ground would solve—by studying the conditions that potentiate needs for a common ground.

For Mumby, these needs stem from an assumed "default condition of opposition and difference." This condition is created by caricatures of scholarly work that reduce all intellectual disagreements to simple, binary oppositions. Binary oppositions favor a rhetorical strategy of putting oneself on the right side of the binary opposition and critiquing opponents for being on the wrong side, and it is these rhetorical practices that create the impulse for constructing common ground.

To eliminate the impulse, we need to think of ourselves as participating in different discourses that significantly blur together "at the edges." Mumby proposes four discourses that exist in the discipline that fulfill this idea: representation, understanding, suspicion, and vulnerability. These discourses relate and group together in different ways depending on what philosophical issue is under consideration, defying any kind of simplistic groupings or oppositions.

The idea of multiple overlapping discourses also problematizes sharp distinctions between self and other, according to Mumby, undermining oppositional rhetorical strategies. Moreover, it directs our attention to the broader discursive field as the common focus of our study. Mumby reviews four problematics that he thinks are good foci for the efforts of a diverse range of scholars in organizational communication: voice, rationality, organization, and the organization–society relationship. These are not intended as a complete inventory but rather as starting points for thinking about things we could study together.

THE COMMENTARIES

The panel that led to this book included the three essayists, Scott Poole, and me. In an effort to expand the dialogue for this volume, we invited a number of scholars to provide brief commentaries. We recruited a list of prominent established researchers and theorists in organizational communication. To this list we added some newer scholars whose work is known to us, in order to represent the perspective of those just beginning their academic careers.

All of the commentators received drafts of this Introduction and the three essays. They were asked to provide essays of about 3,000 words according to the following editorial guidelines:

• The commentaries should focus on ways we can accomplish or develop the common ground described by the essayists. Commentaries might identify creative tensions between the different perspectives, take provocative positions, and/or consider how paradigms have influenced the trajectory of organizational communication scholarship and the relationships between scholars.

• The tone of the commentaries should be constructive. They should neither simply debate points made by the essayists, nor engage in paradigm critiques. Rather, they should focus on value-added, practical advice about how we can construct the common ground or create the conditions it requires.

• The commentaries should take a balanced perspective, consider as much as possible points made in all three of the essays, and avoid picking winners/losers or making final judgments.

• The audience for the book includes students as well as established scholars. Enough context should be given that the commentary is suitable reading for graduate seminars.

• Don't feel obligated to load up your commentary with references. We are most interested in provocative and original ideas.

The commentaries are presented in alphabetical order, as are the essays.

HINDSIGHT

As a consequence of the pace of scholarly book projects, most of this Introduction was written quite some time ago. This is a frustrating thing for yours truly, because as an editor/introducer part of my job is to point out important issues and themes. On the other hand, I (1) want to avoid more than minor tinkering with the Introduction, which was sent out for commentary, and (2) do not want to confuse readers by discussing a lot of material they presumably have not yet read. Fortunately, Poole and Lynch do an excellent job of drawing things together at the end of the volume, leaving me with the need to make only make two brief points in hindsight.

First, as you will see, several of the commentators in this volume do not share the concern (or at least the level of concern) about disciplinary discourse expressed in this Introduction. I confess that I find this puzzling. The panel that gave birth to the book was standing-room-only. I expected more than the usual smattering of people to be interested in the panel, but I could not believe what I saw when I walked into the room. Many in the audience commented to me afterward about the importance and currency of the topic. People even complained that we were thinking of a book project because it would take too long for the papers to see print!

Did people pack that room because they expected a brawl? Maybe people will come to hear Cheney, Miller, Mumby, and Poole no matter what they are talking about. Perhaps a scheduling fluke created downtime for a large number of organizational communication people at the time of that panel, and folks needed something to do. Of course, I am forced to consider the possibility that I am overestimating the problems, and tempted by the thought that some of the book's contributors are underestimating them. I do not have answers to these questions, but I know the discrepancy between what I experienced and what I am reading must be important in some way.

A second hindsight is that the book reproduced the competing perspectives more than I had hoped or expected. This may be in part due to the definition of *incommensurability* I used above. I refer here to the quote from Scherer (1998) that for incommensurability to hold, "an accepted system of reference to objectively evaluate the competing perspectives must be lacking" (p. 150). I believe some of the essayists and commentators took this as an implicit declaration on my part that objectivity is the preferred path to common ground. This is a reasonable and predictable reading, but it is *not* the argument I wanted to establish, and I should have taken steps to head it off.

I did not recognize that the word "objective" in such an important definition for the book project would be a hot-button. On reflection, it is probably one of those "triggers" Fairhurst talks about in her commentary. I wish I had critiqued that part of the definition, suggesting as a replacement: "an agreed-upon system of reference to intersubjectively evaluate alternative perspectives."[7] Among other things, this provides a good lesson about how hard it is to escape the power of institutions, and how vigilant one has to be when trying to do so.

These concerns notwithstanding, readers can look forward to an excellent set of essays and commentaries in this volume. Nearly every contributor calls directly or indirectly for more dialogue between perspectives. The format of the book in itself is has helped generate some (asynchronous) dialogue. The many, many insightful comments made by the contributors will fuel enormous quantities of (synchronous) dialogue in discussions and seminars. All of the contributors suggest theoretical moves and/or concrete scholarly practices that can help establish common ground. By making individual choices to occupy this ground, I believe we can work together across (or in spite of) metatheoretical positions to escape imprisonment in our own rhetoric(s).

NOTES

1. From an AP wire story in the *Arizona Republic,* January 19, 2000. At the time this book goes to press, Pakistan and India are stepping down from military and diplomatic conflict over the Kashmir region of the Himalayas. Both countries have recently disclosed nuclear weapons capabilities and conducted tests.
2. The conference panel, "Finding Common Ground between Metatheoretical Perspectives on Organizational Communication," was at the National Communication Association conference in Chicago, November 1997.
3. This is a common attack against scientific approaches. The argument is that science is amoral at best (and therefore a probable tool of evil) and immoral at worst (therefore evil in itself).
4. See Sokal's web page at http://www.physics.nyu.edu/faculty/sokal/index.html for a comprehensive set of links to commentary about the affair, including the *Lingua Franca* article, and exchanges between Sokal and the editors.
5. And if that person is reading, I want to thank him or her. The thought that I have a "nomothetic dream" has been an unending source of amusement.
6. We decided not include a major essay on postmodernism because it is a relative newcomer to organizational communication. The interpretive, post-positivist, and critical positions have been elaborated in the field over many decades, and there is a large body of communication scholarship for each perspective. The postmodernist position has not yet generated nearly as much scholarship, and in many senses its history is still being written. For the present, then, we are satisfied that the perspective finds voice in many of the essays and commentaries in this book.
7. This is pretty much what I think of as "objective" anyway; thus my complacency toward the word in the early draft.

PART II

THREE ESSAYS

CHAPTER 2

Interpreting Interpretive Research

Toward Perspectivism without Relativism

George Cheney

> Why *shouldn't* truth be stranger than fiction? Fiction, after all, has to make sense.
>
> —MARK TWAIN

PROLOGUE

One of the most useful exercises in discussing any "paradigm," or generally accepted and patterned way of approaching a problem, is to apply that paradigm to itself. As I pondered my role in representing and reflecting on interpretive approaches to research in organizational communication, I realized that such an exercise would be especially interesting for a family of perspectives on research that themselves feature interpretation. That is, I wanted to probe some of the things we mean when we say and do interpretive organizational communication research. Furthermore, I knew that I ought to be provocative, playful, and open-ended in terms of the evocation of meaning. An interpretive perspective on interpretive research should embody some of the very principles and concepts that characterize programs and bodies of research as the result of the so-called interpretive turn. Still, I understood that I better not stop there: I would also need to offer a somewhat *critical* perspective on interpretive research endeavors, in an effort to reveal their limitations and to challenge future scholarship. Continuing to explore different meanings, I could also ask: "What's *functional* about interpretive research?" In sum, and related directly to the very purpose of this volume, I decided to take seriously the call to place the three dominant paradigms, or schools, in dialogue and productive confrontation with one another. What does it mean, for example, to look at interpretive research with an empirical–analytic eye? To take a critical perspective on it? To apply notions of interpretation reflexively to interpretive projects? This essay will thus offer a bit of meta-analysis of the interpretive perspective, a bit of dialectical reflection, and a bit of intellectual prodding. To the disappointment of some readers, the essay is not written as a story, but it does freely employ several different genres of writing (cf. Baxter, 1993; Browning, 1992).

INTRODUCTION(S)

Consistent with the meaning-centered nature of the interpretive perspective, I considered the following options for introducing this essay. Accordingly, you can take your pick. Or, better yet: please review the list of possibilities, and then we will move on to the next part of the discussion.

Option #1: *Multiple Paradigms as Distinctive Voices in the Field*. The interpretive tradition now represents one such voice or one chorus of such voices. We may be inclined toward acceptance of the interpretive (or "historical–hermeneutic") perspective, alongside what might be called the empirical–analytic and the critically oriented perspectives (to use Habermas's [1971] terms). We might then argue for the peaceful coexistence of the three big paradigms—perhaps with a "Good fences make good neighbors" sort of approach.

Option #2: *The Appealing, Reflexive, and Elusive Nature of Interpretation*. Let us take the "social" part of the social sciences and humanities seriously. What if we really looked at ourselves and listened to ourselves in a way that makes our symbolic expressions and maneuverings nontransparent? We might then exclaim: "We have met the object of study, and it is us [sic]!" The autoethnography folks take this reflexivity quite seriously, reminding us of our own roles in what we call research.

Option #3: *"Interpretive" as a Highly Ambiguous Adjective*. On the one hand, that is a problem. "Interpretive" has come to be a slogan whose meaning is usually not questioned or penetrated. But, on the other hand, so what? Ambiguity is an inherent and important dimension of language itself. As Burke (1950) reminds us, we ought to pay attention to "the strategic spots at which ambiguities necessarily arise" and not just to our imperative of precision. After all, the fact that "teamwork" is used today to mean all sorts of things in organizations is an important aspect of its study. One possible resolution ("On the third hand . . . "): we still need to understand how it is that we are meaning and being interpretive.

Option #4: *The Bounds of Interpretation or of Interpretive Scholarship* (e.g., the "Sextext" controversy; see Corey & Nakayama, 1997).

Speaking of genres of interpretation, writing, and presenting research, now we have multiple forms. In this regard especially, recent organizational communication scholarship is pretty different from that of the late 1970s. But are there any limits to the proliferation and exploration of genres? Should there be? If not, how do we compare an "organizational performance" with a journal article? How do standards of quality develop for different arenas and media, and to what extent can the various sets of standards be translated for one another? However we choose to answer these questions, the debate should be allowed to flourish. We may never determine finally "what ought to count as research," but we can, perhaps, come to certain understandings about how to assess work within various communities of investigators.

The above are several ways I considered beginning this essay (and the convention presentation on which it is based). I mention them here because they highlight important aspects of interpretive research and they help to frame the next section. As I continued to explore for myself the meanings of interpretation—not only in reference to organizational communication scholarship but also more generally—I discovered a variety of loci or "objects" (excuse the term; it still works nicely here) of interpretation, as well as many different senses of the term. Let me explain.

FOCUSING ON "INTERPRETIVISM"– IF THAT MAKES SENSES

Loci of the Interpretive Endeavor: The "Elements" of Interpretation

Here the basic question is: What are we *doing/saying* when we declare ourselves to be "interpretivists"? Looking across the range of studies that claim to be interpretive (again, not only within organizational communication), we find these possible emphases. The locus of interpretation may be on any one or more of the following elements of the research enterprise:

The Social Actor

"Everyone's a critic." What we all do is interpret our world, and this attribute makes us very different from billiard balls knocking into one another on a table. With such an orientation toward research, we endeavor to understand the very processes by which meaning is constructed. We employ a metaphor for the person that features interpretive capacity, rather than, say, the processing of information. In this way, we regard our "subjects" as relative equals—as people who themselves have theories about the social world and who can react in meaningful ways to our own. Max Weber's (1968) interpretive sociology took this notion seriously by treating within the universe of "facts" laypersons' images of and experiences in organizations.

The Researcher

"Making sense of social life." What I, as an investigator, do is interpret the world. Data, information, and "the facts" do not merely present themselves to me. I actively construct important aspects of them, from the formulation of research questions and the identification of a research "problem" to the drawing of conclusions. In this way, I ought to be aware of the very processes by which I interpret social data, making every effort to shed light on those as well as on my "objects" or "subjects" of analysis. If my study is especially conscious of the workings of its own methodology, it may include commentary on, say, how I understand key moments in my developing relationship with the organization under study. Today, we find some cultural studies of organizations that include, either as part of the main text or as a sidebar, a narrative about the researcher's relationship to the community being explored (see, e.g., Carbaugh, 1999). The researcher's reflexivity is not only allowed for, it is encouraged.

The Situation

"Life is research, research is life." What I am, really, is an interpreter among interpreters. So, I do not make much of a distinction between my research and the rest of my life experiences or projects. From this perspective, research is understood to be part of the larger stream or *durée* of life. What becomes research is not always known at the outset of what might later be termed "a project." And what may be identified as a research project ought to flow naturally back into other life activities. This perspective aims to dissolve the boundaries between what counts as research and what does not, particularly with a broad sense of what are potential domains for exploration. Researchers who consider mundane activities or their hobbies as ripe for research may well find affinity with this approach. In a way, Nietzsche's (1997) philosophy of identity introduced this perspective by suggesting that a construct such as identity, not to mention its investigation, would need to be considered reflexively. That is, reflection on identity could fold into the very thing or process we call "identity."

The "Text"

"Recognizing the language game for what it is." With this focus of attention, the interpretive scholar seeks to break the transparency of the research product. No longer is the research article, chapter, or book taken for granted. The most important influences here are the linguistic turn in twentieth-century philosophy and some brands of postmodernism. From this language-centered point of view, the range of acceptable genres of writing is opened up to admit alternative forms. The research enterprise is seen as something of a language game. From this perspective, not only should the research report be seen as an argument, but also the very symbolism employed should be treated self-consciously and playfully. The research report should represent, "capture," invoke, provoke, and illuminate. In organizational studies, John Van Maanen (1988) and others have challenged us to consider new ways of relaying our research.

The Research Process

Like life, research is an ongoing conversation. As Kenneth Burke (1969) might put it, "We enter the conversation after it has already started; we try to get the hang of it; we leave it, just as we are catching the drift of it; after us, it goes on." Here the interpretivist is reflecting on the entire research enterprise, looking well beyond her own endeavors. One imperative is that research ought not to occur primarily in artificial controlled settings but rather in settings as naturalistic as possible. Another commitment is that any accomplishment of social research ought to be understood as situated, contingent, partial, and subject to revision. This emphasis of interpretation is simply a way of countering the certainties and arrogance with which conclusions about the social world are often presented. The research process is inherently open-ended, and any good study ought to conclude with some questions as well as some tentative answers. For a researcher to do otherwise is to deceive himself and potentially to mislead the reader or listener.

These five "loci" or emphases of interpretation are not at all mutually exclusive. In fact, I have risked the charge of reductionism to try to separate them analytically in this manner. But my central point is that the process of interpretation may be applied to various parts of that experience we call research. And, with that understanding, we can better appreciate not only what a particular researcher means by "interpretive" but also what basic assumptions are often associated with such a perspective on research. Until recently, of course, there were very few examples of interpretive research that included all of these elements. But the rationales, forms, processes, and outcomes of research are continuing to change.

Conceptions and Enactments of the "Interpretive": The Meanings of Interpretation

The range of meanings for "interpretive" is broader than many researchers appreciate. Although I do not have the space to describe each of the meanings for the term that I have found (and I would fail miserably at trying to weave all of them into a single story!), I would like to offer as a heuristic catalogue the many meanings of interpretive. Along the way, I list some prominent associated authors and key organizing themes. You will notice that I am speaking well beyond the confines of organizational communication in this section, but you will find that most if not all of these meanings have made their appearance or had their subtle influences in the research of organizational communication recently.

Here is what I have found (and interpreted!). I encourage you to add other senses of "interpretive" to the list:

1. Exposition, explanation, commentary, representation (according to *The Oxford English Dictionary*).

2. Impressionistic, or with a stress on the creative powers of the writer-researcher (e.g., a good film review). Such a sense of interpretation may include the technique of "reframing," in terms of ironic or otherwise surprising takes on a message or event. The first two meanings mentioned here are often found in colloquial speech.

3. The human being's capacity to make sense of the world and therefore in certain ways to make it (see, e.g., Winch, 1958, on the nature of social science); regard for sense making itself as an object of empirical investigation (compare Schutz's [1967] and Merleau-Ponty's [1962] versions of phenomenology). I have already said quite a bit about this conception of the interpretive above.

4. A stress on language and symbolism as a creative, action-oriented domain of human activity (see, e.g., the British linguistic philosophers: Austin, 1970; Searle, 1970; and Wittgenstein, 1953; cf. Burke, 1966). This proposition has become a truism in communication studies, but its "commonsensicality" should not blind us to *its* multiple meanings.

5. A focus on the meanings of everyday social actors in contrast to or in dialogue with the terms or constructs of researchers (see, e.g., Weber, 1968; some forms of ethnomethodology). Various approaches to data gathering and data analysis have come to reflect this orientation.

6. A strong interest in intersubjective understanding as a defining or constitutive dimension of our "humanness" (see, e.g., Habermas, 1979). Some would interpret the sixth meaning in terms of a revival of the ancient Greek ideal of *praxis*, in the deep sense of "practical" specifically in regard to the process of interactively achieved though contingent wisdom (cf. Craig, 1999).

7. A category of social-scientific or humanistic research that, in contrast to the "empirical" and "critical" categories, does not try to privilege the position of the researcher (see, e.g., some feminist perspectives—Mies, 1979). This sense of interpretive takes seriously the idea that every piece of research embodies or demonstrates a point of view, but the historical and

cultural situatedness of interpretation itself can be an appropriate object of social-scientific and humanistic study (Gadamer, 1975).

8. A stress on the socially constructed aspects or nature of "(social) reality" (see, e.g., Berger & Luckmann, 1967). Of course, there are multiple ways in which "(social) reality" may be thought to be "(socially) constructed," and the discussion is muddled when some so-called social constructionists use the idea like a slogan that requires no explanation (for help, see, e.g., Orr, 1978; Searle, 1995). More importantly, consider the parallel yet distinctive concepts of collective mind, institutional memory, and distributed cognition (see, e.g., Taylor, 1999), each of which attempts to account for intersubjectivity as what Durkheim would have called "a social fact."

9. "Thick description" and faithful representation of the social interactants and their world from their standpoint and in depth; some versions of ethnography (see, e.g., Geertz, 1973). As suggested, there are multiple philosophies and versions of ethnography, with some being more theoretically oriented and some being more methodologically focused.

10. Awareness of the multiplicity of perspectives within any social situation, unit, institution, or process (e.g., the film *Rashomon*; the story of the blind people and the elephant). This idea has helped to discredit the assumption that any organization is really monolithic in terms of "culture," although granting that some organizations try mightily to present themselves that way.

11. Skepticism toward general, covering-law, or sweeping claims; an emphasis on the particularities of "local" experience (e.g., some ethnographic approaches; some feminist approaches; some postmodernist approaches; see the discussion in Brown, 1977). In this sense, an "ideographic" research approach is sometimes contrasted with a "nomothetic" one. The key difference is to be found in the orientations toward issues of particularity and universality.

12. Systematic reflection on the researcher's own role in the research and the collapse of the "subject/object" split (see, e.g., Taylor, 1979). When we really start to fold the researcher into the domain of research itself, the endeavor can look quite different from most forms of research to which we are accustomed.

13. The "transformation" of social phenomena into "texts," "dramas," and the like, for purposes of either exposition or illumination (see, e.g., Ricoeur, 1993; Turner, 1981)—taking such notions either metaphorically or literally.

14. A profound awareness of the power of labeling in the creation of our world, though not a form of linguistic nominalism that suggests that all or most things do not really exist until they are named (cf. Douglas, 1986; Hacking, 1982).

15. Appreciation for the interrelationships of symbols, including that they make/have "autonomous" dynamics (Baudrillard, 1983), as well as defining patterns or structures (Peirce, 1955).

16. A deep awareness of the arbitrary dimension of language (Saussure, 1959); reflexivity and recursivity, in the sense that the dance of interpretations and "interinterpretations" can be virtually endless (see, e.g., Derrida, 1976).

17. Opposition to "positivism," "empiricism," "objectivism," and "functionalism" (e.g., as often found in the discourses of contemporary organizational communication research). All of these meanings have surfaced in the literatures of the social sciences and the humanities, especially in the second half of the twentieth century. Again, what I have separated here for purposes of analysis often is part of a larger context of assumptions in the actual doing or reporting of research.

As an exercise to follow this list of meanings, you might consider which senses of "interpretive" fit most closely with your own assumptions about social research. Another question to consider is: What makes some research more or less "interpretive" than other research?

Because one of the themes of this essay is the multiplicity of meanings, I am making it difficult to pass judgment on the different senses of "interpretive" or interpretation. Still, I think we should ask any user to *explain* what she means by employing the term. This is why I regularly ask those of my students who seek to be ethnographers to defend their use of that term. Given the varied epistemological, theoretical, methodological, and practical senses of the term *ethnography* alone, we can imagine how the ambiguity expands with "interpretive." Not that there is anything wrong with this ambiguity! And, of course, it cannot be fully channeled into some seemingly precise operational definitions. But, in the interest of dialogue and collaboration, there is a certain responsibility that goes with self-definition and claims to do one type of research or another.

In this way, I find it ironic (and frankly maddening) that some researchers of organizational culture choose to cloak their own assumptions about research, including their methodological procedures and logical paths to conclusions, in mystery. I cannot tell you how many convention and journal submissions I have reviewed over the years that refuse to detail the "inner workings" of a study! The burden of proof is sometimes dismissed as irrelevant ("I'm not doing *that* kind of research"), as unduly constraining ("I'm free to express my own subjectivity"), or on the basis of uniqueness ("No one could possibly replicate what *I* did"). And, of course, there is the practical protest: "I would love to talk more about my methods, but the editor didn't allow me sufficient space to explain them." Whatever the reason given, methodological mystification on the part of interpretive researchers is unsettling because a common complaint of "interpretivism" against empirical-analytic research is that the latter maintains excessive distance between researcher and "subject."

At the risk of being judgmental, I feel the need to add these five "unfortunate" meanings to the list of what interpretive signifies in research:

18. A simplistic synonym for qualitative data analysis. "Interpretive equals qualitative, so I don't have to go near those numbers."
19. What is cool. What is hot. "So you mean I can just hang out in an organization and call it research? Cool!"
20. Never having to explain your methodology; an ironic form of mystification of the research enterprise (as explained above).
21. Unduly blurring the line between "fact" and "fiction." While this sort of "genre bending" sometimes makes an effective point, it can also be used to deceive the reader.
22. Being avant-garde. "Look at those poor functionalists over there. I'm glad we don't have to read *their* work anymore!"

SOME REFLECTIONS ON TWO DECADES OF INTERPRETIVE ORGANIZATIONAL COMMUNICATION RESEARCH: HOW FAR HAVE WE COME?

In this section, I would like to return to a focus on "interpreting interpretive research." With twenty years of interpretive organizational communication to consider, it is useful to summarize some of the general contributions of this work. That is, let us ask specifically just how organizational communication study has been enriched by studies of organizational culture and other lines of research closely associated with the claims and orientation of "interpretivism." What have we noticed, learned, and especially come to understand better? You will notice that some of these contributions are by now taken for granted. Still, they remain important to highlight here.

What We Study

Appropriate "objects" of study include all sorts of organizations and forms of "organizing" (Carlone & Taylor, 1998). We may explore all sectors, industries, activities, and even such boundary-spanning notions as work–nonwork relationships (see Hochschild, 1997a, 1997b). In fact, we can look beyond work organizations themselves to consider professional associations, street gangs, virtual groups, social movements, and more (Glaser, 1994). Finally, we may reverse the "communication *in* organizations" prepositional phrase to consider "organizing features *of* communication," especially in terms of the construction of "voice" and authority in language (see Cooren, 2000; Taylor, Cooren, Giroux, & Robichaud, 1996; Taylor & Van Every, 2000). All of these moves have deepened our understandings of organizational communication at the same time that they have widened our array of options for doing research, though the field is only now becoming multicultural.

How We See What We Study

There are many ways of "seeing" an organization—for example, through the lenses of different fundamental metaphors. Compare the root metaphors of machine, person, family, war, and community (see Koch & Deetz, 1981; Smith & Eisenberg, 1987; Trujillo, 1992). These and other images may shape the work of researchers as well as the activities of laypersons. We now appreciate how any approach to the study of an organization embodies certain assumptions that may not be easy to bring to the level of awareness. And we are much more conscious than we once were of the role of language in the research process—from the formulation stage to the reporting of research results.

What Is Happening behind the Scenes

There are many different forms of life and forms of understanding within a particular organization. Even the most seemingly monolithic or "organized" organization will have a great deal going on behind a unified facade (Frost, Moore, Louis, Lunberg, & Martin, 1991; Martin & Meyerson, 1987). This is not to say that anything can happen or to ignore the material and symbolic constraints that may be present in any situation, but it is to recognize such things as the multiple roles that an individual may play (Mintzberg, 1968), the multiple subcultures that may exist within an "official" culture (Young, 1989), and the inevitability of symbolic transformation (consider, e.g., the evolution of the idea and role of the "consumer"; de Certeau, 1984). Seen both synchronically and diachronically, symbolic systems cannot be assumed to be univocal or stable, although they may have those features at particular places and times.

Different Ways of Doing and Being

There are many different cultural contexts for and many different cultural understandings of what it means to "be" in an organization. Noninstrumental behaviors in the organization are worthy of attention in addition to the ways any organization "does business" (Pacanowsky & O'Donnell-Trujillo, 1982; Smircich & Calás, 1987). The human relations movement, despite its problems, did call our attention to this idea (Rose,

1990). There is much more going on even in the most profit-driven of organizations, and the members of those organizations often do well to recognize that fact (Meyer & Rowan, 1977). Moving beyond the point above,
we may consider diverse conceptions of such taken-for-granted notions as
what it means to "act like a professional" on the job (cf. Clair, 1996). Some
of those seemingly mundane activities in the organization—like weekly
staff meetings that everyone complains about—may in fact serve important
ritualistic functions for many employees (Schwartzman, 1989). In some
cases there are spiritual or sacred dimensions to work processes that can
only be appreciated by the researcher who spends a great deal of time
standing shoulder-to-shoulder with employees, just as the same is now being revealed with respect to certain practices of consumption (cf. Belk,
Wallendorf, & Sherry, 1991; Gabriel & Lang, 1995).

How We Account for What We Do

We now recognize that there are rationalities and not just Rationality. Weber
(1978) taught us this, but we somehow forgot the lesson. The value-driven aspects of work and organizational activity may well get lost in our analyses,
just as they do in the everyday rush toward production (Conrad, 1993). The
fact that emotional dimensions of work experience and paradoxes of organizational pursuits were ignored for so long is strong testimony to the need to
present an image that we know what we are doing (cf. Mumby & Putnam,
1992). Such insights have also reshaped the ways we talk and write about research, opening up the production and consumption of research to many different genres (Goodall, 1989; Strine & Pacanowsky, 1985).

Understanding and Empathizing, not Just Scrutinizing

We have much to learn from penetrating, comprehending, and representing
the experiences of organizational members (Howard & Geist, 1995). When
we really begin to experience organizations and work as various groups of
laypeople do, we can speak to issues that take us far beyond our classrooms
and research enclaves (Cheney & Wilhelmsson, in press). Along these lines,
let us consider research that involves perspective taking, empathy, role rota-
tion, and other ways to yield profound understandings of one another.

These are some of the contributions of two decades of interpretive research in the area of organizational communication, especially in terms of
reshaping the research process and what counts as research. By no means is
this list comprehensive. And it deliberately downplays some of the more
epistemological and theoretical issues because these are treated elsewhere in
this essay. Rather, I am trying to emphasize the ways the research endeavor
has been transformed through the rise of interpretive research. I should

note, also, that some of the points I have listed are not as strictly tied to interpretivism as others. The probing reader can argue that certain of these contributions can be fairly associated with either the empirical-analytic or the critically oriented traditions of research. These would be reasonable claims to make: after all, there is nothing inherent in the empirical tradition to keep us from examining all sorts of "organizing" and organizations. Still, we can identify an *ethos* of interpretive organizational communication research, as it has developed and supported the intellectual and practical expansion for organizational communication. Now, let us consider the interpretive perspective within the larger context of the range of possible perspectives on research.

INTERPRETIVISM WITHIN THE CONTEXT OF MULTIPLE PERSPECTIVES: PERSPECTIVES THAT A NUMBER OF FORMS OF INTERPRETIVISM WOULD THEMSELVES ENCOURAGE

I have already alluded to the fact of the weaknesses associated with any research perspective, paradigm, or theory. To believe that one does not have to lapse into relativism, though. In fact, I like to cite Richard Rorty (1982), who explains that relativism is the position that one claim is just as good as another; no one really believes that. I would like to see someone who really tries to live and act as though relativism were true. Okay, so that is something of a cheap argumentative shot. But it does make a good point: we should not use multiplicity of meanings as an excuse to dismiss evaluation or to escape choice (see R. J. Bernstein, 1976). Seen from another, more practical, perspective, relativism "involves a breakdown in communication, typically temporarily, between individuals, groups, or communities" (Seidman, 1992, p. 75). Mikhail Bakhtin's (1981) concept of *heteroglossia* is useful for this discussion, by encouraging us to consider the range of multiple voices and understandings present in any particular "text" or social situation. At the same time, though, Bakhtin's concept incorporates a notion of *point of view* with respect to plausible and defensible interpretations. That is to say, "heteroglossy" (or, as we might say, "polysemy") has certain limits or operates within certain parameters. While the parameters themselves may be contingent and not absolute, they provide interpreters with places to stand to consider viable and compelling and even bizarre meanings. The particular, peculiar meaning may in fact be the most revealing in a study, but its mere existence does not necessarily make it so.

The heuristic concept of heteroglossia inspires my own treatment of multiple paradigms for doing social research. Each major approach to research—the three categories of empirical-analytic, historical-hermeneutic, and critically oriented—along with their variants and hybrids, have their own blindspots as well as capacities for illumination. As with the even broader category of metaphor, we might liken the use of a paradigm to going into a dark room with a flashlight. Certain parts of the room will be seen clearly, becoming temporary focal points. Other areas will be seen less well, because they will be on the margins of the beam of light. And still other parts of the room will be shrouded in darkness altogether. What is seen will shift as the flashlight itself is moved around. But it is important for the flashlight user to remember that what is seen brightly is not all that there is. To extend this imagery a bit further, we could say that certain flashlights will work better in some rooms than in others. In fact, part of the result depends on whether one really wants to focus on a particular object or get the general picture of the room.

With this image in mind, I would like to comment briefly on what I see as the primary limitations of each of the three major paradigms for doing research. The points will be illustrated with hypothetical or composite examples from organizational communication research. I treat these limitations as partially inherent, distinctive but not unique, and somewhat complementary.

Empiricism's Distanced Reductionism: "Let's Not Get Too Close to What We're Studying, Lest We Lose Our Objectivity"

The empirical-analytic approach in general, and logical positivism in particular, have often been criticized for an insensitivity to the dynamics of language. I do not need to repeat or revisit those arguments here. But I will note that the claims advanced against logical positivism in the middle of the twentieth century do not necessarily apply to the range of research being associated with that label or the terms "empirical" or "post-positivist" today. (Note: Here I am trying to avoid the term "functionalism" altogether because I believe it has been misappropriated from structural-functionalist sociology and unfortunately applied as a "devil-term" that denies the actual "functions" of social institutions and phenomena and militates against opportunities for productive debate.) Within communication studies, especially, there is now a large body of research that follows the prediction-and-control model of empirical-analytic research that is highly attuned to the nature of language and to the role that language plays in the very development and application of constructs. This is not to say that all or even the bulk of such research is explicitly directed toward the isolation and control of variables in social analysis, given that the overwhelming concern for such research is description and explanation. Still, the experimental methodological paradigm remains the implicit prototype of such investigations. Moreover, a desire for prediction is implied in both the key constructs and the inferential statistics commonly used for data analysis.

Much of the research on organizational socialization and assimilation fits the bill here (see, e.g., Bullis & Bach, 1991; Jablin, 1987; Krone, Chen, Sloan, & Gallant, 1997). Loosely speaking, a great deal of that research has been conducted within the empirical tradition, with close attention to the predictive value of knowing certain things about employees and organizations during stages from initial encounter to "business as usual." What such research does especially well is to try to identify key factors in the socialization processes, for both individuals and organizations, while recognizing that the very formulations of the problem by managers and workers are important to incorporate into the researchers' models. Moreover, that research has helped us to make some useful generalizations about the experiences of newcomers in a variety of types of work situations and organizational settings. This research has struck a nice balance between consideration of the individual's experience upon entering an organization and organizational demands and constraints. With the addition of recent efforts to capture the stories told by both individuals and groups about becoming an organizational member (see, e.g., Brown, 1985), as well as critical insights about the restrictive biases inherent in many of our conceptions of jobs and organizational roles (see, e.g., Clair, 1996), the research on organizational socialization has become quite sophisticated and very interesting.

Next, in discussing empiricism's limitations, I would like to stress the ways the empirical-analytic orientation toward research can embody what I am calling "distanced reductionism." By that term, I mean to combine two interrelated limitations: (1) a tendency to overlook the "big picture" for a concern with isolable parts of some "system," and (2) an analytically distant posture that undermines the intersubjectivity between researcher and research participant.

Although the pure experimental model of research, accompanying what used to be called the "hypothetico-deductive" paradigm for doing research, is not especially common in communication studies these days, we can use it as a prototype for a set of assumptions that highlight prediction and control as guiding themes of the research project. That is, some of the basic assumptions of this model are modified and used even in nonexperimental research. Such an orientation, whether it is often acknowledged or not, does embody certain fundamental interests (see Habermas, 1971). Despite any claims to relative or complete value neutrality (which, granted, have generally been softened in recent decades), the guiding interests in prediction and control will help to shape what counts as knowledge in studies where the empirical perspective operates.

In the realm of research methodology, we see the blind spots of the empirical orientation in some elaborate uses of statistical analysis that become far removed from the terms and concepts and feelings of the persons and situations under study. In effect, there are several levels of abstraction that "take" the researcher away from the "subjects." This becomes a serious problem when no feedback loops are employed to reconnect the research findings with the original *sources* of data (see Tompkins, 1994). Within the empirical paradigm itself there are important concerns for validity that are ignored by some researchers in their ambitious attempts to "fit" statistical and conceptual models to data when the real nature of the data can be long forgotten or obscured by an overly rationalized view of the research process. Methodological fetishism can sometimes get in the way of meaningful and practical understanding.

But here I would like to keep our attention on theory and conceptualization more than on method. Let us consider a single example and trace it through the three major research paradigms, so as to appreciate more fully their respective strengths and limitations.

For instance, suppose we are studying employee participation within the context of a monthly meeting in a moderately sized business: an auto parts manufacturer with about 500 employees. The meetings are officially set up to promote "dialogue" between top management and rotating representatives of the rest of the staff, especially in recognition of the forty percent growth in the workforce of the firm over the past five years. About twenty percent of the workforce holds technical or managerial positions; approximately the same number has been to college. The business is an a suburban town of 100,000 people in the Midwest of the United States, with a fairly broad economic and industrial base. Managerial and technical staff members are all self-identified as European American males, except for the HR director, who is an African American female. The nonmanagerial portion of the workforce, eighty percent of employed persons, is fifty percent African American, forty percent European American, and ten percent Hispanic. The business has a nonunion environment, but it is committed to ideas of "employee participation" and "worker empowerment," as manifested in these monthly meetings and in new programs for the team-based restructuring of work processes. Lately, the company has established several "minifactories" in its various production areas, in order to stimulate "entrepreneurship" at the level of the individual work position and work team. Each minifactory therefore maintains its own relations with suppliers and customers, and coordination is achieved at the highest managerial levels. According to top managers, the organization is in a "race," in terms of implementing the most advanced technologies in its production system and by virtue of being a highly "customer-responsive," "quality" organization.

We are a research team with access to the monthly dialogue and quality meetings in the plant. These meetings are convened by the CEO and the HR director. Other top and middle-level managers are strongly urged to attend, but their actual support is variable from person to person. The meetings are designed for about ten percent of the total workforce at a time. "Representatives" of nonsupervisory employees for each monthly meeting are chosen according to a stratified random sampling technique by the HR director.

Although our research agenda is not completely set in place, we are especially interested in *conceptions and enactments of "participation" in these meetings* (cf. Cheney, 1995; Deetz, 1992; Harrison, 1994; Seibold & Shea, 2000; Stohl, 1995). That is to say, we are exploring both interpretations, or "frames," of participation and the specific activities that count or may be counted as participation. Thus, the ways participation is defined by participants are important to us as well as the ways participation "happens" (e.g., through the structure of the meetings, patterns of talk, overt exercises of power, etc.).

Because researchers already know a fair amount about these issues, we may be inclined to try to apply research questions and even directional hypotheses derived from the literature. Operating within the empirical framework, it would be reasonable to address questions such as: "What are the key demographic and social factors predictive of the extent to which individuals will participate in the meetings?" This one could serve as our primary research question. Beginning with the background information outlined above, and adding to that some knowledge of the organization obtained through casual observation, we could develop a list of potential independent variables to predict a dependent variable of "participation." Participation in the meetings would then need to be operationally defined, say, in terms of extended comments made or responses given to questions, or the like. To accomplish this, we might construct our research in two stages, allowing for input from participants into the very process of determining our indicators and measures of participation (see P. Bernstein, 1976). In this way, this study could be quite sensitive to some of the lay constructs employed by the participants in meetings. (Accordingly, what might commonly be termed *empirical research* could well incorporate a dimension of interpretive sensitivity. Indeed, various Q techniques for analyzing data attempt to do this through highly systematic means.) In the end, participation in the meetings would be largely construed as observable, verbal, and perhaps also in terms of some measure of "intensity," "engagement," or "forcefulness." Because of our open access to meetings over a period of one year, let us say, we could expect to witness many different types of interactions and to assemble a large amount of data. Assuming sound methods for coding and analyzing these data, we would then be able to develop a preliminary model to predict employee participation in the meetings. And, depending upon our specific questions, as well as the nature of our analysis of data, we might try to generalize beyond the specific organization under study. Our model of "factors in participation" might well even account for the multiphasic, nonlinear development of a group (see Poole & DeSanctis, 1990), to the extent that certain members of the group would be the same over time and to the degree that information about the meetings became widely shared around the organization.

The brief profile I have given for this hypothetical research project cannot begin to account for the complexities of such a real study in practice. So, the paragraphs above represent something of a caricature. However, I have tried to present sufficient detail to give us something to work with. And I have been careful not to set up a "straw person" in terms of the empirical approach to this research opportunity in an organization. The study I have just described has several important merits, including its clearly defined focus, its careful attention to an array of factors relevant to participation, its systematic approach to potentially relevant factors, its refined methods of data gathering and data analysis, and its structured output.

On the other hand, the same study can be limited in trying to force precision on a concept such as "participation" that is richly ambiguous—and even *purposely* so from the viewpoints of some architects of participation programs. That is, we may miss ways in which both strategic ambiguity and unintended ambiguity function as part of the dynamics of the situation (cf. Eisenberg, 1984). It is not that one or even a cluster of operational definitions for participation lack utility—in fact, they may well be necessary—but such formulations could block us from seeing how our very understandings of participation are molding the situation and are in fact products of the situation at the same time (see Giddens, 1984; cf. McPhee, 1985; Poole, Seibold, & McPhee, 1985). Thus, trying to isolate participation, its antecedents, and perhaps also its effects can lead us to miss important ways in which the meeting serves as the management of meaning on multiple levels—from consideration of the symbolism of the meeting as a whole to specific interactions that take place within it (Markham, 1996). Even though the research is attuned to how the whole issue of participation in meetings is framed, it may rely ultimately on narrowly circumscribed and "inelastic" understandings of this important dimension of the meetings. We risk not appreciating how the very phenomenon we are studying has in fact *changed for the participants themselves* during the course of the investigation and as a result of both planned and unforeseen interactions. In this way, our very models could place undue distance between us and the dynamics of participation in the meetings. Further, if the research project is approached with too much confidence in the conceptualizations and analyses, or uses models of interrelationships of factors that are too linear or too "cleanly" presented, we may fail to recognize how our roles in the research effort have affected the very phenomenon we are studying. Especially in working with a topic such as participation, it can be difficult to fully account for its reflexive nature, that is, that talk about participation itself folds into and affects the process of participation. Thus, we would take on certain advantages and disadvantages in approaching our problem with an empirical-analytic frame.

Interpretivism's Parochialism: "Sometimes We're Looking So Closely We Don't Even Know What We're Missing"

The contours of a primarily interpretive study of meeting participation in this organization have already been suggested. An essential part of the effort, in both conceptualization and methodology, would be to try to capture well the actual meanings held by participants. We would therefore take what participants have to say about participation very seriously. Also, we would probably attempt to approach such meanings with a fairly open mind and open agenda for coding or interpreting data. Taking a creative approach to the understanding of participation, we may envision it operating on *several different levels*: for example, the ways participation is labeled, the specific speech acts that are seen to count as participation, and even how *the meetings themselves* come to symbolize participation or lack of it for certain participants.

An interpretive study of participation in our case would be buoyed by the effective use of data-gathering strategies that place the researcher as much as possible inside the world of the research participants. Indeed, participant observation might become part of the overall approach to the study, depending on access and the specific evolution of the project.

The strengths of such an investigation should by now be apparent: I would especially highlight a focus on the meanings of the members of the organization, an explicit allowance for the multiplicity and dynamism of meanings, and the opening to a richly textured and evolving understanding between researcher and research participants.

However, by taking multiplicity and polysemy seriously, and by placing variant meanings on equal footing, we may become blind to the workings of power in the situation that have helped to create *the very parameters for those meanings*. Some of the basic assumptions about participation, especially on the part of different groups (by class, educational level, ethnicity, and gender) in the organization may exist on what we may call a "deep structural" level and may be appreciated well only through attention to issues of power on a scale that transcends the boundaries of the workplace and organization (see Conrad & Ryan, 1985). For example, perhaps only in the realm of the larger community could we find subtle evidence of characteristic ways of talking and dealing between the several racial groups. And even within this wider arena, certain patterns may be so ritualized or disguised as to conceal the historical reasons for certain ways of relating (cf. Lukes, 1974; Scott, 1990). Our research participants, in whom we have so much confidence and with whom we have built solid and trusting relationships, may themselves be unaware of the extent to which their own activities and conceptions of work and self are shaped by some larger institutional forces (du Gay, 1996). While responding freely to certain work situations—such as the monthly meetings—organizational members may at the same time be "importing" dominant meanings from larger social contexts (see Mumby, 1997b). For some participants, "participation" may be something one does only when permitted to do so or when motivated by someone else. For others, it might involve a two-sided game composed of active public participation and denial of that very participation in other conversations behind closed doors (Cheney et al., 1998). For still other organizational members, participation may be something best achieved through "active" *non*involvement (cf. Marshall & Stohl, 1993).

An interpretive approach to this study might in fact be able to capture some of the subtleties of the meeting environment as I have discussed it, but those aspects could also easily be overlooked—that is, by a form of interpretive investigation that took itself too seriously. Oddly, by taking our roles as researchers—perhaps even as participant–observers—too seriously, we may overestimate our own insight into the entire situation. If the research effort unfolded so that we gave too much attention to the thrill and progress of our own relationships with the organization, or if we adopted an "every meaning is sacred" sensibility, we might miss opportunities to probe more deeply into the very power dynamics that shape what we take to be a sheer multiplicity of meanings. This is true despite the occasional interpretive move to situate (or contain) a power-centered interpretation as one among many possible perspectives (see, e.g., Friedman, 1989; Trujillo, 1992)—as an essentially political perspective that is on the same analytical and epistemological plane with other competing perspectives. Some forms of interpretive research also view it to be anathema to make value judgments on what is being investigated, along with taking extra care not to impose the researcher's own meanings on the situation. In this way, interpretivism often tries to steer an investigative course between empirical distance and critical arrogance. Still, important risks accompany the "middle way," as we have seen.

Criticism's Arrogance: "The Critic Always Knows Best"

By now, it should be obvious that I have structured this discussion so that each paradigm is used to critique the one presented before it. The interpretive perspective on research has been used to reveal the limitations of a chiefly empirical-analytic approach to our case. Likewise, we are now sliding into the critical perspective, as we consider what is not well appreciated by the interpretive perspective. This is but one way for such a story of "paradigmatic blindness" to be told. (Consider, for example, the recognized similarities between certain brands of empirical research and certain types of critique: both can lapse into a problematic form of objectivism through their retention of a realist epistemology; cf. Putnam & Cheney, 1983; Redding & Tompkins, 1988.) It would be easy to think at this point in the discussion: "Okay, here comes the triumph of the critical approach—

just like Habermas [1988] presents it as 'the foremost among equals'!" But that is not my design here, and I wish to make an effort to avoid that kind of conclusion for our case study.

Let me simply conclude in a somewhat open-ended way, by suggesting the limitations that could accompany a critical reading of our case. I would take the following to be the hallmarks of a critically oriented perspective on social research: (1) an explicit concern for making value-based assessments; (2) paying special attention to relations of power in whatever situation is under study; and (3) penetrating and ongoing questioning of basic assumptions (both practically and theoretically speaking). Deetz's (e.g., 1992) and Mumby's (e.g., 1997a) research, both independently and together, embody these three assumptions in fairly complete terms. So does Buzzanell's (e.g., 1994) and Clair's (e.g., 1993). All of these researchers of organizational communication are careful to raise provocative, value-driven questions and yet present answers that are in some ways tentative, contingent, and open to multiple views. In fact, Mumby (e.g., in press) has explained his project of "postmodernist feminism" in terms similar to what I have outlined here. The critical research "camp" divides on the issue of emancipation and the extent to which that goal is constitutive of the perspective; it also divides over the practical question of how best to achieve emancipation, if at all possible (see Fay, 1987).

I have no space here to detail different approaches to the functions, processes, and outcomes of critique, just as I could not do justice to the multiple forms of what I have called for terminological convenience "the empirical-analytic approach." However, it is worth noting that the third assumption of criticism listed above can be pushed very hard and far so as to undermine the other two principles. This is precisely what happens with some brands of postmodernism: through unceasing questioning, the value claims of the research effort and the claims to relatively definitive knowledge of power relations by the researcher themselves become suspect or at least need to be expressed with a large measure of uncertainty (on this issue, cf. Baudrillard, 1983, and Foucault, 1984). Ironically, though, some approaches to postmodern critique in effect try to establish their own metaposition, from which all other epistemological standpoints are critiqued (see the discussion in Rosenau, 1992).

To return to our case: A critical sensibility could well lead us toward a greater appreciation of relations of power—in both their overt and hidden dimensions—than either of the other two approaches. In contrast with the empirical-analytic approach, as typically practiced, the critical approach could enable us to move beyond mere observables and thus allows us to make provocative judgments about "what's really going on" in the situation—as understood from some reasonably coherent, value-based standpoint (e.g., featuring interpretation in terms of class, gender, ethnicity, managerial/technical/professional expertise, or some other source of power relations and group dominance). In its response to the interpretive perspective, the critical posture on the problem would attempt to organize the multiplicity of meanings in such a way as to account for their existence and (perhaps) bring them together under a single explanatory framework. Thus, the fact of interpretive diversity with respect to "participation" might be seen as a product of the successful propagation of a myth about "freedom of expression" inside the organization. The ambitious critic might actually trace the origins and development of such a myth, showing how it has come to operate with a scope of influence well beyond the level of awareness of most if not all organizational members. Even allowing for some cynicism and resistance on the part of employees, a model of the myth's persistence could be seen as something that prevents any coherent opposition from forming among employees vis-à-vis managerial initiatives (cf. Burawoy, 1979; Graham, 1995; Grenier, 1988; Jermier, Knights, & Nord, 1994; Willis, 1977).

Such a critique of participation in our case would indeed be provocative. It might even prove revealing for some organizational members, if we, the researchers, created the opportunity to present them with our analysis. However, the merits of this perspective on the study could be restricted in several ways. First, such an analysis could presume an overall understanding of the situation that is monolithic and too stable. This is precisely why some postmodernist and feminist approaches to criticism have emphasized the fragmentary and dynamic nature of meaning in many social situations, even in cases where domination by one group or one ideology seems so sure (Fraser, 1989). Second, such an approach would share with an empirical-analytic posture a decided distance between researcher and "subjects"—in this case, perhaps, insistently privileging the interpretations of the researcher over those of the participants—along with risking a kind of objectivism. Third, depending on the strength of our commitments to our brand of the critical research perspective, we might unknowingly suppress certain meanings (or forms of "evidence") that counter our view. In an effort to advance the "counterfactual" argument, as many critical researchers do, one incurs both a tremendous burden of proof and a risk of the over-zealous pursuit of one's case (cf. Lukes, 1974; Scott, 1990). Again, this danger is not unique to the critical perspective, but self-seduction does tend a somewhat different form for the researcher operating within each of the three paradigms.

RECIPES FOR PARADIGMATIC SURPRISE:
PERSPECTIVES BY INCONGRUITY

Through this exploration of the interpretive perspective on organizational communication, I have tried both to interpret that perspective and to suggest its important similarities and differences with respect to the two other major paradigmatic points of view on research: the empirical-analytic and the critically oriented. To understand the interpretive perspective more deeply, we should place it in direct dialogue and productive confrontation with the other perspectives. In this way, we can inspire new forms of research, such as are already appearing in the field. I appeal to Burke's (1945) term *perspective by incongruity* in this section of the essay because it so eloquently captures the creative dimension of some paradigm-spanning research efforts. The point is not simply to explore *what is possible or what is conceivable*, interesting as such mind or discussion exercises might be. Rather, I think our research has a lot to gain by directly addressing the complementary strengths and weaknesses of different approaches to social investigation. To illustrate my point, I consider three different ways that more than one paradigm could be related to one another. Under each type of relation, I offer illustrations from the pages of recent research reports.

When Paradigms Speak to One Another

At the outset, it is important to recognize the array of possible relationships that can be produced "when paradigms collide." Schultz and Hatch (1996) express this point well with a triangle of conceivable "metatheoretical positions with respect to multiple paradigms." The three points of the triangle are incommensurability, integration, and crossing. The first position is described by Schultz and Hatch as the most common in that researchers have generally tended to dismiss the claims of paradigms other than the one to which they themselves are wedded or within whose range of vision their research programs are operating. I would add that in some cases researchers do not even reach the point of articulating a principle such as *incommensurability* because either (1) they are not fully aware of the claims of competing perspectives (by holding caricatures of them) or (2) they simply do not recognize the competing claims that originate from outside their own strongly held ideology as valid.

Schultz and Hatch (1996) continue by describing the strategy of *paradigm integration*. They describe this as a strategy that "ignores differences" in the interest of synthesis and the construction of an overarching position. While this strategy is certainly one that can be identified in certain pieces of research (we see this very often in theoretical exposition), again, I would say that Schultz and Hatch oversimplify the options that they quickly review before moving to their presumably superior form of paradigm dialogue—what they term *crossing*. I would emphasize that not all attempts at substantial integration ignore meaningful differences between and among distinct paradigms (see, e.g., Fairhurst, Jordan, & Neuwirth, 1997; Scott, Corman, & Cheney, 1998). In fact, we might say that creative theory building and methodological triangulation is sometimes impeded by the assumption that any attempt at real integration involves either cooptation of one paradigm by another or analytical sloppiness. In an ironic way, by their attempt to elevate their paradigm-crossing set of strategies, Schultz and Hatch may be guilty of some of the same conceptual sins they point out in other research.

Under the category of *crossing*, Schultz and Hatch identify three options or techniques. These are worth comment here because of the possibilities for interparadigm research they illuminate. The first is a *sequential* relationship between paradigms. One of the clearest examples of this in the field of communication is Bowers's (1968) controversial essay on the "prescientific function of rhetorical criticism." Arguing from a basically empirical-analytic perspective, Bowers explained that rhetorical criticism (as what we might term an interpretive–critical enterprise) is best suited to explore social situations (and important messages) in an exploratory way, thus setting up further research for the investigation of directional hypotheses under testable experimental or quasi-experimental conditions. Although Bowers was clearly favoring the empirical-analytic endeavor as the culmination of a multistage research effort, his essay does offer a very good example of how we may place different paradigms in logical, linear relationships with one another, for the purposes of pursuing particular forms of research. With respect to research on organizational values, for instance, we might be creative in considering not only that an interpretive phase could give way to an empirical one, but also that an empirical one could give way to an interpretive one. Similarly, each or both could be framed or informed, preceded or followed by a critical take on the matter (cf. Cheney & Frenette, 1993; Gioia, Donnellon, & Sims, 1989; Zorn, Page, & Cheney, 2000).

Schultz and Hatch's (1996) second strategy is termed *parallel*. This involves the simultaneous development of different paradigmatic approaches to the same problem. Such studies are becoming more and more common in communication studies, though the development of parallel models or approaches is often done under the umbrella of one overarching paradigm. Schultz and Hatch cite Hassard's (1991) study of the British Fire Service, in which he applied theoretical concepts and methodological entailments representing each of Burrell and Morgan's (1979) four paradigms (cf. Deetz, 1996; Mumby, 1997a; Putnam, Phillips, & Chapman, 1996).

Such a metaposition yields useful research exemplars as we have in Papa, Auwal, and Singhal's (1995, 1997) multifaceted study of the Grameen (Rural People's) Bank of Bangladesh. Their 1995 article offered parallel applications of the theories of coorientation (Cronen, Pearce, & Harris, 1979), concertive control (Barker, 1993; Bullis & Tompkins, 1989; Tompkins & Cheney, 1985), and feminist criticism (see, e.g., Buzzanell, 1994; Calás & Smircich, 1999a; Martin, 1990) to a single though extensive case study. In this case, the coorientation model itself may be seen to bridge the empirical and interpretive categories of research, while the other two theories are critical–interpretive (broadly speaking). It is interesting to note that the parallel strategy itself can implicitly support the idea of incommensurability, as suggested by Martin's (1992) analysis of various types of organizational culture research. This is a point not clearly recognized by Schultz and Hatch in their discussion, despite their reference to Martin's study.

The "most favored" technique of Schultz and Hatch's (1996) paradigm-crossing strategy is what they call "paradigm interplay." This perspective involves living in and with gray areas: "*Interplay* refers to the simultaneous recognition of both contrasts and connections between paradigms and, thus, to both the differences and similarities between paradigms that are emphasized by the parallel and bridging strategies, respectively" (p. 534). This heuristic device is distinguished for treating paradigm boundaries as permeable. Different paradigms are explored vis-à-vis one another with respect to both connections and contrasts. Furthermore, Schultz and Hatch take an overarching postmodernist position (as they term it) in order to make their playful suggestions with respect to multiple paradigms: "In interplay, the researcher moves back and forth between paradigms so that multiple views are held in tension" (p. 535). This is a noble analytical goal, but it is quite difficult to achieve in practice. Schultz and Hatch illustrate the utility of such a perspective on paradigms through a meta-analysis of organizational culture research. Among other things, they claim that the notion of interplay allows for research to take into account both the "categorical" and the "associative" modes of analysis that characterize "functionalism" and "interpretivism," respectively. While I do not have the space to further explicate Schultz and Hatch's model of interplay (let alone describe its limitations, such as the seeming transparency of language in their system), I should emphasize that their essay moves us into *a broad and nuanced discussion of the various kinds of relationships we can imagine or articulate between different paradigms.*

When Paradigms Appropriate One Another

Through reference to Schultz and Hatch's (1996) model, I have already discussed a variety of ways that paradigms can be seen from "above," from a metaperspective on their interrelationships. Now, I would like to highlight two specific ways in which I see "paradigm dialogues" occurring in organizational (communication) research. The first is what might be seen in political terms as a strategy of cooptation, but I prefer to stress its creative, productive aspects. The essence of this strategy is that phenomena and concepts typically identified with one paradigm are profitably addressed by the employment of a different paradigm. This is one way of getting beyond, or at least sidestepping, the incommensurability problem. In my view, this strategy also offers a way of overcoming unnecessary barriers that have been set up between paradigms, schools of thought, and programs of research (e.g., the simplistic notion that no numbers have any place in an "interpretive" research report).

In their study of "antecedents and outcomes of interpretive diversity in organizations," Contractor, Eisenberg, and Monge (1994) offer an excellent example of what I am calling the strategy of *appropriation* of one paradigm's territory or resources by another. Using advanced tools of network analysis to examine not only communication connections but also shared meaning, Contractor and his colleagues focus empirical attention on the issue of "interpretive diversity" among an organization's members. At first glance, this is a surprising conceptual and methodological move, precisely because the whole issue of interpretive diversity, fragmentation, and dynamism has generally been thought to be part of the distinct province of interpretive scholarship and the study of organizational culture from that viewpoint (see, e.g., Bantz, 1993; Brown, 1990; Goodall, 1989; Kreps, 1989; Trujillo, 1985).

In this case, we find the pathways between paradigms to be opened up through such a creative venture. Contractor and colleagues (1994) systematically examine certain hypotheses about relationships between demographic and communication-related variables, on the one hand, and interpretive diversity, on the other. *The researchers made the interesting finding that it is not the fact of more communication but rather the similarity between communication patterns that is the better predictor of shared interpretations of the organization's mission.* In relating their findings, Contractor et al. explained the importance of the distinction between perceived and actual interpretive diversity, in that many interactants who communicated often with one another were likely to *assume* shared meanings that were not really held in common (cf. Chiles & Zorn's [1995] somewhat parallel analysis of employee empowerment). This kind of study has important implications for the study of networks, culture, and meaning in organizations. Moreover, the work can now be further enriched with close attention to issues of ambiguity, manipulation, and dynamism in language use.

When Paradigms Become One Another

With this final category, I wish to focus attention on the ways that a line of research or even a particular study can develop over time so as to cross paradigmatic boundaries. Especially interesting in this respect are cases where an in-depth study is revisited and reinterpreted.

The most famous study, or series of studies, in all of organizational studies remains the Hawthorne experiments, conducted by a group of researchers from Harvard University at the Hawthorne Western Electric plant near Chicago from 1928 until 1935. This research, which was to some extent conducted with operational assumptions under scientific management, attracted a lot of attention almost immediately and eventually became known as the "turning point" that ushered in the human relations movement. Giving its name to an "effect" whereby the influence of observation on behavior in social research is acknowledged, the Hawthorne series of investigations has been credited for bringing into full view the idea that *social as well as economic motivations are important in the lives of workers.* I will not review here the most famous or the least famous components of that research, but we should remember that the studies have been variously interpreted and reinterpreted over the seven decades since they became well known (cf. e.g., Carey, 1995; Mayo, 1929–1930; Roethlisberger & Dickson, 1939; Rose, 1990). The studies have been criticized for a simplistic bifurcation of motivational types, sloppy methodology, blindness to issues of power, elitism, sexism, and *over*interpretation.

Perhaps the most comprehensive study of the Hawthorne experiments is Gillespie's provocatively titled *Manufacturing Knowledge* (1991). Gillespie goes to painstaking lengths to document the various stages of the study, and not only from the perspective of the research team. Beginning with the assumption of multiple interpretations—operating both within the context of the Hawthorne studies *and* in terms of the various research reports since—Gillespie makes even more problematic than previously the way that the famous research is essentialized in a cluster of lessons about human motivation at work. Remarkably, by scrutinizing a variety of documents from research notes to workers' diaries, Gillespie is also able to uncover details of relationships among workers and between workers and the researchers. Gillespie's reanalysis of the famous relay assembly tests, from which the research drew its most-cited conclusion about the importance of social factors in human motivation and especially of the need for humane attention to workers and work processes, is extremely revealing. Gillespie shows not only that a number of workers were well aware of the experimental manipulations in the research and of how the resulting effects were being understood by the researchers, but also how several workers who were especially influential on the shop floor reframed the entire situation as an opportunity to make gains in terms of their demands for better working conditions. As Gillespie explains at some length, *these pivotal workers carefully managed relations with their colleagues, with the researchers, and with management, helping to create a situation whereby favorable responses to their demands would be most likely.* Using insights like this one, Gillespie punctuates the development of the "knowledge" of the Hawthorne studies with multiple perspectives and twists and turns on what is typically presented as a story with a single plot line.

Gillespie's (1991) fascinating analysis of the Hawthorne studies is not without flaws itself: for example, there are several places where his conclusions could be questioned for having insufficient data to support the warrants. But, his research offers a beautiful example of the transformation of an experimental (or, more correctly, quasi- or intendedly experimental) form of research through the combined lenses of interpretive and critical scholarship. Along the way, something of an empirical-analytic spirit is maintained, in that the original research methods are critiqued from within that paradigm. In addition, *Manufacturing Knowledge* demonstrates well an open-ended, "conversational" approach to the research enterprise. New claims, new interpretations, and even new data enter the process of "deciding" what the research means or ought to mean. Indeed, it would be useful now for some researcher (with a lot of time on her hands) to do a comprehensive meta-analysis of the various studies of Hawthorne. The Hawthorne studies are being successively reframed and in a sense remade by subsequent visits to those famous experiments, but in ways that maintain the original research effort as an important point of reference.

PUTTING THINGS IN PERSPECTIVES:
A PROLOGUE TO FURTHER DISCUSSION

I wish to conclude this essay with a partially open-ended epilogue (renamed "prologue"), structured through a series of challenges to interpretive organizational communication scholarship.

First, I would inquire again about the *bounds* of interpretation. In Burke's (1945) terms, "Which is the container and which is the thing contained?" To interpret the matter with Venn diagrams: Just how big is the domain of interpretive activity? Is it as large as that of communication, for example? If so, what is *not* interpretation? Do we run the risk of so diluting interpretation's meaning that it ceases to have heuristic or practical value? Should we even *try* to "locate" the interpretive endeavor? Do we even need to worry about these questions?

Second, what can we say about the domain of interpretation *within the context of organization?* That is, what do we lose as well as gain by stressing the interpretive aspects of organizational life? Here, I find it helpful to revisit the classic sociological debate over social structure and individual agency. Clegg (1994) captures the tension between what he calls "structure and subjectivity" by reinterpreting the works of Weber (1968) and Foucault (1984) in light of one another. Clegg praises Foucault for "liberating" organizational studies from an "overstructuralized" account of persons as vehicles of organizational structure (in Weber's ideal typical bureaucracy) while not falling into excessive reliance on a notion of *Verstehen* (understanding) that tends to act as if structure does not exist (a view that can be found in parts of Weber's corpus). Interpretive organizational communication scholarship often drifts toward the latter "pole," preferring a Goffmanesque (e.g., 1956) view of individuals as actors who *create* an idea of their roles as scripted (at least to some extent) by larger social forces. The question then becomes, What is or ought to be the role of structure in interpretive studies of organizational communication?

Third, let us *apply the perspective of interpretation to itself.* In a world of unstable and multiple meanings, how do we settle on an interpretation as "solid," even for a little while? How do we thus "position" interpretation? This issue is addressed fairly clearly in the writings of Mouffe (1992), who speaks in terms of "nodal points" in popular or vernacular discourses (such as politics) where meanings become "stuck" or "unstuck." I find this heuristic device to be applicable, though, not only to discourses under study but also to the discourses of interpretive research *itself.* Indeed, the entire complex of discussions over the "real meaning" of the Hawthorne studies can be usefully subjected to this idea.

In communication studies, Taylor's (1997) research on the cultural and organizational dimensions of the nuclear weapons research facilities at Los Alamos, New Mexico, also provides a compelling example of what I am talking about here. Taylor's research simultaneously adopts "synchronic" and "diachronic" perspectives on the key narratives told at the Bradbury Science Museum, revealing how single dominant stories come to the forefront of explanations for a while but also how they may be supplanted by subsequent plot lines that capture the imagination of listeners and readers. Taylor's commentary on the institutionalization of "cultural memory" can help us to understand better how such processes take place in social research itself. Indeed, we may take Taylor's analysis to further our reflection on how "interpretivist" claims come to be part of the received wisdom of scholarship and how, in taking certain claims for granted (e.g., about the "social construction of reality," as commonly uttered in a sloganlike manner, without attendant explanation), interpretive research sometimes constrains its own imagination and development.

Fourth, interpretive scholarship needs to *come to terms with the material world.* Again, we confront the distinction between interpretation and noninterpretation. To what extent, if at all, should research about organizational communication try to "stand outside" the domain of interpretation? Especially, how should we understand the roles of materiality, "constants," and "nonnegotiables" in the world of work, business, and organizations? Speaking generally, I would say that interpretive organizational communication scholarship has suffered somewhat from a case of "symbol worship," occasionally to the point of nearly denying "there's anything else out there" (Cheney & Bullis, 1999). With no room at all to delve into the intricacies of debates over ontology and epistemology, I can at least say that a modified form of interpretivism that takes the "pre- or noninterpreted world" more seriously would be a welcome development in organizational communication. This is one of the most difficult issues interpretive scholarship faces, and it has yet to be dealt with in a systematic and subtle way within the subfield of organizational communication (cf. Berger & Luckmann, 1967; Hall, 1982; Popper, 1972; Searle, 1995). Cooren (2000), following the lead of Latour (1993), has shown how both material and symbolic "objects" are necessarily "translated" and negotiated language processes. But even this useful perspective on textuality runs the risk of minimizing the roles of material constraints and resources.

Cloud's (1994, 1996) critique of the "materiality of discourse" thesis urging theorists and critics to consider not only the ways in which symbolism shapes what we call reality but also how reality sometimes crashes our symbolic celebrations, has sparked extensive debate within rhetorical studies. For instance, Cloud's studies of labor movements reveal how available material resources can constrain even the most creative and ambitious of labor communication campaigns. Just as certain postmodernist takes on the situation would emphasize the latent possibility for "symbolic reversals" and overturns of the definition of the situation by labor (cf. Foucault, 1978; Hayden, 1998), in its relation with management, so does Cloud's research remind us of material parameters for symbolic maneuverings. The symbolic and the nonsymbolic are, in very real senses, mutually constraining. It is time for a parallel analysis in organizational communication.

Fifth and finally, I would again place "interpretivism" within the context of other perspectives. What new forms of research can we imagine? To list just a few "blurred genres" (Geertz, 1983): critical ethnography, the science of interpretation, folk empiricism, symbolic analyses of technological systems, and the interpretive strategies of critique.

My part of the story ends here. What is your conclusion?

CHAPTER 3

Common Ground from the Post-Positivist Perspective

From "Straw Person" Argument to Collaborative Coexistence

Katherine I. Miller

During my career as an organizational communication scholar, I have been lucky enough to work in a variety of exemplary institutions of higher education. At all these institutions, I have had fine colleagues and students with which to work. Fortuitously, though, I have landed in a department that is, to my mind, unmatched as a place to do organizational communication scholarship. For in our department of Speech Communication here at Texas A&M University, I am blessed with three highly productive and thoughtful senior colleagues in the subdiscipline of organizational communication who have made, and continue to make, important contributions to the field: Linda Putnam, Scott Poole, and Charley Conrad. Luckily for me, my colleagues are also nice and generous with their time, and when I asked them to do me a favor in the preparation of this chapter they cheerfully complied (though Charley told me that the assigned task was "impossible" as well as "morally bankrupt").

Specifically, I asked Linda, Scott, and Charley to consider the classic Burrell and Morgan (1979) typology that has inspired many of the "paradigm dialogues" in organizational studies, as well as the revision of this typology that was put forth by Stan Deetz (1996), and to "place themselves" on these typologies with comments on their comfort with the placement and the task. The Burrell and Morgan typology divides sociological scholarship along the dimensions of objective to subjective and regulation to radical change, resulting in the four quadrants of functionalism, interpretivism, radical humanism, and radical structuralism. Deetz's alternative typology uses the dimensions of dissensus to consensus and local/emergent meaning to elite/a priori meeting, resulting in the quadrants of normative scholars, interpretive scholars, postmodern scholars, and critical scholars. These typologies are presented in Table 3.1.

The results of this exercise were interesting. Scott placed himself near the center of both typologies, straddling the horizontal axis and commenting that he also used interpretive approaches. Linda placed herself on the Deetz framework on a "project by project" basis, with these projects placing her in as many as three different quadrants of the typology. She noted, though, that her "experience with these quadrants is that the assumptions that underlie them are more important than the major dimensions and the divisions among the perspectives." Charley questioned the underlying utility (and even morality) of typologies such as these, commenting that "the greatest weakness of all research paradigms is the way in which they constrain researchers' vision. . . . When a researcher can place him*self* or her*self* in a category system, deterministic readings are inevitable, since

TABLE 3.1. Two Typologies of Organizational Theory and Research

Burrell & Morgan's (1979) typology	
Radical humanists	Radical structuralists
• Subjective approach to social research • Nominalist ontology • Anti-positivist epistemology • Sociology of radical change	• Objective approach to social research • Realist ontology and positivist epistemology • Sociology of radical change
Interpretivists	Functionalists
• Subjective approach to social research • Nominalist ontology • Anti-positivist epistemology • Sociology of regulation	• Objective approach to social research • Realist ontology • Positivist epistemology • Sociology of regulation
Deetz's (1996) typology	
Postmodern scholars	Critical scholars ("late modern")
• Dissensus relation to dominant social discourse • Local/emergent origin of concepts and problems	• Dissensus relation to dominant social discourse • Elite/a priori origin of concepts and problems
Interpretive scholars ("premodern")	Normative scholars ("modern")
• Consensus relation to dominant social discourse • Local/emergent origin of concepts and problems	• Consensus relation to dominant social discourse • Elite/a priori origin of concepts and social problems

anything else would involve an abandonment/fragmentation of her/his identity."

So what do we learn from this? Clearly, we learn that dimensions and quadrants that look neat and clean on the outside are not nearly so tidy from the inside. Instead, for practicing scholars, these boundaries are blurry, they are straddled based on particular views of the world, they are even "jumped" as the needs of specific research projects evolve. But perhaps the most important insight here is that these typologies *can* serve as a straightjacket, constraining researchers to "think like a critical theorist" or "do research in the interpretivist tradition" or "be a good post-positivist," rather than explore research questions that are important for an understanding of organizational communication processes.

Concerns such as this, of course, were the impetus for this book, and for this chapter. We *do* jump across traditions, we *do* straddle metatheoretical camps, and (unfortunately) we *do* let paradigmatic "definitions" constrain our work. This chapter is an attempt to allow for comfortable jumps and straddles and to loosen up some of the constraints. Admittedly, this chapter emanates from one area of these typologies: the area that is labeled as "functionalist" in the Burrell and Morgan scheme, as "normative" in the Deetz scheme, and as "post-positivist" in this chapter. My hope, though, is that by addressing issues of how researchers in this quadrant actually approach the social world and knowledge about that world, we can both move beyond "straw person" views of this paradigm, as well as allow for increased jumping and straddling among paradigms. Thus, this chapter will first trace historical developments in positivism, to provide a picture of "the way we were." I then consider how times changed in the 1970s and 1980s, how post-positivists in organizational communication typically approach research and theory today, and how we might reduce incommensurability both through enhanced understanding of alternative positions and through metatheoretical bridges such as structuration theory.

THE WAY WE WERE

Many writers have argued that a positivist philosophy, and the scientific forms of inquiry that stem from such a philosophy, has dominated social science inquiry throughout much of the twentieth century. For example, in classic works on the philosophy of science, Suppe (1977) and Kolakowski (1968) outline the philosophy of positivism and its critiques that have had a great deal of sway in intellectual discussions in the twentieth century. Much of the prominence of positivist viewpoints can be attributed to "physics envy," or a desire to emulate the methods and philosophies of the physical sciences. As the argument went, if the social sciences were to "mature" and become fully realized "paradigms" of research, scientific inquiry and systematic theory building were necessary. As Richard Bernstein (1976, p. 24) states, in the 1950s and 1960s, there was "basic unanimity about the nature of empirical theory in the social sciences; about the importance of such theory in attaining or approximating scientific explanations; and about the importance of developing testable explanatory theories, if the social sciences [were] to mature as the natural sciences have done." These standards of positivist empirical research and the development of axiomatic and testable theories were held throughout a variety of social research disciplines, including psychology, sociology, political science, economics, and communication. In this section, I will briefly trace the roots of positivism in philosophical circles, then consider the ways in which positivist modes of thought were vigorously adopted by the social scientific community.

Philosophical Roots: Positivism[1]

The term *positivism* is now widely used as a term of derision within many disciplines of social research. However, this usage often sets up positivism as a caricature that can be easily ridiculed by those preferring an alternative philosophy of science. Indeed, Phillips (1992, p. 95) argues that the term *positivism* "has ceased to have any useful function—those philosophers to whom the term accurately applies have long since shuffled off this mortal coil, while any living social scientists who either bandy this term around, or are the recipients of it as an abusive label, are so confused about what it means that, while the word is full of sound and fury, it signifies nothing." Thus, it is instructive to take a very brief look at the history of the positivist movement by first distinguishing between two "brands" of positivism— classical positivism and logical positivism—and then discussing how these philosophical schools of thought were adopted by social scientists. Much of this discussion is drawn from presentations of the positivist movement by Phillips (1992) and Diesing (1991).

Classical Positivism

The term *positivism* was coined by Auguste Comte (1798–1857), a French philosopher who argued that branches of knowledge must pass through three intellectual stages: "the theological or fictitious state, the metaphysical or abstract state, and the scientific or positive state" (Comte, 1970, p. 1). The progressive nature of these three stages of knowledge suggests that religious and metaphysical explanations are less acceptable than those based on scientific evidence and that, as a result, fields such as physics are at a "higher" level than fields that do not fully comport with scientific ideals. In classical positivism, the foundation of knowledge was to be found in empirical or observable phenomena and knowledge was assumed to be formulated through the use of formal logic and embodied in scientific laws. It is through a "well-combined use of reasoning and observation" that it is possible to come to "a knowledge of the final causes of phenomena" (Comte, 1970, p. 2). Thus, classical positivism was a foundationalist position that advocated the primacy of empirical data and formal theory in the generation of knowledge about the physical and social world.

Logical Positivism: The Vienna Circle

The logical positivist movement was embodied by a group of scholars who met during the 1920s and 1930s in the area around Vienna, Austria. Known as the "Vienna Circle," these scholars included Moritz Schlick, Rudolf Carnap, Otto Neurath, Herbert Feigl, Friedrich Waismann, Kurt Gödel, and Victor Kraft. Later influential members of the logical positivist movement included Hans Reichenbach, Carl Hempel, and Alfred Ayer. In laying out their highly influential philosophy of science, the logical positivists began by making a critical distinction between *science* and *metaphysics* via the "verifiability principle of meaning." This principle stated that "a statement is held to be literally meaningful if and only if it is either analytic or empirically verifiable" (Ayer, 1960, p. 90), or, as Phillips more colloquially puts it, "if it can't be seen or measured, it is not meaningful to talk about" (1992, p. 100). Thus, scientific statements are those statements that can be verified through the senses, and all other statements—metaphysical statements—are meaningless.

After making this clear distinction (and rejecting all metaphysical considerations), the logical positivists turned their attention to explicating the syntax and semantics of scientific language. For example, a great deal of attention was devoted to constructing an ideal language for science, to describing various kinds of scientific statements (e.g., observation statements, theoretical statements, and correspondence rules), and to clarifying the relationships among these statements (see Diesing, 1991, pp. 6–10). Logical positivists also considered the question of what counts as confirmation and disconfirmation of scientific statements and theories. Consider the statement "All leopards have spots." Clearly, one cannot "prove" this statement true, as one cannot observe all of the leopards in the world. This led some (see, e.g., Popper, 1959) to argue that the goal of science should be falsification rather than verification, though many logical positivists felt that there were problems with a falsifiability principle too (see, e.g., Carnap, 1937).

Throughout all of these efforts, the logical positivist movement was one of accounting for an ideal of science—science as logical positivists believed it was meant to be. As Diesing (1991) summarizes:

> This movement approaches science from far above, from the ideal of perfect knowledge. . . . Thus the treatment of testing begins with the idea of complete verification. . . . Explanation is defined first as deduction from

true, verified laws with all relevant circumstances specified. . . . Theory is defined first as a fully axiomatized structure of axioms, postulates, definitions, and theorems. . . . Actual sciences are interpreted as approximations to the ideal. (pp. 24–25)

Positivism in Social Research

Of course, the men who made up the "Vienna Circle" were not social scientists. They were philosophers of science—or more specifically, philosophers of *physical* (and to some extent *biological*) science. The ideals the Vienna Circle developed for a positivist science, however, were quickly adopted by theorists and researchers in fields of social research. Many scholars trace this adoption of positivist principles through the work of classic sociologists such as Talcott Parsons and Robert Merton. For example, Merton, in 1942, proposed that the scientific communities share certain values that allow them to maintain unity and deal with external threats (see Diesing, 1991, chap. 6; Merton, 1973, chap. 13). These four values were (1) universalism, the value for judging truth claims by preestablished and impersonal criteria; (2) communism, the value for viewing research products as belonging to a scientific community of scholars; (3) disinterestedness, the value for impartiality in the promotion of social scientific ideas; and (4) skepticism, the value for questioning beliefs and submitting them to scientific scrutiny. Though these values move beyond the positivist interest in philosophy and logic, they emphasize the importance of progress and scientific scrutiny in the study of social processes.

The frameworks of these seminal sociologists soon percolated into the values held by social researchers working in the trenches of academic institutions. For example, the fruition of these positivist ideals can be seen in textbooks on theory development in the social sciences that were published in the 1960s and 1970s. These books—including Robert Dubin's *Theory Building* (1969, 1978), Jerald Hage's *Techniques and Problems of Theory Construction in Sociology* (1972), and Hubert Blalock's *Theory Construction: From Verbal to Mathematical Formulations* (1969)—exemplify a view of sociological theory that is consistent with many of the basic tenets laid out by the philosophers of the Vienna Circle. That is, the theorist is instructed to clearly define concepts both operationally and conceptually, to join those concepts in systems of causal relationships, and to support their theoretical systems through replicable scientific procedures.

Similarly, Hassard (1993) traces the development of positivist thinking in the area of organizational analysis. Hassard argues that, in addition to Parsons and Merton, scholars such as Bronislaw Malinowski, A. R. Radcliffe-Browne, and Philip Selznick wed concepts of positivist philosophy with functionalist and systems concepts. According to Hassard, this joining of systems theory and positivism led to a hegemony of systems thinking in organizational theory, as evidenced in both the publications of leading journals and the presentations of best-selling management text-books. He concludes that "the systems approach attained an intellectual hegemony in organizational theory for almost half a century, mainly through professing a prior claim to empirical explanation" (p. 19).

Finally, within our own discipline, many writers tracing the history of organizational communication theory and research have also noted the widespread influence of positivist thinking during the middle part of this century (see, e.g., Putnam & Cheney, 1985; Redding, 1985; Redding & Tompkins, 1988). For example, Redding and Tompkins (1988) identify an important *applied-scientific* phase in organizational communication schol-arship that flourished during the period from the late 1940s to the 1970s in which "emphasis was placed on measurement, variable-analysis, and hypothetico-deductive designs intended to test competing perspectives" (Taylor, Flanagin, Cheney, & Seibold, 2000). The influence of positivist val-ues and methods can clearly be seen in these theoretical and research em-phases. In short, during the middle part of the twentieth century, scholars in a variety of social research disciplines—including organizational commu-nication—largely agreed with the sentiments of David Easton (1967), a po-litical scientist:

> All mature scientific knowledge is theoretical. . . . The higher the level of generality . . . the broader will be the range of explanation and understand-ing. . . . Clearly, if (social) science could arrive at . . . a general theory, the understanding of (social) life that it would give would be both profound and extensive. There is no need consequently to point out that such a theory would be desirable. (p. 4)

BUT TIMES CHANGE

It should be clear from the last section that the work of positivists thrived in the early and middle decades of this century. Indeed, this school was so well entrenched that the terms *philosophy of science* and *positivism* were virtually synonymous. Furthermore, the influence of positivism spread from beyond the limited horizons of philosophers of scientists, and gained a great deal of influence over social research disciplines ranging from soci-ology to psychology to political science to communication.[2]

Amazingly, though, by the 1960s, positivism was all but dead and new views of the philosophy of science had ascended. What happened? What were the factors that led to the demise of positivism? Several explanations help shed light on the downward spiral of this intellectual movement. We will first consider the "philosophical fall" of positivism and then consider the demise of positivism (and other related "isms" such as functionalism and empiricism) in fields of social research.

The Demise of Positivism in Philosophical Circles

Several explanations can be put forth in exploring the arguments that prompted the ultimate rejection of positivism by philosophers of science. First, increasingly, both practicing scientists and philosophers of science began to argue for the "theory-laden" nature of observation. This position posits that "some value orientations are so embedded in our modes of thought as to be unconsciously held by virtually all scientists" (Phillips, 1992, p. 142). For example, Sandra Harding (1987) argues from a feminist perspective that there is a male bias in fundamental aspects of scientific thought, and Stephanie Shields (1975) found that a great deal of research on sex differences over the last century has been influenced by historical biases. More generally, N. R. Hanson's classic work *Patterns of Discovery* (1965) argued that observation is always influenced by the observer's theoretical perspective and background knowledge. Hanson's classic example of this phenomenon is his suggestion that if Tycho Brahe and Johannes Kepler were drawn together at dawn, one would see the sun moving above the horizon and the other would see the earth rotating to reveal the sun. Thus, values and theoretical perspectives constitute lenses through which we view the world, and these lenses cannot be eliminated in any portion of the scholarly process.

If one accepts the position that all observations—in the physical and social sciences—are influenced by the theoretical stance of the observer, it is impossible to maintain the clean distinction between observational and theoretical statements that was so important to logical positivists. Furthermore, the theory-laden nature of observation cuts to the heart of the verifiability principle of meaning, for it is no longer possible to allow sensory experience to be the final arbiter of meaningfulness. A rejection of the verifiability principle in essence means a rejection of the entire logical positivist movement. As Diesing (1991, p. 15) explains:

> Once the two languages [observational and theoretical] had been distinguished, it proved difficult to keep them apart. Some philosophers argued that most scientific observations nowadays are made through instruments, and the instruments embody a theory by which we interpret the observed fuzzy lines and patches as moons of Jupiter, microbes, or Brownian motion. Thus even "observation terms are themselves for the most part theoretical terms whose credentials we have come to accept at face value" (Rozeboom, 1962, p. 339).

Consequently, there could be no pure and direct observation language.

Finally, the logical positivist movement was seen as more and more detached from the actual workings of science. Logical positivists concentrated on the syntax and semantics of science, not its pragmatics. In other words, in their quest to map out an ideal for science, the logical positivists had little to say about what scientists actually did or what theories actually

looked like. Other philosophers of science began to take a different tack by
addressing how science actually proceeds as hypotheses are proposed and
tested, theories are built and modified, research programs thrive or degenerate (see, e.g., Agassi, 1975; Feyerabend, 1962; Kuhn; 1962; Lakatos,
1970). These investigations were seen as far more relevant than the "quib-
bling over syntax" that occupied the attention of most logical positivists.

The Demise of Positivism (and Related -Isms) in Social Research

So positivism in its classic forms was largely dead by the middle of the
twentieth century. One might argue, though, that few social scientists attended the wake, for most scholars in social research fields such as psychology, sociology, and communication continued to both work and teach in
ways that embraced the goals of universal explanation, and the procedures
of operationalism, value-free inquiry, and the scientific method. It was not
until the 1970s that changes really started percolating in social research
fields, and scholars began to argue against the tenets of positivism (or functionalism, or naturalism, or empiricism, depending on your preferred nomenclature). One major impetus in these discussions was Kuhn's publication of *The Structure of Scientific Revolutions* (1962). Though Kuhn was
not writing about the history of the social scientists, nor addressing a social
science audience, his book had the effect of spurring social researchers into
a period of self-examination. In the late 1960s and throughout the 1970s,
increasing attention was paid to such questions as "Do we have a paradigm?," "What is it?," and "Should we reject it?" At a macroscopic level,
these questions led to "fragmentation" (Hassard, 1993) in fields that had
before walked lockstep in a positivist formation. For individuals, these
changes led to transformative journeys "from positivism to interpretivism
and beyond" (Heshusius & Ballard, 1996). In short, the times definitely
were a changin'.

   In the field of organizational communication, the clearest demarcation
for these changing times was the Alta Conference of 1981. As Taylor and
colleagues (2000) summarize, "During that summer a group of young communication scholars met at a mountain retreat just south of Salt Lake City
to consider where the field had been and where it should now be going."
This conference was the first gathering of organizational communication
scholars to collectively consider alternative approaches to functionalism
such as interpretive and critical theory and research. This is not to suggest
that scholars in organizational communication did not consider these approaches before this time, but this conference—and the book that resulted
from the conference (Putnam & Pacanowsky's [1983] edited volume, *Communication and Organizations: An Interpretive Approach*) was a water-
shed event that changed the thinking and behavior of many organizational
communication scholars.

As the Alta scholars gathered in the crisp mountain air, however, traditional research and theory—investigations that could be traced back to positivist philosophies—were still the dominant mode of inquiry in organizational communication. Given this hegemony, how were interpretivism and critical theory to gain a foothold? How could the case be made for alternative modes of theory and research? Perhaps the most influential argument for interpretivism that emerged from this conference and during this time period was Linda Putnam's (1983) introductory chapter to the Putnam and Pacanowsky volume. Indeed, Putnam's chapter, "An Interpretive Perspective: An Alternative to Functionalism," won the National Communication Association Woolbert Award as an article having a profound impact on subsequent scholarship in the communication discipline. I would also be willing to wager that very few graduate students in organizational communication get past their first topical course without reading and discussing this seminal work.

In her essay, Putnam (1983) puts forth an incredibly persuasive and compelling argument for an interpretive perspective in organizational communication theory and research. The picture she paints of interpretivism is rich, complex, and varied. Here are but a few examples. Interpretivists conceptualize collectivities as "symbolic processes that evolve through streams of ongoing behavior" (p. 35). Interpretivists believe that individuals "act and interpret their interactions with a sense of free will and choice" (p. 36), and they take a pluralistic view that avoids "catering to one viewpoint at the cost of the other" (p. 38). Furthermore, interpretivist theories "aim for in-depth understanding and explanation of a particular phenomenon" (p. 46). These hallmarks of interpretivism are certainly compelling. Indeed, it is hard to read Putnam's descriptions and *not* want to view organizational communication from an interpretive point of view.

But how is the "other side" of the fence depicted? Following Burrell and Morgan (1979), Putnam (1983) used the term "functionalism" to describe the contrast to interpretivism, but it is also likely that similar descriptions would be provided of positivists in organizational communication. After many readings of Putnam's presentation, I have come to conclude that functionalists in this chapter are portrayed—perhaps by rhetorical necessity—in a somewhat "stylized" manner. Here, again, are a few examples. Functionalists see collectivities as "static" and "immutable" (p. 34), assume that individuals "absorb and respond to externally controlled events rather than to their own self-interests" (p. 36), "endorse a pursuit of universal laws" (p. 40), see communication as a "tangible substance" (p. 39), and "cling to a unilaterial model of causality" (p. 41). A wide range of characterizations of interpretivism and functionalism from Putnam's chapter are presented in Table 3.2.

By presenting this view of functionalism, Putnam sets up a clear contrast with interpretivism. The contrast of interpretivists and functionalists

TABLE 3.2. Functionalists versus Interpretivists

Functionalists	Interpretivists
Treat social phenomena as concrete, materialistic entities—social facts	See reality as socially constructed through words, symbols, and behaviors
See collectivities as external to individuals with their properties	See collectivities as symbolic processes that emerge through streams of ongoing behaviors
Collectivities are static and immutable	Social structures are sets of complex relationships that originate in human interaction
Social reality exists "out there," external to the individual, and it takes form prior to any human activity	Reified structure is symbolic in representation of previous and potential relationships
Individuals are products of their environment who respond to external stimuli in mechanical ways	Individuals create their social environment
Humans are reactive participants who absorb and respond to externally controlled events rather than to their own self-interests	Humans are proactive creative agents who exercise free will in interaction
Assume a unitary view of organizations in which organizations are cooperative systems in pursuit of common interests and goals	Adopt a pluralistic perspective by treating the organization as an array of factionalized groups with diverse purposes and goals
Individuals are instruments of purposeful-rational action aimed at technological effectiveness and organizational efficiency	Individuals negotiate their goals, actions, and meanings to achieve a common direction, but they never abandon their different aims
Primary unit of analysis is the organizational entity; social, psychological, and economic characteristics are static properties	Primary unit of analysis centers on the values, goals, and interactions that create and sustain coalitions
Have a conservative orientation, frequently biased toward management, organizational efficiency, and the status quo	Build multiple treatments of organizational reality into their purview and paint a "composite" picture of organizational life
Communication is a tangible substance that flows upward, downward, and laterally within the container	Communication is meaning-centered by conceptualizing social reality as constructed through words, symbols, and actions
Endorse a pursuit of universal law, stable patterns, and value-free conclusions	Aim to understand social phenomena by extracting the unique dimensions of situations rather than by deducing generalizable laws
Cling to a unilateral model of causality	Consider complex and circular causality
Inquire from the outside	Inquire from the inside

Note. Data from Putnam (1983).

is not a value-neutral one, though. As Tompkins (1997) argues, "The functionalists were the bad guys and gals in black hats. The interpretivists wore the white" (p. 368). I believe this villification of functionalism was a necessary move for Putnam's argumentative focus at the time—and the ensuing years have proved that it was undoubtedly an effective move as well. When interpretivism was emerging as a valued approach to social research, it was important to set up clear contrasts with the status quo of positivist-inspirted approaches. Thus, for rhetorical purposes, a caricature of positivism is a useful prong in an argument *for* an interpretive approach to organizational communication. The picture Putnam paints of functionalism was also probably representative of the modus operandi of many (though clearly not all) organizational communication researchers during the 1960s and 1970s.

Unfortunately, the rhetorical power of Putnam's descriptions of functionalism and interpretivism has not dissipated as interpretive and critical approaches gained a foothold, then continued to gather strength in organizational communication. As Tompkins (1997, p. 370) summarizes, interpretivism became a "God-term" (Burke, 1950), and functionalism became a "Devil-term." Now, many years later, writers of organizational communication textbooks still rely on these stylized descriptions of paradigmatic camps in organizational communication (see, e.g., Pace & Faules, 1994, chap. 1) and we teach these distinctions in both undergraduate survey courses and graduate seminars. However, as Tompkins concludes, "The world is a bit more complex than that" (p. 370). Interpretivists do not always wear white, and functionalists (or post-positivists or empiricists) do not always wear black. It is not my intention here to soil the white garb of interpretivism. However, I would like to rescue from villification those organizational communication researchers who conduct research within a tradition that has its roots in positivist and scientific traditions. The metatheoretical commitments of these researchers—whom I will label "post-positivists"—are considered in the next section.

THE WAY WE ARE

If positivism, in its classical and logical forms, is largely rejected, what philosophical foundation should take its place as a framework for social research? As should be clear from the discussion above of the move from "functionalism" to "interpretivism" in organizational communication, a great many social researchers have argued that flaws in the positivist foundation require a radically different philosophy of science, one in which the realist ontology, objective epistemology, and value-free axiology of positivism are vehemently rejected and replaced with forms of inquiry that honor nominalism, subjectivism, and omnipresent values. The positions of these scholars form the interpretive and critical schools of organizational communication scholarship that are well represented in other chapters of this volume. However, there are many organizational communication scholars who believe that a rejection of positivism (in its "classical" and "logical" forms) does not require a rejection of realism, objectivity, and the scientific *goal* of value-free inquiry. However, these scholars *do* reject the notion of absolute truth, the unassailable foundation of observation, and the assumption of an always steady and upward accumulation of knowledge. In these rejections, scholars have forged a new philosophy of science that D. C. Phillips has called "post-positivism" (1987, 1990, 1992). The metatheoretical tenets of this position are discussed below in terms of ontological, epistemological, and axiological commitments.

Ontological Commitments

Scholars following debates on "paradigms" in organizational studies and social research are familiar with the ontological distinctions typically drawn among realists, nominalists, and social constructionists. To briefly (and simplistically) summarize, a *realist* stance (sometimes called an "objectivist" position) sees both the physical and the social world as consisting of structures that exist "out there" and that are independent of an individual's perception. That is, for a realist, an organizational hierarchy is a social "fact" that can be considered by social researchers. At the other end of the ontological spectrum is the *nominalist* stance (sometimes called a "relativist" or "subjectivist" position) that assumes "that the social world external to individual cognition is made up of nothing more than names, concepts and labels which are used to structure reality" (Burrell & Morgan, 1979, p. 4). A third—some would say intermediary—point on the ontological map is the *social constructionist* position (see, e.g., Berger & Luckmann, 1967) that has been highly influential in social research during the last several decades. According to this position, social reality is seen as an *intersubjective* construction that is created through communicative interaction. As Leeds-Hurwitz (1992, p. 133) states, "In this view, social reality is not a fact or set of facts existing prior to human activity . . . we create our social world through our words and other symbols, and through our behaviors."

Both the realist and the social constructionist positions make contributions to the ontology of the post-positivist. Researchers in the post-positivist tradition are largely realists in that they support "the view that entities exist independently of being perceived, or independently of our theories about them" (Phillips, 1987). However, this realism is tempered by the argument that humans cannot *fully* apprehend that reality and that the driving mechanisms in the social and physical world cannot be *fully* understood. As Smith (1990, p. 171) states, "Realism is essential . . . because it poses 'at least in principle, a standard by which all human societies and their beliefs can be judged: they can all have beliefs about the world which turn out to be mistaken' (Trigg, 1985, p. 22)."

Phillips argues, however, that a post-positivist ontology does not deny the notions inherent in approaches advocating a "social construction of reality" (Berger & Luckmann, 1967). Rather, Phillips draws the distinction between *beliefs* about the reality and the objective reality (1990, pp. 42–43). Making this distinction allows a post-positivist scholar to appreciate (and investigate) multiple "realities" that are constructed by social collectives through communicative interaction. That is, a post-positivist scholar could study the ways that beliefs about the imminent end of the world influence the behaviors of mountain survivalists, members of cults, and fundamental religious groups. However, the fact that a social group has arrived at certain beliefs about the world does not make those beliefs about the social or physical world necessarily true. As Phillips notes, "It is clear that Freudians believe in the reality of the id and superego and the rest, and they act as if these are realities; but their believing in these things does not make them real" (p. 43).

I would further argue that post-positivism is consistent with social constructionist views in two important ways. First, many post-positivists would argue that the *process* of social construction occurs in relatively patterned ways that are amenable to the type of social scientific investigation undertaken by post-positivists. Individuals have "free will" and "creativity," but they exercise that free will and express that creativity in ways that are often (though not always, certainly) patterned and predictable. In the field of mass communication, Barbara Wilson (1994) argues convincingly for this point regarding her own study of children's responses to the mass media:

> I believe that children's interpretations and responses are as richly individualistic as snowflakes. However, I also believe that there are common patterns that characterize a majority of young viewers and that those patterns are as predictable and explainable as the basic process by which all those unique snowflakes are formed from water. (p. 25)

Second, many post-positivists would argue that social constructions are regularly "reified" and treated as objective by actors in the social world. Thus, it is reasonable to study the impact of these "reified constructions" on our communicative lives. Tompkins (1997) has made this argument with regard to his organizational communication research with the National Aeronautics and Space Administration (NASA):

> The engineers, scientists, managers, bureaucrats, and other kinds of members did *not* believe in a socially constructed world. They believed the rockets they made did in fact go to the moon. Moreover, they believed that

NASA and the contractor firms who worked for them were real. They believed that these organizations could succeed or fail by objective criteria
and that their bosses could hire or fire, reward or penalize individiuals—actions with *real* consequences. (p. 369)

Thus, a social constructionist ontology is consistent with a post-positivist
position that emphasizes both the patterned nature of the social construction process and the regular and predictable effects that reified social constructions have on organizational members. Being a post-positivist does *not*
mean believing in a hard, immutable, and unchanging social world. Rather,
it entails believing in regularity and pattern in our interactions with others.
The ways in which these regularities and patterns are studied within the
post-positivist tradition are considered in the following section.

Epistemology and Axiology

Post-positivist assumptions about the grounds of social knowledge (i.e.,
epistemology) and the role of values in the production of social knowledge
(i.e., axiology) are largely based on the ojectivist tenets that have guided
positivist social research throughout this century. These assumptions—
worded in a strict objectivist terminology—include the interlinked notions
that (1) knowledge can best be gained through a search for regularities and
causal relationships among components of the social world; (2) regularities
and causal relationships can best be discovered if there is a complete separation between the investigator and the subject of the investigation; and (3)
this necessary separation between the knower and the known can be guaranteed through the use of the scientific method.

As they have done with ontological assumptions of realism, however,
most post-positivist scholars in social research today have tempered these
epistemological and axiological bases to what Guba (1990) has termed
"modified objectivist." Post-positivist theorists generally hold to the first
assumption listed above. That is, the search for knowledge remains cen-
tered on causal explanations for regularities observed in the physical and
social world. This is clearly consistent with the ontological position outlined above. It should be noted, though, that the regularities and causal relationships studied by post-positivist scholars are rarely simplistic and often
involve a multiplicity of factors and over-time relationships (see Miller,
2000).

Beyond this first assumption, however, post-positivists have largely rejected the second tenet above regarding the necessary distinction between
"knower" and "known." Instead, many post-positivists have concluded
that "the hope for a formal method, capable of being isolated from actual
human judgment about the content of science (that is, about the nature of
the world), and from human values seems to have evaporated" (Putnam,
1981, p. 192). Because this assumption of value-free inquiry is rejected,

post-positivists have similarly rejected blind obedience to the scientific method. Instead, objectivity is seen as a "regulatory ideal." In other words, a post-positivist will use methods that strive to be as unbiased as possible and will attempt to be aware of any values that might compromise neutrality. However, because the possible fallabilities of the scientific method are recognized, the post-positivist will also rely on the critical scrutiny of a community of scholars in order to safeguard objectivity and maximize the growth of social scientific knowledge. Thus, though there are no claims to absolute truth and value-*free* inquiry, there is the belief that progress can be made if researchers exercise care in their theorizing and research and are critical of theoretical assertions and empirical justifications. Thus, the position of post-positivists is far less dogmatic than that of their positivist predecessors. As Phillips (1990) summarizes:

> The ideal that is embraced seems to be this: Seekers after enlightenment in any field do the best that they can; they honestly seek evidence, they critically scrutinize it, they are (relatively) open to alternative viewpoints, they take criticism (fairly) seriously and try to profit from it, they play their hunches, they stick to their guns, but they also have a sense of when it is time to quit. It may be a dirty and hard and uncertain game, but with no fixed algorithms to determine progress, it is the only game in town. (pp. 38–39)

Of course, for most post-positivists working in organizational communication scholarship today, post-positivism is *not* the only game in town. Indeed, the rise of interpretive and critical approaches in organizational communication has been little short of meteoric (see, e.g., the review of Taylor et al., 2000). The question then becomes, Can the discipline of organizational communication move beyond the stage of caricature and claims-staking that marked the period when interpretivism and critical approaches were gaining a foothold? And, if we can move beyond these potentially destructive tendencies, where do we move to? How do we deal with a plurality of metatheoretical viewpoints in our discipline? In the metaphors of cultural theorists, will we develop into a discipline best characterized as a "melting pot" in which we join our metatheoretical commitments into one view of organizational communication theory and research, or should we be a "salad bowl" in which various approaches to scholarship coexist but maintain separate and distinct qualities? These issues will be considered in the final section of this essay.

SO WHERE DOES THIS LEAVE US?

To this point, I have argued that the hegemony of positivist approaches in social research during the middle portion of this century led proponents of interpretive and critical positions to present caricatures of researchers working in traditions with positivist roots. This straw-person image of positivism (and its progeny) could then be beaten down in order to enhance the contrast between paradigms, and to provide a stronger justification for interpretive and critical positions. These distorted views of what post-positivist researchers believe and do, however, are no longer useful as a rhetorical tool in sensitizing audiences to the value of critical and interpretive approaches. In organizational communication research, critical and interpretive approaches are clearly accepted as valid modes of scholarship in organizational communication. Thus, it is now important to move beyond these straw-person views and develop more accurate (if I dare use such a post-positivist term!) views of how we theorize and investigate organizational communication processes. I hope, in previous sections of this essay, that I have advanced that cause by more fully describing how post-positivists got to where they are today and what contemporary researchers in the post-positivist tradition hold as their basic ontological, epistemological, and axiological assumptions.

But does enhanced understanding of post-positivism (and, similarly, of interpretivism and critical theory) mean that we can move beyond the problem of paradigm incommensurability? To answer this question, it is instructive to first consider ways in which "incommensurability" has been considered in the literature.

Views of Incommensurability

One view of incommensurability presented in recent discussions of paradigms in organizational study is largely a philosophical one (see Lueken, 1991; Scherer, 1998; Scherer & Dowling, 1995). As Scherer (1998, p. 150) explains, a situation of incommensurability is found with relation to three conditions. These conditions were explicated in Steve Corman's Introduction to this volume, but they are worth reiterating here:

> First, there have to be at least two (radically) different systems of orientation. Second, these systems of orientation must be competing with each other concerning a way of acting or using language, e.g., the definition or solution of a concrete problem, so that coexistence of the different perspectives is not possible. Third, an accepted system of reference to objectively evaluate the competing perspectives must be lacking. Though a pluralism of perspectives is a necessary condition for incommensurability, as long as there are accepted standards available to reasonably decide between competing perspectives, we do not consider the perspectives incommensurable. . . . A situation of incommensurability occurs only when such standards are absent. (p. 6)

This view of incommensurability deals largely with the logical inconsistencies between various systems of orientation and with the inability of some "metasystem" to mediate among these fundamental differences in orientation. This approach can be illustrated with respect to organizational communication studies. Specifically, if the metatheoretical commitments of post-positivists, critical theorists, and interpretivists are seen as contradictory, *and* these three approaches to organizational communication are seen as "competing" for the same scholarly "turf," *and* there is no "higher" system that can be turned to in order to adjudicate among these foundational positions, *then* incommensurability would be said to exist among theoretical and research approaches in organizational communication.

In contrast, other views of incommensurability emphasize the concept of shared symbol sets and common vocabularies, rather than logical inconsistencies among systems of explanation. This symbolic approach to incommensurability leads to the conclusion that when paradigms are incommensurable, "meaningful communication" is impossible (Jackson & Carter, 1991) and that, like the allegory of the Tower of Babel, it is a "single, shared language that allows work to proceed and its absence halts all joint efforts" (Kaghan & Phillips, 1998, p. 192). This view of incommensurability draws on interpretations of Kuhn's (1962) work on paradigms, as well as Burrell and Morgan's (1979) interpretation of that work in their consideration of scholarly paradigms and sociological and organizational analysis. To apply this view to organizational communication scholars, incommensurability would exist if scholars in interpretive, post-positivist, and critical camps could not understand each other or often "talked past each other" in intellectual interaction.

These two views of incommensurability suggest different possible resolutions of the incommensurability "problem" in organizational communication. These different "solutions" to the incommensurability issue will be explored next.

Reducing Incommensurability 1: Talking to Each Other

I will begin with the second notion of incommensurability discussed above: the idea that incommensurability exists when proponents of various theoretical positions cannot talk to each other in a meaningful way. Solutions to incommensurability in this respect suggest that we need to, at a basic level, be able to "translate" from one paradigm to another, or at a more fundamental level, come to an enhanced understanding of the presuppositions and work and life experiences of those in another paradigm. In this view, reducing incommensurability does *not* mean that proponents of various paradigms typically work together on problems, or even agree with each other in any fundamental way. It does suggest, though, that there should be both motivation and effort to understand the life world of another and there should be the motivation to support the legitimacy of these various approaches. In the nomenclature of Bochner and Eisenberg (1985) that was further developed by O'Keefe (1993), it is not important to have a *coherent* discipline (i.e., one that agrees on assumptions, priorities, and methods), but it is critical to have a *cohesive* discipline (i.e., one that provides support for other members, regardless of their specific beliefs and practices).

Is it possible to resolve incommensurability in this way? I would argue that it clearly is. First, even Thomas Kuhn—who could reasonably be argued to be the "founder" of the incommensurability thesis in social research—found that incommensurability in this sense of shared understanding could be overcome. Kaghan and Phillips (1998) explain:

> Kuhn (1970) provides an illustration of this . . . when he discusses how he finally came to comprehend Aristotelian physics as a coherent system of ideas and could begin to *think* like an Aristotelian (and presumably speak and practice as an Aristotelian as well). Though the paradigm (i.e., theories, formal methods, tacit practices, and exemplary problems) that underlies Aristotelian physics is very different than the one that underlies modern physics, Kuhn managed—through reflection and communication with the writings of the Aristotelians—to come to some understanding of the Aristotelian approach. Though his understanding did not make him a proponent of the Aristotelian approach, he could recognize the relative merits and demerits of both the Aristotelian approach and the approach of modern physics. (p. 201)

Second, as experts in organizational communication, we *should* be particularly adept at dealing with issues of symbolic translation and understanding. This may just be an instance of learning to "practice what we preach" in adopting practices that will enhance the possibility of shared understanding within the organization that is our discipline. Recent work on organizational dialogue can provide some useful pointers (see, e.g., Anderson, Cissna, & Arnett, 1994; Eisenberg & Goodall, 1997; Isaacs, 1993). Dialogic approaches do not emphasize necessary *agreement* with another's position, but rather the attempt to understand another's frame or interpretation. For example, Isaacs (1993, p. 25) defines *dialogue* as "a sustained collective inquiry into the processes, assumptions, and certainties that compose everyday experience." Thus, dialogue requires examination of both our *own* assumptions and the assumptions of others, and the suspension of judgment during the dialogic process. As Hilmer (1997) summarizes:

> The purpose of dialogue is to learn how to think together, to surface fundamental assumptions and gain insight into why these assumptions arise, in order to become aware of how meaning is created collectively. The goal of dialogue is to learn to talk to each other. (pp. 9–10)

Reducing Incommensurability 2: A Bridging Perspective

The above considerations for reducing incommensurability deal with incommensurability in its second sense, or, to quote the warden in *Cool Hand*

Luke, with "a failure to communicate." But even if we deal with these communication problems through dialogue and enhanced understanding, this still does not mean that we have any level of agreement or can actually *work together* in a meaningful way. If we are to move beyond dialogue and understanding in the reduction of incommensurability, and to the notion of agreement and shared practices, we must consider the first approach to incommensurability discussed above and finding a metatheoretical perspective capable of embracing the assumptive bases and the practices of various approaches to organizational communication theory and research.

Though there have been objections in the literature (see, e.g., DeCock & Richards, 1995), I find myself drawn to and encouraged by the direction proposed by Dennis Gioia and his colleagues (Gioia & Pitre, 1990; Weaver & Gioia, 1994, 1995; see also Gioia, Donnellon, & Sims, 1989) in arguing for a multiparadigmatic approach to theory development. In their first piece on this topic, Gioia and Pitre (1990) largely accept the separation of paradigms of organizational analysis, but examine the borders or "transition zones" between various paradigms and suggest strategies for bridging these zones. Weaver and Gioia (1994, 1995) go further, arguing that it is not just possible to bridge paradigms through these transition zones, but that paradigms of organizational study are actually commensurable. In stating the case for paradigm commensurability, Weaver and Gioia (1994) posit that various paradigms of inquiry serve to "selectively bracket" social phenomenon. They maintain that structuration theory (Giddens, 1976, 1979, 1984) provides a means for understanding this selective bracketing and a point of connection between the assumptions of interpretivists and functionalists. Weaver and Gioia (1994) explain:

> Structuration provides a basis for seeing how organizational scholars can invoke different assumptions, pursue different goals, ask different research questions, and use different approaches, but nonetheless be engaged in inquiry with commonalities despite such diversities. . . . Structuration theory shows just how the selective of bracketing of social phenomenon can occur. (pp. 577–578)

Weaver and Gioia then go on to argue that structuration theory's central construction of the "dualism" can serve to break down oppositional dichotomies and illuminate "positions, processes or entities whose various aspects may be temporarily bracketed" (p. 578). For example, in proposing the "duality of structure," Giddens (1976) argues that social structures "are both constituted 'by' human agency, and yet at the same time are the very 'medium' of constitution" (p. 121). Thus, the structuration process, by considering both the *process* of social structure constitution and the ways these constituted structures then frame practices, provides a fertile ground for both post-positivist and interpretive theorists. Furthermore, Giddens's critical social goals provide one framework through which critical theorists can interrogate power, politics, and ideology as they play into the constitution of social structure.

This use of structuration theory as a "metatheoretical bridge" does not begin to take into account the richness nor the details of structuration theory as laid out in Giddens's many writings. Nor is it intended to. Rather, this use of structuration theory is intended merely as an orienting framework. That is, the recognition of the central concept of the action–structure duality can "offer a conceptual scheme that allows one to understand both how actors are at the same time the creators of social systems yet created by them" (Giddens, 1991, p. 204). This conceptual scheme, then, provides the "space" within which post-postivists, interpretivists, and critical theorists can work on important conceptual and research issues in organizational communication. This work will often take place "side by side" but could also occur collaboratively. The important point is that structuration theory provides a framework in which there is no priority given to one of these three theoretical approaches. This use of structuration theory as an orienting framework is similar to Robert Craig's (1999) recent proposal that we use the concept of "communication as constitutive" as a metatheoretical framework for communication theory. As Craig argues, a constitutive model of communication—similar to a structurational model of organizations—is a "metamodel that opens up a conceptual space in which many different models of communication can interact" (pp. 126–127).

Interestingly, scholars within the field of organizational communication are poised to take a leading role if structuration theory is used as a bridging metatheoretical framework among interpretive, critical, and post-positive paradigms. Organizational communication scholars have been vocal proponents of structuration theory for many years. For example, this framework has been used to enhance our understanding of the political nature of organizational cultures (Riley, 1983), for organizational communication structures (McPhee, 1985), group decision making (Poole, Seibold, & McPhee, 1986), and communication network participation (Corman & Scott, 1994). Thus, it seems reasonable to maintain the hope that, as a discipline, we can deal with the incommensurability problem both through dialogue and enhanced understand and through the use of metatheoretical frameworks that allow for productive work within several paradigmatic assumptive bases.

CONCLUSION

Common ground among post-positivist, critical, and interpretive paradigms is possible in the theorizing and research of organizational communication. But it is only possible when we clearly understand the "lay of the land"—the assumptive bases and the practices of post-positivist, interpretive, and critical theorists. There are probably few organizational communication researchers today who would feel at home as part of the Vienna Circle, and it is important that we acknowledge the tenets of *post*-positivism rather than vilify the tenets of *logical* positivism. Through the dialogic processes of perspective taking and mutual understanding, and through bridging metatheoretical frameworks such as structuration theory, productive collaboration is possible among organizational scholars from a variety of perspectives.

NOTES

1. The discussion of positivism in this section, as well as the discussion of the demise of positivism and descriptions of post-postivism in subsequent sections of this essay are based largely on chapter 3 of my book *Communication Theories* (Miller, 2000). It should be emphasized, however, that the term *positivism* is used to denote general trends in theorizing, and that a more detailed account could make distinctions among positivism, empiricism, functionalism, and the belief in the value of quantification.
2. As Feagin (1999) has recently pointed out with regard to the field of sociology, much of the dominance of quantitative research at major institutions and in major journals can be attributed to the institutional power of major funding agencies. However, Feagin argues convincingly that this quantitative bias in the major journals and institutions was not representative of the sociology field as a whole.

CHAPTER 4

Common Ground from the Critical Perspective
Overcoming Binary Oppositions

Dennis K. Mumby

I have rather ambivalent feelings about the underlying premise of this book. On the one hand, I have considerable sympathy with the notion that the development of a common ground among a community of scholars is necessary for the health of that community. Theory development and research flourish in a context where researchers share basic assumptions about what counts as appropriate knowledge claims. The idea of a "community" suggests commonality and a shared language that permits academics to communicate with one another in developing a robust body of research. In addition, I identify with Steve Corman's frustration at the divisiveness that frequently results from the clash of competing perspectives. As the CRTNET debate over "Sextext" (Corey & Nakayama, 1997) demonstrates, there is a fine line indeed between scholarly debate and name calling.

On the other hand, I do not feel totally sanguine about the merits of such common ground. Academically speaking, we live in a polyglot community where multiple languages and dialects articulate many different (and often incommensurable) knowledge claims. In the context of organizational communication studies, these multiple voices have in the last twenty years produced a diverse body of research that has greatly enriched our understanding of the complexities of organizational life. Ironically, the kind of common ground for which Steve Corman yearns was very much a feature of organizational communication research in the 1960s and 1970s—a period characterized by a kind of homogenizing tyranny with extremely narrow criteria for what counted as significant research. Given a choice between the "common ground" of the 1960s and 1970s, and the "incommensurability" of the 1980s and 1990s, I would have no hesitation in choosing the latter.

However, I do not wish to deny the importance of the case for common ground made by Steve in the Introduction, but rather I want to warn against the possibility of an "extorted reconciliation" (Adorno, qtd. in Jay, 1984, p. 14) that can easily accompany efforts to find a common voice with which to speak. In the tradition of critical theory, I do not want to simply accept uncritically the idea that "common ground" is de facto an unproblematic and positive state for organizational communication scholars to achieve. Too often such common ground arises from membership in a disciplinary "club" which, as Deetz (1992) has pointed out, can have the dual meaning of requiring adherence to membership rules and functioning as a big stick to coerce appropriate behavior. As such, the question of common ground is a political issue as much as it is an epistemological issue. Anyone who doubts this has only to read Blair, Brown, and Baxter's (1994) "Disciplining the Feminine" to see the lengths to which the arbiters of "good scholarship" will sometimes go to regulate club membership.

Thus, in this chapter I want to address "the politics of common ground." That is, from a critical perspective, I want to ask: How can we come to grips with the assumptions and interests that underlie issues of consensus and incommensurability? How can we move beyond the current—apparently debilitating—state of affairs in our field? To this end, in the first section of this chapter I briefly discuss the critical perspective and suggest how it can help us to address the issue of common ground. In the second section, I adopt a deconstructive mode and examine some of the entailments of the very idea of "common ground." In the final section, I suggest what common ground from a critical perspective might look like.

DOING THEORY AND RESEARCH FROM A CRITICAL PERSPECTIVE

The critical perspective has developed enough of a tradition in the field of organizational communication that it is no longer necessary to explicate its principal elements in great detail. Indeed, many excellent overviews of the critical perspective are now available (see, e.g., Alvesson & Deetz, 1996; Alvesson & Willmott, 1992; Clegg, 1989; Deetz & Kersten, 1983). In addition, the fact that most textbooks devote at least a chapter to critical research suggests that it has become an accepted part of the organizational communication canon (see, e.g., Daniels, Spiker, & Papa, 1998; Eisenberg & Goodall, 1997; Miller, 1999). As such, it is difficult for critical scholars to continue to argue that they occupy a marginal position in the field. While a position of academic marginality gives one a certain amount of li-

cense to critique the "dominant paradigm," the critical perspective now occupies a position that requires a more nuanced and textured response to the
current state of the field.

What issues, then, does the critical perspective address? Clearly, any
critical orientation must address the dynamics of power and politics. For
critical researchers, this focus operates on two levels. First, there is a concern with power as it operates in the context of social relations amongst individuals and groups. Since its inception with the work of Marx (1967) and
later with the Frankfurt School (Horkheimer, 1982; Horkheimer &
Adorno, 1972) and Marxist cultural studies (Morley & Chen, 1996), critical researchers have attempted to explain the social and communicative
processes through which conditions of hegemony arise (Gramsci, 1971). In
other words, how does a particular social group or class come to hold sway
over other groups or classes? While Marx explained this relationship primarily in coercive terms with the emphasis on capitalism as an intrinsically
exploitative political and economic system, subsequent generations of critical scholars have attempted to explain the exercise of power as a dynamic
process of consent (Althusser, 1971; Gramsci, 1971).

In both media studies (see, e.g., Dow, 1990; Fiske, 1986) and organizational communication studies (see, e.g., Collinson, 1992; Deetz, 1992;
Mumby, 1988, 1989), researchers have attempted to explicate the dynamic,
discursive processes through which structures of meaning and identity
"spontaneously" arise. Particularly in the last twenty years, critical researchers have come to recognize that "power" is a multifaceted phenomenon that cannot be explained in terms of simple, causal relations (Mumby,
2000). Indeed, in organizational communication studies, there has been a
widening of research focus, with increasing emphasis on power as a dialectical process of domination and resistance. In this sense, there has been an
important shift away from seeing the social actor as a "cultural dupe" who
is at the mercy of ideological processes, and toward a perspective that takes
seriously the social actor as a complex, often contradictory, but always active participant in the construction of dialectics of control (Giddens, 1979).
Thus, a number of empirical studies have examined the various ways in
which social actors discursively construct organizational identities that are
simultaneously constraining and enabling, debilitating and empowering
(Burawoy, 1979; Collinson, 1988; Trethewey, 1997; Willis, 1977).

In sum, the first level at which critical theorists and researchers conceptualize power is via a close examination of the everyday communicative
process through which meaning construction and human identity formation occur. In this sense, the critical perspective is centrally concerned with
the politics of everyday life. That is, it engages in analyses of the ways in
which the shaping of human interests, values, and possibilities occurs at the
most mundane of levels (for organizational communication scholars, the
interest lies in understanding the mundane features of organizational life).

In addition, a focus on the microlevel features of communicative behavior is complemented by linking such analyses to larger, macrolevel social, political, and economic processes. For example, David Collinson's (1988, 1992) critical analysis of shopfloor humor is *both* an examination of the organizational subculture of a group of semiskilled workers *and* an analysis of the complex relations among class, gender, patriarchy, and capitalism. By linking the micro- and macrolevels of analysis, Collinson is able to show (1) the fundamentally political dimensions of everyday interaction, and (2) the importance of understanding organizations not as self-contained entities, but as both medium and outcome of larger economic and political processes.

The second, and complementary, level at which critical scholars examine power might be described as a focus on the "politics of epistemology." At this level, critical scholars are concerned with the values and interests that underlie knowledge claims. A central tenet here is that no claim to knowledge is value-free, but rather rests upon a set of (frequently hidden, sometimes even to the researcher) assumptions about how the world works and the appropriate methods for uncovering this process. The early Frankfurt School theorists such as Adorno and Horkheimer were critical of both "scientistic," reductionist Marxism, and traditional, bourgeois science. The former, they argued, reduced society to mechanistic, causal forces that incorrectly predicted the inevitability of proletarian revolution, while the latter they saw as the handmaiden of capitalist forces, perpetuating bourgeois ideology despite its claims to value neutrality.

Many years later Jürgen Habermas (1971, 1984) provided a more subtle analysis of the politics of epistemology by showing how all knowledge claims are rooted in three "quasi-transcendental" human interests: (1) the *technical* interest, embodying humans' desire to predict and control the natural world; (2) the *practical* interest, representing the human orientation toward understanding and establishing community through social interaction; and (3) the *emancipatory* interest, reflecting the human proclivity for self-reflection leading to autonomy and empowerment. These three "knowledge-constituting" interests are embodied in the natural and social sciences, hermeneutics, and critical theory, respectively. Habermas claims that while in an ideal society all three forms of knowledge are represented equally, the technical interest has come to dominate, subsuming the other interests under its worldview.

Placed in the context of organizational communication studies, Habermas's theory of interests gives us some insight into the ways in which the politics of epistemology has traditionally played itself out in our field. For the most part, the dominance of the technical interest has meant that knowledge claims—regardless of their content or area of research—are framed largely in terms of issues of efficiency, control, and predictability, and thus have a strong managerial bias. Indeed, even alternative perspectives are not immune from this framing process. For example, in the early

1980s, scholarship on organizational culture seemed to represent a major paradigmatic shift in terms of the kinds of knowledge claims researchers could make about organizations (representing, in Habermas's terms, the reassertion of the practical interest). However, it did not take long for this line of research to take a distinctly managerial turn, such that the construct of "culture" was transformed into a tool for increasing organizational effectiveness and productivity. Articles with titles such as "Implications of Corporate Culture: A Manager's Guide to Action" (Sathe, 1983) and "The Culture Audit: A Tool for Understanding Organizations" (Wilkins, 1983) suggest the general tenor of this appropriation process.

Such was the rapidity of this reframing of the notion of culture that by 1987, Smircich and Calás (1987) were moved to announce that the concept of "organizational culture" was "dominant but dead." In other words, although organizational culture research had proliferated greatly, its cooptation as a managerial, functional perspective meant that it had lost its critical edge, and hence its ability to enable us to "think otherwise" about organizational life. I would suggest that Smircich and Calás rather overstate the demise of any critical edge to the organizational culture literature, but their point is an important one. There is a rather salutary lesson to be learned about the power of the dominant, technical interest to ideologically define the limits and terms of what it means to "know something." To borrow Deetz's (1992) term, the dominant ideology of "managerialism" powerfully shapes definitions of what is, what is good, and what is possible, both in everyday organizational life and in the realm of theory and research (Therborn, 1980).

Taken together, these two complementary conceptions of power and politics describe the critical perspective's principal focus. That is, its central concern lies with understanding, explicating, and critiquing the various ways in which political and ideological limits are placed on social actors' abilities to fully realize their identities as active participants in meaningful dialogue communities (including organizations). Such limits exist at the levels of both everyday practice and epistemology. On the one hand, how are constraints placed on people's ability to engage in meaningful dialogue and participatory processes? On the other hand, how does the dominance of the technical interest function to artificially limit our understanding of the world? The critical perspective attempts to unpack the processes by which both forms of power operate.

As a political construct embodying particular interests, the notion of "common ground" represents a challenge to the critical perspective in that it embodies both possibilities and limitations. On the one hand, it represents the possibility for dialogue and the overcoming of seemingly impervious barriers between different perspectives. In this sense, it suggests a means by which to overcome the problem of incommensurability. On the other hand, it suggests the danger of the subsumption of diverse perspectives beneath a single, overarching, and possibly totalizing worldview. In this latter sense, it may represent a false consensus that limits possibilities for understanding organizational phenomena. In the next section I deconstruct the very notion of "common ground," exploring both its limitations and its possibilities.

DECONSTRUCTING "COMMON GROUND": OVERCOMING BINARY THINKING AND REDUCTIONISM

In his Introduction, Steve Corman refers to the debate between Jeffrey Pfeffer and John Van Maanen (Pfeffer, 1993, 1995; Van Maanen, 1995a, 1995b) as an example of the increasing stridency caused by the "paradigm wars." While I suspect that the tone of the debate is just as much a consequence of the rhetorical style of the two protagonists—for Van Maanen style *is* theory—it also speaks to the larger issues involved in the common ground/incommensurability problematic.

Jeffrey Pfeffer (1993) argues that in the field of organization studies paradigm consensus is necessary for the systematic advancement of knowledge. He equates paradigmatic consensus with technological certainty, in which there is "a wide agreement on the connections between actions and their consequences [and that] certain methods, certain sequences and programs of study, and certain research questions will advance training and knowledge in the given field" (p. 600). Pfeffer states further:

> A substantial amount of the variation in the level of paradigm development is a consequence of the social structure, culture, and power relations that characterize the discipline. . . . [T]here are forces at work that tend toward stability of whatever system is in place. A field in which control is concentrated in the hands of a comparatively small elite is one in which power is much more institutionalized and control by the dominant paradigm is quite likely to be perpetuated. By contrast, an area of inquiry characterized by diffuse perspectives, none of which has the power to institutionalize its dominance, is one in which consensus is likely to remain elusive and the dispersion in resources, rewards, and activity will be great. (p. 615)

In his response to Pfeffer, Van Maanen (1995b) argues that the former wants to engage in a "Stalinist purge of our low-consensus field . . . whereby we might invest authority in a few, well-published elites within our ranks who would be willing if not eager to institutionalize some topical and methodological strictures to guide our work. A high-consensus paradigm—or better yet, a Pfefferdigm—could thus be imposed" (p. 133). Van Maanen suggests that his own work positions him as a weed in Pfeffer's carefully pruned and manicured academic garden. In typical fashion, Van

Maanen offers the following rejoinder to Pfeffer's call for paradigm consensus:

> But whether I am a tulip, wildflower or weed, I want to suggest here that this sour view of our field is—to be gentle—insufferably smug; pious and orthodox; philosophically indefensible; extraordinarily naive as to how science works; theoretically foolish, vain and autocratic; and—still being gentle—reflective of a most out-of-date and discredited father-knows-best version of knowledge, rhetoric and the role theory plays in the life of any intellectual community. (p. 133)

For Van Maanen, theories are worthwhile not because they mirror reality, but because they generate it. In this sense, "Theory is a matter of words, not worlds; of maps, not territories; of representations, not realities" (1995b, p. 134). From this perspective, our writing as scholars is a rhetorical performance with a persuasive aim.

As I mentioned above, it is clear from this exchange that the question of singular versus multiple disciplinary voices is just as much a political issue as it is a knowledge issue. Indeed, when one reads Pfeffer's (1993) argument he appears less concerned about the quality of the knowledge claims made by management researchers than he does about the field of management developing political, cultural, and economic capital in relation to other fields (he identifies economics as a field that, by attaining paradigm consensus, has moved from marginal to central academic status). Similarly, Van Maanen's argument for greater pluralism is an attempt to destabilize Pfeffer's efforts to articulate and institutionalize a particular epistemological position that would, by definition, marginalize Van Maanen.[1]

For our purposes, the question is how we can steer a path between the Scylla of Pfeffer's advocacy of a narrow institutionalized orthodoxy, and the Charybdis of Van Maanen's self-consciously iconoclastic, "style is all there is" position. Steve Corman is right to point out that much of the stridency of this debate and others like it is predicated on a dualistic form of thinking that operates according to an absolutist totalizing way of thinking. Such a binary "either/or" way of characterizing the field of organizational communication obscures its many nuances and also undermines the possibility for engaging in genuine dialogue among different perspectives.

Indeed, one could argue that the very idea of building "common ground" suggests a default condition of opposition and difference. That is, the argument goes that as a field (not just organizational communication, but the field as a whole) we seem to have reached a particularly agonistic point in our development where we have a Babel of voices, none of which seem to be doing a particularly good job of establishing dialogue and making connections with each other. Following from this, this Babel is seen as problematic. Good research can only be conducted and fields can only be strengthened if we operate from a shared set of assumptions about research and theory development.

However, too often in our field, this so-called multivocality is reduced to a simple binary opposition. This opposition takes various forms: subjectivism versus objectivism (Burrell & Morgan, 1979); social constructionism versus positivism (Stewart, 1991); interpretivism versus functionalism (Putnam, 1983), modernism versus postmodernism (Habermas, 1981), and so forth. But in order to arrive at this binary opposition, much oversimplifying and caricaturing of the respective positions has to take place. In her chapter, Kathy Miller points out very ably how the more rigid, dogmatic forms of logical positivism have come to stand as a straw person for all theoretical positions that fall under the rubric of "post-positivism" and that believe in some form of material reality.

The reverse also happens. Even though interpretivism, critical theory, postmodernism, and poststructuralism are distinct theoretical projects with varying—sometimes overlapping, sometimes oppositional—intellectual histories, they are frequently collapsed together (by both supporters and critics alike) as representative of a generic social constructionist position that sees reality as completely relativist and existing only in the heads of individuals. For example, in an article entitled "Poststructuralism and Language: Non-Sense," Don Ellis (1991) argues that "little could be more contrary to a theory of communication than principles that emerge from post-structuralism and the critical theory that it spawns." He goes on to argue that "post-structuralists very much want to cling to the idea that reality exists in the human mind and nowhere else" (p. 219). Two critiques can be leveled against Ellis here. First, his conflation of poststructuralism and critical theory represents a confounding of two epistemological projects that have separate philosophical trajectories. Poststructuralism both builds on and critiques the work of Saussure, and is partly a reaction to disillusionment with Marxism, particularly in the wake of the failed May 1968 "revolution" in France.[2] In this sense, poststructuralism is anti-Enlightenment and anti-modernist. Critical theory, on the other hand, has strong Kantian underpinnings with its focus on self-reflection and enlightenment, and of course represents a reworking and continuation of the project of Marxism. Second, given their emphasis on the material qualities of discourse and its pivotal role in the construction of human identity, most poststructuralists would be extremely surprised to learn that they are accused of the heresy of locating reality exclusively in the human mind!

Much of the apparent lack of common ground, then, seems to arise out of attempts by advocates of a particular position to marginalize "opposing" perspectives through caricature. The favored rhetorical strategy is to set up a simple binary opposition with one's own perspective as the privileged, sophisticated and, of course, reasonable position, and then to present a one-dimensional view of the "opposite" perspective, showing how adherence to this position will ultimately lead to the demise of one's field of study. Indeed, we seem to have reached a point where the extreme positions in this binary opposition are represented by, on the one hand, a "space cadet idealism" (there is no reality other than that we create in our heads), and, on the other hand, "dumb-as-a-post positivism" (if you can't count it, it isn't real) (Robbins, qtd. in Slack & Semati, 1997, p. 208). But oppositions are appealing and, as Derridean deconstruction suggests, language is built on binary opposites, in which the meaning of the privileged present term is dependent on an absent marginalized other term. Even though we might critique these simple binary oppositions and argue that, of course, we need to think about theory and knowledge production in a more complex and nuanced fashion, such binaries become hegemonic in insidious ways.

For example, in her chapter, Kathy Miller refers to Linda Putnam's (1983) important article entitled "Interpretivism: An Alternative to Functionalism," and rightly lauds it for its influence on the emergence of the interpretive approach to organizational communication. As Kathy notes, though, Putnam treats functionalism in a rather stylized manner in the process of making her case for interpretivism. What Kathy fails to mention, however, is that the assumptive framework in Linda's article is appropriated wholesale and unquestioningly from Burrell and Morgan's (1979) widely read book, *Sociological Paradigms and Organizational Analysis*. Such has been the widespread acceptance of Burrell and Morgan's metatheoretical framework that Deetz (1996) is moved to argue that although "many grids had appeared before in sociology and after in organization studies, . . . none have gained the almost hegemonic capacity to define the alternatives in organizational analysis" (p. 191).

However, when we look at Burrell and Morgan's (1979) articulation of these alternatives, what do we find? Burrell and Morgan's power to "fix" and reify our assumptions about theory development revolves around two binary oppositions: a regulation/radical change dichotomy, and—more significantly—a philosophical dualism between subjectivity and objectivity. Burrell and Morgan argue further that the four paradigms that result from these two dimensions are mutually exclusive and represent fundamentally different ways of seeing. So much for developing common ground.

For the purposes of this discussion let me ignore the regulation–radical change dimension and focus briefly on the subjective–objective dimension. I think it is more significant for the whole question of how we articulate a common ground among perspectives, and why we seem to have so much trouble doing that. Furthermore, I think it is a particularly significant issue for us as organizational *communication* scholars. That is, because Burrell and Morgan come out of a sociological tradition they completely ignore scholarship that is produced in our field. Given this fact, it seems curious that their framework has achieved the level of acceptance that it has. One could even make the case that it is precisely the definitional power of their framework—particularly their interpretivism–functionalism opposition—that has contributed greatly to the divisiveness we are now experiencing as a field.[3]

As Deetz (1996) points out, at issue is not whether we can develop common ground between so-called subjective and objective perspectives; rather, the problem is the very perpetuation of the subject–object dichotomy itself. In the wake of the linguistic turn, this dichotomy can be viewed as a rhetorical construction rather than as an accurate representation of the status of knowledge claims. In a fundamental sense, Burrell and Morgan's (1979) hegemonic framework is itself subject to the hegemony of dominant conceptions of knowledge: a conception in which the privileged term in the subject–object dichotomy (objectivity) positions its opposite (subjectivity) as "other," feminized, marginalized, and second class. Reversing the valence does not solve the problem. Privileging subjectivity over objectivity does not fundamentally change the way we conceptualize theory and research, nor does it move us any closer to developing common ground.

So how do we do this? First, following the linguistic turn, we have to abandon the binary, Cartesian, dualist logic of subjective and objective forms of knowledge, and recognize instead that all forms of knowledge are intersubjectively generated via a set of shared understandings of different research communities. In this sense, there is neither an objective world waiting to be discovered, nor ideal worlds that exist solely in people's heads.

Deetz (1996) suggests an abandonment of talk about separate and incommensurable paradigms within organization studies, and argues instead for a characterization of our field as consisting of different discourses that are internally inconsistent, overlapping, and blurred at the edges. Thus, rather than talking about subjective versus objective approaches to organizations, Deetz argues that we should see theory development as being either local and emergent from specific research contexts, or as characterized by a set of a priori concepts that are brought to the research situation. In addition, knowledge discourses can be characterized as either existing in a consensual harmonious relationship with the dominant discourse, or in a relationship of difference and dissensus. In Deetz's model, this means that, for example, both the "normative" or functionalist discourse and the critical discourse are characterized as elite/a priori because of their application of already existing concepts to human behavior. Similarly, both the interpretive and the dialogic (postmodern) discourses are described as local/emergent because of their rejection of universal knowledge claims.

The shift from speaking in terms of mutually exclusive "paradigms" to arguing for overlapping "discourses" potentially helps us to reframe our relationship to each other as members of a scholarly community. Rather than viewing ourselves as practicing a form of epistemological apartheid (and of course seeing our own paradigm as the one that is both the most reasonable and the most persecuted), we can instead see ourselves as engaged in complementary ways of understanding the world. From this perspective, it is permissible to move between discourses, drawing on the various intellectual traditions that comprise these discourses. For example, in my own work I have engaged in theorizing that draws on interpretive, critical, and postmodern writings. While such a combination may represent intellectual heresy to some, it strikes me as perfectly appropriate given that these perspectives all share an epistemology that—with some variation—is social constructionist in orientation, giving discourse a constitutive role in the construction of both the material world and knowledge claims about that world.

In fact, as communication scholars, it seems to me that the road to a common ground lies with a more explicit recognition of our shared focus: the study of human communicative behavior. While this may appear to be something of a truism, I have always been surprised by the degree to which the *act* of communication (as opposed to the antecedents or derivatives of this act) is ignored as an object of study by our field. This is partly a product of our hybrid, perhaps parasitic, status in the academy. Because we lack clear identity and recognition as a field, we tend to draw heavily on definitions and explanatory constructs of human behavior that have been generated by other fields such as sociology and psychology. As such, we have problems developing common ground when we overlook the phenomenon that binds us together, and instead allow other fields to dictate our self-definition.

How, then, can we cultivate this shared focus while at the same time overcoming the kind of binary oppositions that I mention above? In my own work (Mumby, 1997a), I have argued that current research in both communication studies generally and organizational communication more specifically can be characterized by four distinct but related discourses. Rather than framing them in a series of oppositional relationships, I situate the four discourses on a continuum, and see them as representing increasingly transgressive positions toward any simple correspondence theory of the relationship between communication and the external world. The four discourses are therefore presented not as mutually exclusive and hermetically sealed, but as having blurred boundaries that bleed over into one another. If Geertz (1983) can speak of "blurred genres," it seems equally appropriate to think in terms of "blurred discourses of knowledge."

The first three of the discourses represent different iterations of modernist thought, while the fourth discourse is postmodern in its orientation. The four discourses are briefly reviewed here.

A DISCOURSE OF REPRESENTATION

This discourse is an inheritor of the Cartesian dualist tradition, treating language and communication as neutral modes of representing already coherent ideas about the world. In this sense, the relationship between communication and the world is seen as relatively unproblematic and transparent. In terms of the politics of epistemology, language is seen as value-neutral, and hence the role of the researcher is one of making neutral, detached observation statements about an objectively existing world. As Kathy Miller points out in her essay, however, the extreme positivist version of this position has largely been rejected by social scientists, who now embrace a more nuanced "post-positivist" perspective. However, methodologically speaking, most social scientists still appear to implicitly accept the notion that rigorous truth claims can only be made through the careful bifurcation of observer and observed, knower and known. As such, one of the basic principles of Cartesian dualist thought—the radical bifurcation of subject and object—is preserved.

A DISCOURSE OF UNDERSTANDING

This discourse originated with the German idealist tradition and the Kantian notion that the mind is an active contributor to the construction of knowledge about the world. In the context of current approaches to organizational communication studies, this discourse underpins all of the research that comes out of the interpretive perspective, taking seriously the idea that communication is not simply a conduit for ideas about the world, but actually constitutes that world. Thus, the discourse of understanding is premised on a dialogic, social constructionist approach to society. Such a discourse undermines any representational correspondence model of communication in that it makes problematic the bifurcation of subject and object, knower and known. Just as social actors are conceived as collectively constructing their worlds through discourse, so researchers are seen as actively engaging with the people that they study in producing truth claims about the world. Politically speaking, it is impossible for researchers coming out of this tradition to claim a neutral position regarding the knowledge that they produce, given that they are not simply conduits of those knowledge claims.

A DISCOURSE OF SUSPICION

The third discourse invokes an even more radical challenge to any representational model of knowledge and communication. Devotees of this discourse politicize the social constructionist perspective by arguing that ostensibly consensual processes of collective meaning formation obscure deep structure conflicts and contradictions that systematically limit the possibilities for genuine dialogue and community among social actors. Thus, the politics of everyday life and of representational practices are made explicit in this discourse. Although it falls under the rubric of modernism, the discourse of suspicion is also more skeptical about the Enlightenment project as a force of emancipation and freedom. Rather than accepting at face value the idea of the progressive development of a freer and more rational society, theorists in this discourse question the preeminence of rationalization processes in society and the distortion of human identity that results (see the discussion of Habermas above). The critical theorists of this discourse therefore argue that the modernist project can only be furthered by uncovering the deep structure interests that lead to the privileging of some discourses over others (in both the everyday and the academic sense). Recognizing the multiple human interests that lead to multiple forms of knowledge claims lays the groundwork for a more open and democratic society.

A DISCOURSE OF VULNERABILITY

The final discourse embodies some of the more recent developments in postmodern thought, and refers to the way in which the postmodern intellectual has given up the "authority game" as a uniquely positioned arbiter of knowledge claims (Said, 1994). Thus, the traditional understanding of the sovereign knowing subject as the wellspring of knowledge is "decentered" and displaced. Where even Habermas's critical project still places the reasoning rational subject at the center of his theory (albeit in a transformed way through a linguistic model of rationality), postmodern discourse deconstructs the idea of a coherent subject. Where the modernist subject retains a certain autonomy and coherence, the postmodern subject is portrayed as constructed and disciplined through various discursive practices and knowledge structures (see, e.g., Foucault, 1975, 1979, 1980a).

BEYOND BINARY OPPOSITIONS

In the context of attempts to create common ground among scholars, the point of this characterization of our field is twofold. First, it moves beyond any simple attempt to think about our field in binary terms. While not glossing over significant differences between perspectives, it nevertheless highlights their interconnections. For example, the first three discourses are conceptualized as differing positions within the larger metanarrative of modernism, and thus all three share a belief in the emancipatory possibilities of knowledge within the Enlightenment project. Similarly, while the fourth discourse (characterized as postmodern in orientation) rejects the tenets of the modernist project, it shares with the second and third discourses a view of communication as constitutive of human identities and systems of meaning.

Second, from a critical perspective this taxonomy helps to make problematic any straightforward conception of the relationships among communication, the social world, and knowledge claims about that world. All knowledge claims are political in the sense that they come out of a particular set of interests that make certain assumptions about what knowledge is and embody certain values about the workings of society. All acts of representation are political acts in their articulation of a worldview that engages us in a particular manner and asks us to make sense of the world in a certain way.

Looking at the world from a critical perspective, are there specific issues or points of focus that provide possibilities for the kind of common ground that is the impetus for this book? In the next section I suggest four themes, or "problematics," around which the field of organizational communication can generate some consensus.

DEVELOPING COMMON GROUND

As a representative of the critical perspective, my concern is that as scholars we generate a set of research issues that facilitate common ground without sacrificing the kinds of difference and multivocality that make our field so rich and diverse. As I indicated in my introduction, I am not interested in returning to the atheoretic, narrowly method-driven research of the 1960s and 1970s. It also seems that any contribution I can make to common ground among us must—given my orientation—thematize power issues.

As such, I see three initial premises upon which we can begin to build common ground as a field of study. First, we are uniquely placed to study *human communication processes* of organizing. While other fields like management may pay lip service to the importance of studying organizations as complex communicative processes, scholars in such fields often lack the conceptual tools to take this idea seriously. Second, and relatedly, we have to take *ourselves* seriously and build a body of work that is qualitatively distinct from other fields that study organizational phenomena. We are not management or sociology, and we should not allow those fields to define the parameters of what we do.[4] Third, and finally, we should develop research agendas across perspectives that explore organizations as political structures that embody diverse interests and values. In other words, the critical perspective can help us to move beyond relatively one-dimensional views of organizations as homogeneous entities with coherent and consensual agendas, goals, and value systems.

Based upon these initial premises, and drawing on the earlier work of Mumby and Stohl (1996), I present four central "problematics" that can help move our field toward common ground. While these problematics get their impetus from a critical orientation, I argue that they are by no means unique to this perspective and can be addressed from multiple epistemological points of view.

The Problematic of Voice

Given their politicization of organizational communication processes, "voice" becomes a central issue in the work of critical researchers. In this context, voice refers to both the voices with which researchers speak (and implicitly to the audiences they address), and to the different voices of various organizational interest groups that speak through our research. In our field we speak differently and address different audiences than scholars in fields like management, where a relatively monolithic managerial voice predominates. Our field is increasingly characterized by multiple voices that challenge dominant ways of seeing and thinking about organizations, and which breach conventional rules about who can legitimately construct organizational knowledge.

For example, Allen (1996) writes from a black feminist perspective suggesting how, as an African American female academic, she is inscribed very differently into organizational structures and processes than her white male counterparts. Interestingly, her essay speaks with the dual voice of one who is organizationally "other" and of one who is not comfortable with traditional managerial models of organizational socialization processes. Allen's critique suggests the need for organizations to change to meet the needs and expectations of members, rather than organizations working to adapt members unquestioningly to the formers' goals and expectations. Working from a very different epistemological viewpoint, Lamude, Daniels, and White (1987) provide compliance-gaining research with a different voice by examining workers' strategies in getting managers to conform to their wishes. While these two lines of research differ in many ways, their commonality arises out of their expansion of the range of organizational voices heard. In both cases, the usual "targets" of managerial theory and practice are given space to articulate their own organizational interests.

In broad terms, the issue of voice boils down to the following questions: How can we as organizational communication scholars provide insight into the practices of traditionally marginalized groups or forms of organizing? How can we show from a communication perspective that what appears natural and normal about organizational practices is actually socially constructed and obscures other organizational possibilities? When George Cheney (1995, 1999) studies the Mondragón system of worker cooperatives, for example, he is addressing precisely these questions.

Ultimately, the issue of voice is integrally bound up with the relations among communication, ethics, and democracy. As organizational communication scholars, we can all basically agree that communication is not a neutral process of information transmission, but is rather constitutive of organizing and has political consequences that both enable and constrain the possibilities for collective behavior. The question of who gets to speak about and for organizations is clearly an ethical issue once we move beyond a purely instrumental view of organizational life. If we conceive of organizations as playing a significant role in the construction of personal and group identities and in perceptions of the wider society, then issues such as whistleblowing, participation in decision making, and workplace harassment cannot be framed simply in managerially defined economic terms.

The Problematic of Rationality

A second way in which we can generate common ground is through a greater recognition of our plural understandings of rationality. In particular, by making problematic any singular notion of rationality, we productively undermine a particularly dominant organizational construct—that of effectiveness. Not only does organizational communication scholarship expand and challenge notions of whose interests should provide measures of effectiveness, but it ideally renders problematic the very ground on which effectiveness is based. In short, organizational communication studies characterized by common ground should exist at the intersection of a production tension among technical, practical, and emancipatory interests (see discussion above). Such a tension provides richer understandings of "effectiveness" than those found in fields dominated by a managerial voice.

For example, greater participation in organizational decision making may not be effective in narrow technical, managerial terms (due to increased deliberative time, more complex decision structures, and increased levels of conflict). However, when one expands definitions of organizational effectiveness to include criteria such as personal growth, increased community identity, more robust conceptions of organizational democracy, and so forth, one broadens the interests upon which organizational rationality is founded. In short, one of the ways in which organizational communication scholars can build common ground is through challenging the exclusively technical rationality of managerialism and focusing instead on how practical and emancipatory forms of rationality expand our understanding of organizational life.

The Problematic of Organization

Probably the clearest way in which organizational communication researchers can establish common ground is through their making problematic the very notion of "organization." This problematic is closely tied to attempts in our field to rearticulate traditional conceptions of the communication–organization relationship (Smith, 1993). Some exceptions not-

withstanding, the dominant conception of this relationship among management scholars is that communication involves the linear transmission of
information along relatively stable hierarchical channels. As Axley (1984)
has pointed out, this concept of communication operates according to a
"conduit" metaphor, the dominance of which in management theory and
practice leads to certain dangerous assumptions about the nature of "communication in organizations." For example, it promotes the idea that communication is an unproblematic transference process in which the message
sent equals the message received. Such an assumption fosters a common-
sense view among organization members (including managers) that communication is an uncomplicated process that does not have to be worked
at, and that miscommunication is an exceptional occurrence.

The focus of organizational communication scholars on the relationship between communication and organization enables us to problematize
and hence "make strange" both notions (Smith, 1992; Taylor, Cooren,
Giroux, & Robichaud, 1996). For us, organization is a precarious, ambiguous, uncertain process that is continually made and remade. In Weick's
(1979, 1995) sense, organizations are only stable rational structures when
viewed retrospectively. Communication, then, is the substance of organizing in the sense that through discursive practices organization members engage in the complex construction of diverse meaning systems.

This shift from treating organizations as reified structures to a focus
on communication practices and processes has generated myriad research
agendas throughout our field, encompassing many different theoretical perspectives. Whether we study the communication experiences of organizational newcomers and transferees (Kramer, 1994), the relationship between
face-saving and controlling poor performance (Fairhurst, Green, &
Snavely, 1984), perceptions of fairness and coworker communication (Sias
& Jablin, 1995), sexual harassment in the workplace (Clair, 1993), or the
role of narrative in organizational power relations (Helmer, 1993; Mumby,
1987), we share a common concern with problematizing and explaining organizational phenomena in terms of a communication framework. Regardless of our perspective, we share a belief in communication as the ontological foundation of human collective behavior (Shepherd, 1993).

The Problematic of the Organization–Society Relationship

The fourth problematic underscores the recognition that organizational
boundaries are permeable and in flux and that the dividing line between organizations and society is blurred and perhaps nonexistent. The interest of
organizational communication scholars in explicating the dynamic relationship between society and organizations can be seen in the recent publication of several case studies (see, e.g., Giroux, 1993; Tompkins, 1993), the
emergence of a bona fide perspective for studying groups (Putnam & Stohl,
1990), and research on globalization and organizational communication

processes (Wiseman & Shuter, 1994). In all these studies the boundaries between organizations and their environments are indistinct and permeable. Indeed, organizational communication scholars are well positioned to study the dynamics of globalization because our view of communication as an embedded, collective, and emergent process can capture the complex interplay among organizational, national, political, and global factors.

One excellent example of research that addresses these relations is Papa, Auwal, and Singhal's (1995) study of the Grameen (Rural) Bank in Bangladesh. Their exploration of the ways in which the Grameen Bank successfully mobilized a large number of poor and landless Bangladeshi women into an organizational framework, enabling them to generate income and improve their socioeconomic conditions, blurs the boundaries between organizations and the organization of society. By invoking a pluralistic theoretical framework that encompasses coorientation theory, the theory of concertive control, and critical feminist theory, they include a study of the broad social context of Bangladesh as well as a close analysis of the micropractices of daily organizing.

Finally, the organization–society relationship has been further problematized in our field by recent work on the relationship between organizations and democracy (Cheney, 1995; Deetz, 1992; Harrison, 1994). Although traditionally organizations have been studied as if they are exempt from the democratic principles that guide behavior in other spheres of society, communication researchers are beginning to study organizations as important sites of participation and decision making that have effects far beyond the immediate context of the organization. As I indicate above, concern lies not with how participatory practices improve efficiency (narrowly defined), but rather with how a communication approach to workplace democracy can enhance our sense of community and identity. As Cheney (1995, p. 196) simply puts it, "What would organizations be like if we really created and maintained them for persons?"

CONCLUSION

The four problematics discussed above are not intended to provide an exhaustive agenda for building common ground, but rather are meant as heuristic points of departure for thinking about how we can make connections across epistemological and methodological differences. Whether one is a post-positivist, an interpretivist, a critical theorist, or a postmodernist, these four problematics can potentially help to frame how we think about organizational communication as a human phenomenon.

Other possibilities abound. In her chapter Kathy Miller mentions structuration theory (Giddens, 1984) as an example of a perspective that transcends theoretical differences. Certainly Giddens's work has had strong transdisciplinary and transtheoretical appeal, spawning research agendas that range from the systems-oriented work of Scott Poole and his associates (Poole & DeSanctis, 1990), to more critically oriented studies, including work on narrative and organizations (Helmer, 1993; Mumby, 1987). Relatedly, Poole has himself made a persuasive case for new systems theory as a way to synthesize the sometimes antithetical relationship between old systems research and the interpretive turn (Poole, 1997).

While such efforts raise interesting possibilities, I want to end with the cautionary note that began this chapter. Attempts to create common ground should not be confused with synthesis and the erasure of difference. For example, the systems appropriation of structuration theory that has produced such an important body of research in our field seems to largely erase the critical edge that I see as key in Giddens's work. The central role that Giddens gives to power and domination in the reproduction of social systems disappears in the application of structuration theory to small group processes, for example.

Difference and dissensus, then, do not eliminate the opportunity for dialogue but provide the context for its very possibility. Dialogue is by definition a dialectical process in which people from different perspectives challenge each other's assumptions and worldviews. In some ways, too much consensus and common ground can be dangerous because it erodes the possibility for critique and transformation, and heightens the possibilities for the hegemony of a single discourse. Ultimately, the trick is to maintain a constructive tension between consensus and common ground on the one hand, and dissensus and difference on the other.

NOTES

1. Of course, one should not overlook the irony that both Van Maanen and Pfeffer occupy highly prestigious positions at elite institutions (MIT and Stanford, respectively). Thus, regardless of which of them secures the epistemological high ground, neither is in much danger of being marginalized. Indeed, the fact that Van Maanen occupies a chair at the Sloan School of Management suggests that he is unlikely to be the victim of "intellectual herbicide."

2. It is important to note that Burrell and Morgan (1979) make no attempt to privilege or make an argument in favor of any of the four paradigms in their analysis. Indeed, they are careful to indicate that their intent is to provide an overarching, *descriptive*, metatheoretical framework that enables comparison of research across paradigms. In this sense, the different valences and connotations that have become associated with the various paradigms in the last twenty years are not intrinsic to Burrell and Morgan's analysis.

3. Foucault, for example, is distinctly anti-Marxist in his writings (see, e.g., Foucault, 1980b), and Lyotard (1984) explicitly rejects the "metanarrative" of critical theory (particularly the work of Habermas) as "terrorist" in its assumptions.

4. I have long been frustrated by the fact that while scholars in our field draw extensively from research in management and sociology the obverse rarely occurs. Indeed, it seems that our scholars get cited only when they publish in management or organization studies journals.

PART III

COMMENTARY

CHAPTER 5

Commentary on Common Ground in Organizational Communication

George A. Barnett

Throughout my academic career I have been a vocal (though not necessarily articulate) spokesperson for the incommensurability thesis. While describing the organizational structure of the International Communication Association, Jim Danowski and I (Barnett & Danowski, 1992) reported that the most important factor that differentiated the membership was a scientific–humanistic dimension. We also found that the divisions that may be characterized as "humanistic" clustered separately from the ones that took a scientific approach to the study of communication. In discussing these findings, we stated:

> The science-versus-humanities cleavage is perhaps too fundamental to produce a single unified offspring from the merger of the orientations. The epistemologies of the sciences and the humanities are not only different but not compatible. This is not to suggest that one is superior to the other. Both help us understand the human condition. However, the orientations differ even as to what constitutes knowledge. Further the skills necessary to make knowledge claims from either orientation require years of training. Time devoted to training in one set of skills limits an individual's capacity in the other. Rather than encouraging jack-of-all-trades and experts in none by training students with a little bit of knowledge (a dangerous thing), we should focus their education on a single epistemology either scientific or humanistic, and provide in-depth training in that orientation. (p. 281)

As Steve Corman correctly stated in his introduction to this volume, my tone was very dismissive of the critical and interpretive perspectives in the volume of *Organization <—> Communication: Emerging Perspectives* on the renaissance in systems thinking (Barnett, 1997). It was, perhaps, a response to the equally dismissive tone of Pacanowsky and O'Donnell-Trujillo (1982) regarding the accomplishments of the systems perspective.

Most recently, during my keynote address to the first International Conference on Speech Communication in Taiwan (Barnett, 1998), I urged the participants to resist the siren song of postmodernism, calling this perspective socially irresponsible, divisive, and unable to provide an accurate account of the human condition. Furthermore, rather than resolving social conflict, taking this point of view would only serve to exacerbate these problems.

Certainly, these are not the views of a person seeking common ground among post-positivists, interpretive, and critical theorists, and postmodern scholars. But how should a scholar respond, when he receives reviews, as I did recently, rejecting a paper advocating the use of objective computer-based content analysis procedures for public relations because no serious feminist scholar would ever use such methods? This is but one negative review my research has received. I raise it only to show how absurd the review process can be when scholars become entrenched in their paradigmatic camps. However, in the spirit of this volume, I am burying my paradigmatic hatchet and I will explore those areas where I believe a shared perspective can be brought to the study of organizational communication.

At a minimum, I agree with Kathy Miller that incommensurability can only be reduced through dialogue among scholars from the different perspectives. Convergence theory, with which I am associated, argues that communication is a process in which individuals share information with one another in order to reach a mutual understanding (Barnett & Kincaid, 1983; Kincaid, Yum, Woelfel, & Barnett, 1983; Rogers & Kincaid, 1981). When two or more participants share information, its processing may lead to mutual understanding, mutual agreement, and collective action. Convergence theory views organizations as emergent properties of the interactions of the individuals engaged in the process of communication. Therefore, by merely participating in this dialogue I am working to achieve a common ground. However, I have my doubts about the extent to which this dialogue is possible. I am not sure that all organizational communication scholars speak the same language. To be honest, it took me considerably longer to read Dennis Mumby's and George Cheney's essays than Kathy Miller's essay because I was uncomfortable with the language of critical theory, postmodernism, and interpretive scholarship. Still, upon completion of my reading and with some time for reflective thought, I can see some linkages among the perspectives that I was not aware of before reading.

Beyond the first step of dialogue the next step would be to move to the level of borrowing the concepts from one perspective and using the epistemological principles that one is comfortable with to study organizational communication issues normally not associated with that perspective. This falls far short of Kathy Miller's call to find a metatheoretical perspective that embraces the assumptions and practices of the various approaches used in the study of organizational communication. However, to borrow George Cheney's (Chapter 2, this volume, p. 18) "neighbor" metaphor, there is nothing wrong with borrowing a tool or a cup of sugar from the person on the other side of the fence—especially when it allows us to fix a broken (or to build a new) theory or make the explanatory pie a little sweeter.

My research on organizational culture and socialization theoretically draws heavily from the interpretivist perspective but operationalizes the notion of collective meanings in terms more familiar to postivist scholars. Typically, one stage in examining an organization's culture is to conduct in-depth open-ended interviews with a large stratified random sample of the organization in order to gain an understanding of what everyday life is like for members of that organization (see Barnett, 1988). Special attention is paid to their perceptions of the organization's values; its language, rites, and rituals; and how the goals (mission) of the organization are communicated to its members. By sampling from throughout the organization (horizontally across the functions, and vertically from top to bottom in the hierarchy), I try to gain the members' multiple perspectives and to avoid managerial bias. One can clearly see the influence of interpretivist scholars in this practice. But at this point, the positivist in me takes over and the texts of these interviews are transcribed and "objectively" content-analyzed using a variety of computer programs to determine the central tendencies of meaning. After all, culture is an ordered system of meanings and symbols shared during the process of communication. It is an emergent property of the interaction of a group, best represented by a measure of central tendency. The content analysis makes determining the organization's culture possible.

Cheney (Chapter 2, this volume, p. 38) borrows Schultz and Hatch's (1966) notion of sequential crossing to describe this approach to paradigmatic integration. First, I engage in organizational research using the interpretive paradigm, and then, once the data are "objectified" through the process of transcription, I switch to the positivist paradigm.

Another example of crossing the fence to listen to one's neighbor's theoretical critique of research is in the area of semantic network analysis (Doerfel & Barnett, 1999). This research represents a response to the criticism, primarily by interpretivist scholars, that structural analysis ignores the content of communication and the meanings of the messages communicated through network linkages. Semantic network analysis attempts to answer the question "What is the communication structure of an organization that emerges from the members' interactions based on the shared meanings of messages as expressed in their language?" The source of the messages to be interpreted, or, in the language of post-positivists, content-analyzed, to determine the degree of shared meaning (overlap) may be obtained through in-depth interviews or open-ended surveys. They may also come from the text of published documents (annual reports, mission statements, or human resources materials) or electronic media (web pages or advertising). Thus, what results from a semantic network analysis is a picture of the organization as an emergent property of the interactions of its members rather than a description of the organization dictated from above by management or one designed to be the most efficient at achieving its externally imposed goals.

More closely approaching a common metatheoretical paradigm are the post-positivist and the critical perspectives. Establishing common ground between the positivist and critical perspectives need not be an issue of epistemology. After all, Karl Marx was a dialectical *materialist* and not a dialectical *idealist*. One of Marx's greatest contributions to the social sciences was the positivist notion that social class (social structure) can be objectified, that is, operationalized by the variable of ownership of the means of production. Individual behavior was determined by one's position in the social structure, membership in either of two social classes, the bourgeois who owned the means of production or the proletariat who did not. Further, the individual was not free to act other than as a member of his social class. The proletariat (at this stage in history, *lumpenproletariat*) had no alternative, lacking class-consciousness that could lead to empowerment. If a member of the bourgeois attempted to act in a manner that was not proscribed by his class, he would soon find himself reduced to a member of the proletariat—for example, if his human resource policies were more progressive (i.e., he paid his employees a living wage, allowed them to work shorter hours, and included health benefits).

The mechanism for social change that Marx proposed was that members of the bourgeois who did not successfully compete would lose the ownership of the means of production and become members of the proletariat. The fallen bourgeois would communicate alternative world conditions to the *lumpenproletariat*. This knowledge would empower them by raising their class-consciousness. The proletariat would then rise up and take over the means of production and the power of the state. Further, they would eliminate those institutions that produced and distributed messages reinforcing false consciousness (e.g., the church).

It does not take any great paradigmatic leaps from my overly simplistic description of Marxist theory (the foundations of critical theory) to the post-positivist theories currently employed in the study of organizational communication. Two communication theories that readily come to mind are social influence theory (Rice, 1993) and organizational media theory (Danowski, 1994), although neither could be characterized as "critical." Regarding the former, Marx clearly describes how an individual's position in the social structure determines his/her attitudes, values, beliefs, and knowledge, as well as a society's culture. Further, the interpersonal influence of the fallen bourgeois (opinion leaders) on members of the proletariat is suggested as the primary mechanism by which organizational structure and culture may be changed. Regarding the latter, Marx describes religion and the bourgeois press in much the same way as the mass media is currently characterized: as an opiate placating its members/readers/viewers and reinforcing false consciousness, resulting in consumerism, sexism, and the maintenance of the existing social structure.

Rather than any epistemological conflict between the post-positivists and the critical theorists, I believe that the primary source of dispute among these two paradigms is axiological. There is disagreement over the role of values in social research. This is not to suggest that some or even the majority of critical scholars do not reject positivist methods for the objective measurement of the social structure and its impact on such phenomenon as the role of the mass media on society, national development, and globalization as tools of oppression.

Critical scholars take the position that the *primary* role of social research should be to promote social justice through the amelioration of societal inequities. Post-positivists primarily search for knowledge by attempting to separate or at least minimize their values from the object of study. However, since post-positivists cannot claim value-free inquiry, let me suggest the role of the social scientist as advocate. Post-positivists should be free to express their values and to use their expertise to further these values. As Kathy Miller correctly articulated, no serious "positivist" today actually believes that research is value-free. However, the use of objective research may be perceived as more credible in arguments to change the objective conditions of those working in organizations. Let me describe an example.

Recently, I was hired as an organizational communication consultant to describe the values of a large financial institution (note the relevance of the interpretative paradigm to this research). Over 600 interviews were conducted that asked a diverse sample of employees (the organization calls them "associates") to describe the values of the organization, which value they viewed as most important, which they perceived as most detrimental, and to suggest any new value they thought would improve the organization. A content analysis indicated that the employees felt that the organization's culture overly valued intense competition.

One new value the associates suggested for the organization was "family." When asked to explain what they meant by this value, they indicated that they often have to place the financial institution over their family and that this created great conflict. In my role as advocate for the employees of this company, I indicted that the organization should relax its emphasis on competition and institute a number of family-friendly practices. I believe that because I presented the results of the research with all the trappings of objective positivist research that I was more credible as an advocate for the employees. Further, if one is willing to put aside the source of funding for the research, the recommended changes are consistent with the values of critical theory. They would improve the quality of work life for the organization's employees.

Over the last decade most of my academic research has focused on the role of communication in the process of globalization (Barnett, 1999). Theoretically, it draws heavily on world systems theory, a critical theory that focuses on the unequal distribution of power and wealth in the capitalist world system (Chase-Dunn, 1989; Wallerstein, 1976). It argues that an identifiable social system, the global economic system, exists beyond the boundaries of nations. All countries are linked in the world capitalist system, and any change in an individual country is a result of events in the world system. Economic relationships are politically enforced, and as such are relatively stable. This integration is a result of the interdependence and dynamic interaction among nation-states of unequal power. My contribution to this theory is to expand its focus to demonstrate how international information flows reinforce the existing structure. It is not uncommon for world systems scholars (including myself) to employ tools typically associated with positivism, for example, statistical and mathematical models on social and economic data gathered by organizations such as the International Monetary Fund and the World Bank to provide evidence to support the theory's propositions.

In summary, I see the distinction between the critical and post-positivist paradigms as a false dichotomy. Once the positivist roots of the critical perspective are made explicit and the positivist myth of value-free research denied, then I perceive there is little to prevent the two neighbors from sharing common ground and developing a metatheoretical perspective capable of embracing the theories and methods of both perspectives.

So why do we not see these linkages among the paradigms? First, we tend to read only within our paradigm and do not read those associated with the other paradigms. My students are exposed to only one perspective. My course in organizational communication is a course in communication systems. Due to the time constraints of a semester, it does not cover interpretative or critical theory except in readings on organizational culture. Second, journal editors tend to send manuscripts to reviewers that share his/her paradigmatic worldview and remove the paradigmatic perspectives they do not agree with. I once published an article on media/cultural imperialism where the editor removed the portions of the Theory section that dealt with critical theory, reducing it to a traditional positivist media effects study. Third, as scholars, much of our identity is bound up in our research. When someone criticizes our research perspective, we perceive that he/she is attacking our sense of self. We defend ourselves by denying the legitimacy of the alternative view. Creating common ground becomes impossible.

In closing, I offer a question: Is a single metatheoretical perspective that completely combines all perspectives possible? I do not think so, not unless it is so abstract and vague as to have no heuristic utility. Still, this volume has gone a long way to establish a dialogue among often antagonistic perspectives. The creation of a common paradigm will not be possible unless the dialogue established in this volume continues. Let me be the first to turn my academic sword into a plowshare. I hope the few seeds that I have tossed into our common garden will grow fruitfully.

CHAPTER 6

On the Destiny
of Acceptance Frames

Organizational Communication
Discourse

Charles Conrad

> Each frame [for confronting contradictions] enrolls [one] for
> "action" in accordance with its particular way of drawing the
> lines. Out of such frames we derive our vocabularies for the
> charting of human motives. And implicit in our theory of
> motives is a program of action, since we form ourselves and
> judge others (collaborating with them or against them) in
> accordance with our attitudes
> —KENNETH BURKE (1937/1959, p. 92)

For me the most striking aspect of the preceding chapters is the contrast between Steve Corman's angst about the substance and tenor of contemporary organizational communication discourse and the positions taken by
the other authors. Although every author condemns petty bickering and
name calling, Dennis is at least as worried about the stultifying effects of
methodological and epistemological orthodoxy, while George and Kathy
see compensating advantages in diversity and eclecticism. Of course, there
are many possible explanations for this difference. It may be a function of
the differing intellectual climates that existed during our years as graduate
students and assistant professors, those times in one's career when disciplinary dissension is most troubling and when "fitting in" is most important. Most of the authors of response chapters received their PhDs prior to
1981 and got to watch at close hand some really vicious battles between
advocates of the social scientific and the humanistic perspectives. Dennis,

George, and Kathy Miller (as well as Kathy Krone) received their PhDs in 1985, when the ashes were still smoldering; Steve did not receive his until 1988, when the embers were cool and revisionist accounts had redefined the highly emotional tirades of the 1970s into lively but reasoned methodological disputations. For someone raised in the former environments, a little name calling is pretty tame stuff; for someone nurtured during the latter epoch it may be disconcerting indeed.

Or it may be that experience, like knowledge, is inevitably local— Steve's University of Illinois was a haven of goodwill and eclecticism, while George's, Kathy Miller's, and Dennis's departments (Purdue, Michigan State, and Southern Illinois, respectively) were hotbeds of methodological dissension and debate. Or it may be that Steve simply has been reading too many organizational sociologists and business administration professors. Unfortunately, none of these explanations is adequate—the first is too biographically deterministic to be credible; the second too revisionist to be acceptable; the third too simple to be meaningful.

More important, these explanations gloss over some trends in organizational communication discourse that are indeed troubling. On the one hand, it is true that many organizational communication scholars draw on a variety of theoretical/methodological perspectives when their research question(s) warrant doing so. And, as Stan and George suggest, many of us have drawn on multiple perspectives at different points in our careers.[1] Our intellectual community's capacity for reflexive thought and our commitments to "happy eclecticism" (Goldhaber & Barnett, 1988) may indeed allow us to avoid the "crisis" facing our colleagues in sociology (Feagin, 1999; Harris, 1999; Hirsch & Lounsbury, 1997; Miller, 1999; Whyte, 1999).[2]

On the other hand, Steve's analysis and the experiences of other disciplines provide sufficient evidence to conclude that a cautionary tale is in order. I would like to discuss two processes that warrant our being concerned, and then use that discussion to examine George's, Kathy's, and Dennis's recommendations. The first process involves social science in general; the second is based on my reading of the interpretive/critical turn in organizational communication scholarship.

TWO SOCIAL/ORGANIZATIONAL THEORIES?

Sociologist Alan Dawe has observed that, historically, social theorists have developed two antithetical views of human action.[3] On the one hand is a theory of "social system" that is articulated through a pessimistic (Dawe, 1978, p. 370) language of objectivity and externality. Social actors are viewed as choice-making beings, but their definitions of situations, relationships, purposes, and selves are imprinted on them through powerful processes of socialization (Dawe, 1978). Action is not wholly determined by external pressures, but deviations from social norms occur only as the result of flawed acculturational processes or individual error. Advocates of the doctrine of social system created a language of moral authority in which the group/organization/community was supreme. The central problem in the doctrine of social system is the "problem of order" (Dawe, 1978, p. 370). Constraint is viewed as necessary for social collectives to exist at all. It is separated from action, and therefore is self-generating and self-maintaining (Dawe, 1970).

In contrast is a "doctrine of social action," a more optimistic perspective (Dawe, 1978, p. 373) that is expressed through a language system of subjectivity and voluntary, creative action. In this perspective, human beings are autonomous agents whose actions create both their own selves and their societies. The social world emerges through the actions and interactions of its members. This does not mean that social actors are not constrained by their societies. Indeed, actors simultaneously create meanings and meaning systems and are constrained by those systems. But, constraint is not "external to and superordinate over man [sic] but, quite simply, in the actions of other actors; that is, in humanly constructed structures of power and domination" (Dawe, 1978, p. 373). The central problem of the doctrine of social action is that of control: How can one view humans as individual, choice-making beings and simultaneously (1) explain similarities in patterns of action across individuals, or (2) adequately examine processes of behavioral regulation?

Both doctrines are problematic because they provide only a partial explanation of human action. In addition, each doctrine contains purifying tendencies (Burke, 1950). The doctrine of social system tends to shift toward a deterministic/objectivist extreme, while the actionist doctrine tends to shift toward pure voluntarism/subjectivism (Bhaskar, 1979; Dawe, 1978). Both tendencies are sufficiently pervasive that their adherents have developed additional constructs that guard against them. The concepts of "internalization" and "role" added a measure of individuality, subjectivity, and choice to systems doctrines, and the concepts of "symbolic interaction" and "meaning systems" allowed advocates of actionist doctrines to confront the problem of control. However, both sets of adaptations are illusory because they do not change the underlying logics of the doctrines (Dawe, 1970; Ebers, 1985; Harris, 1980; Lukes, 1974; Turner, 1992).

For communication scholars in general and organizational communication scholars in particular, it is the subjectivist tendency that is most pronounced. We focus on examining communicative *processes*; indeed, our collective mantra is that our commitment to process research defines us as a community of scholars and differentiates what we do from other strains of organizational studies. This commitment makes a shift toward structural determinism highly unlikely, and simultaneously makes a shift toward pure voluntarism/subjectivism more likely. The kind of neo-positivist research that still dominates industrial and organizational psychology and mainstream U.S. management research is virtually absent from contemporary organizational communication research (see, e.g., Miller's survey, Chapter 3, this volume). Our discipline's tendency to ignore or deemphasize social/material structure (Aune, 1994; Cloud, 1994) and to valorize models that define structure out of existence (primarily postmodernism) give evidence to the voluntarist/subjectivist tendencies of our doctrine of social action.[4]

INTERPRETING THE INTERPRETIVE/CRITICAL TURN

For many of us, the 1981 Alta Conference was a very important moment in our careers. My recollections of the discussions at Alta are substantially different than what seems to be the "received view" of the event. I recall relatively little discussion—perjorative or otherwise—about traditional social science.[5] What I do remember is a great deal of talk about the ways in which the interpretive and the critical perspectives could enrich organizational research. I will admit that my memories may very well be distorted by the usual processes, plus the effects of age and parenthood. But I believe the two publications that emerged from the conference provide evidence to support my memory of Alta as primarily an affirmation of critical/naturalistic research rather than as a three-day indictment of positivism.

Of the thirteen essays in Putnam and Pacanowsky's (1983) edited volume, only two (one by Linda Putnam, the other by Linda Smircich), deal at length with neo-positivist research. Weick's opening chapter critiques organizational communication research, generally on quasi-positivist grounds (we do not specify boundary conditions, make inexplict comparisons, do not delineate causal relationships between talk and action, etc.), and suggests directions for research. Bantz's overview of naturalistic research and Deetz and Kersten's introduction to critical organizational theory discuss the potential contributions of those perspectives. Most of the remaining chapters suggest that alternative frames could enhance our conceptualization of key constructs like climate (Poole and McPhee), decision making (Tompkins and Cheney), organizational culture (Bormann), managerial roles (Trujillo), organizational socialization (Kreps), and power (myself). The book concludes with a brief comparison of naturalistic and critical research by Len Hawes and a short story by Mike Pacanowsky based on his police research.

The other Alta-related publication is a special issue of *Western Journal of Speech Communication* (Pacanowsky & Putnam, 1982). Mike Pacanowsky and Nick Trujillo's introductory essay chastises previous review essays for bemoaning the lack of a dominant paradigm in organizational communication research; briefly critiques traditional social scientific research for maintaining an "illusion of objectivity" and for excessively adapting methodological choices to "pragmatic" (read "managerial") concerns; and proposes organizational culture as an alternative perspective. Stan Deetz's article foreshadows that analysis that he and Astrid Kersten will present in the Putnam and Pacanowsky–edited book. The following essays are exemplars of interpretive research (by Don Faules and Loyd Pettegrew), and include Terri Albrecht and Vickie Ropp's call for and illustration of method triangulation. Linda Putnam's concluding essay examines Burrell and Morgan's typology at length. Although each text does include critiques of positivist and neo-positivist research, they spend much more space affirming and advocating interpretive and critical research on their own terms.

However, the received view of the Alta Conference is not that it was predominantly an affirmation of interpretive and critical perspectives. As Kathy Miller's chapter indicates, that *legacy* implies that the conference largely involved a debunking[6] of traditional social science, and the key footnote used in that interpretation is Linda Putnam's chapter in *Communication in Organizations* (1983). That chapter usually has been interpreted outside of the broader context of the conference and the book in which it appeared (Putnam & Pacanowsky, 1983; see also Weick, 1987, and Tompkins, 1997). How and why a debunking/rejectionist interpretation of the Alta Conference (and the Putnam chapters) became dominant is an important question that I will not try to answer here. But there is ample evidence that it *has indeed become dominant*. Less oppositional readings of both texts are possible, as are more positive justifications of critical/interpretive research (see, e.g., Anderson, 1987; Cheney, Chapter 2, this volume; Eisenberg & Riley, 1988; Lincoln, 1985), but those are not the choices that our discursive community has made.

Debunking entails a particular frame of reference. In *Attitudes toward History* (1937/1959), Kenneth Burke noted that a rhetoric of debunking, while allowing actors to be opportunistic,

> makes co-operation difficult. . . . The debunking frame of interpretation becomes a colossal enterprise in "transcendence downwards" that is good for polemical, *disintegrative* purposes, but would make that man [*sic*] a fool who did anything but spy upon his colleagues, watching for the opportunity when he himself might "sell out" and "cash in." . . . When the genius of pure debunking prevails, the qualifications of comic charity drop away. . . . And the man imbued with such a scheme of motives is as embittered when he *does* sell out as when he *can't*. His own *self-indictment* is implicit in the thumbs-down system of motives by which he indicts all mankind. (original emphasis, pp. 92–94)

Of course, debunking is not an unalloyed evil. It does define and orient ideas, individuals, and groups (Burke, 1962, 1966). But it is problematic in three ways: (1) it provides an illusory basis for unification, since, as Burke repeatedly said, talking about who we are not is hardly the most effective way of talking about who we are; (2) it keeps us from understanding where our symbol systems are taking us—for example, from recognizing that a debunking orientation increases that likelihood that we will uncritically affirm other rejection frames while hypercritically examining integrative frames; and (3) it limits our ability to engage in the kind of transcendent thought that is necessary for cooperative action. If the interpretive/rhetorical turn in organizational communication research is an exercise in the rhetoric of debunking, and I believe there is sufficient evidence to suggest that it may have been, then Steve Corman's fears regarding incommensurability are not unwarranted.

IMPLICATIONS

Kathy Miller concludes her chapter by differentiating forms of incommensurabilty: those that result from logical contradictions among perspectives and those that stem from their advocates' inability to talk to one another. She suggests that by engaging in meaningful *dialogue* and by valorizing integrative perspectives we can offset at least the second form of incommensurability. Dennis draws a parallel conclusion (albeit for very different reasons), arguing that organizational communication scholars are unified by their focus on communicative *processes*, so that if we only take ourselves seriously and develop multiple research agendas that "embody diverse interests and values," any tendencies toward "binary thinking (subjectivism vs. objectivism)" can be overcome. George rightfully criticizes the "distanced reductionism" of empiricism, the parochialism of interpretivism, and the arrogance of critical theory.[7] His alternative is to employ what Kenneth Burke called a "perspective by incongruity"—in this case, the intentional "crossing" across paradigms through sequential, parallel, and interplay-oriented techniques.

At first glance all three sets of advice promise to confront and perhaps even overcome the dynamics of action–structure dualisms and the rhetoric of debunking. But a closer look suggests that these integrative moves may be "easier said than done." The one assumption that all three authors share is that dialogue—"talking to one another," in Kathy's terminology—will do much to bridge differences. However, if we do indeed speak "different languages," as Kagan and Phillips (cited in Kathy Miller's chapter) suggest, meaningful dialogue is particularly difficult, especially if we mistakenly *think* that we are speaking the same language. And "talking" also requires that we "listen" to one another.[8] Dennis's analysis of the dualism between subjectivism and objectivism provides useful advice about how we can avoid exacerbating dualistic tendencies (through substituting "overlapping" and/or "blurred" discourses for dualistic ones), but it does not develop a program for eliminating or avoiding them.

In addition, perspectives that do seem to bridge the action–structure dualism have had a limited impact. Examples include phenomenology, Pierre Bourdieu's (1988) concept of "habitus," institutional theory, and Giddens's theory of structuration.[9] However, phenomenology quickly disappeared after its appearance in Deetz (1992); and neither institutional theory nor Bourdieu's efforts to integrate functionalism/structuralism/constraint and "concepts of action, meaning and subjectivity" (1988, p. 2) have captured the attention of organizational communication scholars. Structuration has been much more popular, of course, but the extent to which structuration actually avoids the problems of the dualism still is an open question (Barbalet, 1987; Bryant & Jary, 1991; Callinicos, 1985; Layder, 1985, 1987), and the uses made of structuration theory by organizational communication scholars suggest that it also may be prone to the processes that Dawe argued are characteristic of other "integrative" construct systems (Conrad & Haynes, forthcoming).

Perhaps more important, Dennis's discussion of "problematics" in developing common ground (based on Mumby & Stohl, 1996) suggests just how difficult it may be to implement an integrative program. If his conceptions of "voice" and plural "rationalities" are to be taken seriously (and I believe that he intends them to be), they entail serious consideration of a wide range of "technical" rationalities, including functionalist organizational theory (e.g., Jeffrey Pfeffer), advocates of managerialism (e.g., Milton Friedman), as well as structural Marxism. How one simultaneously valorizes multiple voices/rationalities and rejects traditional "conduit" metaphors of organization is not made clear, but it does illustrate just how difficult it is to develop truly integrative perspectives. Both integration and transcendence requires some starting point, some shared definitions or assumptions. If paradigms are indeed incommensurable, that starting point simply may not exist. Arbitrarily excluding some perspectives may make integration/transcendence possible while simultaneously rendering it meaningless.

Perhaps the most promising approach is George's affirmation of "perspective by incongruity." It involves taking ourselves and our perspectives very seriously, which entails focusing attention on our *own* points of view and recognizing, sometimes painfully, where our own frames are taking us (Burke, 1937/1959, p. 310). Perspective by incongruity does involve a kind of "debunking," but it is a debunking of our*selves*, rather than of others. It requires us to recognize that when we adopt a frame that enables us to go "far enough" to answer the questions we ask, it also gives us the power to go "too far" (p. 101). But it is the first step in adopting a wider, "comic" frame that can reduce the pressures of opportunism "by a broadening, or maturing" of thought (p. 102).

NOTES

1. However, I do not want to overstate the case. Even eclectic scholars tend to become more focused on particular perspectives as their careers progress. For example, each of the organizational communication faculty members in my department has published research from a variety of perspectives during his/her career. But I think it is unlikely that I will resurrect my interest in loglinear analysis, Linda Putnam will rediscover lag sequential analysis, Scott Poole will activate his extensive knowledge of Marxist thought, or Kathy Miller will become a critical theorist (although she recently published her first rhetorical criticism of organizational discourse [Miller, 1998]).

2. Perhaps reflecting the severity of these disputes in sociology, Hirsch and Lounsbury (1997) refer to "eclecticism" as a "conspiracy of silence" in which actionist and structure-oriented scholars simply ignore one another.

3. A more extensive development of the ideas presented in this section are available in Conrad and Haynes (forthcoming). See also Reed (1988) and Hirsch and Lounsbury (1997).

4. Perrow (1986) and Zucker (1988) have observed similar trends in organizational sociology.

5. Admittedly, there was an opening session on Burrell and Morgan's typology by a bunch of organizational theorists. This discussion is summarized in Putnam (1982).

6. I am using Burke's terminology, but I believe Mumby's concept of "binary thinking" is quite similar. Symbolic of the dominant interpretation is the Charles H. Woolbert Research Award that Linda Putnam received from the NCA in 1993. Intended to award a publication that has had a lasting impact on communication research, it was given for her chapter in Putnam and Pacanowsky (1983), not for the book as a whole or for the conference.

7. My own view is that no particular framework—neo-positivist, interpretive, or critical—has a monopoly on parochialism, arrogance, determinism, or a tendency to construct "straw person" representations of the others.

8. Listening works best if audiences are exposed to multiple perspectives in the same media. I suspect that the proliferation of outlets for organizational communication research may be working against that goal. As part of the long-awaited *Handbook of Organizational Communication,* Julie Haynes and I surveyed organizational communication research published between 1985 and 1995 in an effort to identify "key constructs" (Conrad & Haynes, 2000). One of the most striking findings in that research involved the placement of different "paradigms." The major journals of the discipline—those published by ICA, NCA, and regional associations—had published a number of what typically would be called "neo-positivist" or "functionalist" studies. Little interpretive research appeared in those outlets, and the research that was published was grounded in integrative perspectives like structuration or "unobtrusive control/identification." Almost no critical work was published by the journals we surveyed. A great deal of excellent interpretive and critical research was being published by organizational communication scholars, but almost all of it appeared in edited collections or, to a lesser extent, in journals outside the discipline. As important, a citation analysis of these publications indicated that there was little dialogue across the different perspectives/outlets. Some neo-positivst researchers cited interpretivst criticisms of their perspective and often indicated that they had adapted their research designs to respond to those critiques. Some intepretivists cited critical theorists; others acknowledged social scientific research that was related to the topic of their research. Otherwise, there seemed to be three separate and independent discourse communities. (Ironically, these communities corresponded roughly to the three "pillars" of research in organizational sociology [DiMaggio & Powell, 1991].) In 1999, I repeated the analysis using journal articles published after 1995 (Conrad, 1999). Traditional social scientific research is alive and well ($n = 45$) and increasingly concentrated in journals that at not sponsored by ICA or NCA, primarily *Management Communication Quarterly.* Some interpretive and integrative research also is being published in journals ($n = 7$ and $n = 5$, respectively), as is

critical organizational communication, including postmodernist and feminist perspectives (n = 14), primarily in NCA-sponsored journals. Consequently, throughout the 1985–1999 period different research paradigms appeared in different outlets. Although some journals publish a variety of research (most notably *Management Communication Quarterly*, which has the smallest circulation of the journals we surveyed). By and large, we still seem to be "preaching to our preferred choirs."

9. Dynamic systems theory (Barnett & Thayer, 1997) and process theories (Poole, Van de Ven, Dooley, & Holmes, 2000) also are promising perspectives not discussed by Miller, Cheney, or Mumby.

CHAPTER 7

The A Priori of the Communication Community and the Hope for Solving Real Problems

Stanley Deetz

As a graduate student in 1972 at the ripe old age of 23, I thought I had come upon the solution to a significant problem. At this point I was transforming myself from an economist who had taken more stat courses than I often admit, to an interpretivist fueling already explosive fights in my doctoral committee and personally entering into a core tension in the social sciences. I was already an odd duck in a communication department, strange enough to feel that my back-to-back courses in foundations of set theory and Husserlian phenomenology should fulfill my methodology core requirement. The essay I wrote then for a class and published (after being a little annoyed with the "B" I received) (Deetz, 1973) still stands in many ways as my take on the question that led to this volume. In my own battle against the subjectivism embedded in both science and humanism, interpretive and normative sciences (understanding and explanation) were to be seen as complementary (not supplementary, exclusive, or integrated) tasks.

Here, I will not repeat that argument. Instead, I want to briefly give my view of tensions in the field, argue for complementarity over integration as a goal, discuss the metatheory of communication that might guide discussion across perspectives, and suggest we worry less about paradigm dialogue and more about solving problems together.

ON TENSIONS IN THE ACADEMY

In some ways I am glad another generation reclaims this tension. In some ways I more fear that we might produce a generation of Teflon-coated cosmopolitans gliding from perspective to perspective (like an intellectual food fair or academic singles bar) unaffected and without commitments than balkanization and new encampment. But I sometimes tire of the hand-wringing and starting over. Choice of method should not be driven by a dislike of numbers, philosophy, or people, but by understanding problems and having hopes for the world. I can respect and be moved by prophets of most any sort and I distrust priests of most.

Perhaps my expectations for the relations among scholars are less than others have. I do not expect unconditional love and respect from colleagues. I expect good researchers to be committed and to push ideas to their limit. I expect to be one-sided at times, but if I stay connected to the world and my colleagues either it or they will set me straight. I trust my community and its discussions more than any of my methods or momentary insights. I trust them enough that I never shy from giving my best insights as clearly as I can.

Have we been unfair to each other at times? Probably, but life is not always fair. I have often been asked whether I thought taking more radical stances hurt my career and even whether young researchers could do this kind of work and get tenure. I always answer honestly: First, I am more surprised that they let me do my kind of work at all than that some people do not like it (that does not mean that I do not sometimes get awful manuscript reviews, but everyone does). Second, tenure is about picking serious questions and pursuing them intelligently. If you do that and do not get tenure, be happy to get to go to a better institution (that does not mean that some people's lives do not get screwed up by biased and nasty people).

Contrary to Steve's introductory portrayal, I do not think we are in a particularly dismissive or tense time as an area of study. Perhaps I am tougher.[1] But I find the battles today are far kinder and gentler, and more importantly, more filled with mutual learning than many in the past or those in the other disciplines and areas of study. Some battles are not very helpful, like the recent response in *Communication Monographs* (Kramer & Miller, 1999). But generally, organizational communication studies, and even management studies, tolerates and often embraces fairly radical perspectives as well as cultivates their current traditions. Our handbooks and journals have been surprisingly balanced over time. We sometimes swing one way, but then we swing back.

I think this arises from our pragmatic orientation. I recall years ago while I was on a consulting job a young manager objected loudly to some of my ideas, complaining that they seemed Marxist to him. Before I could answer, a senior manager retorted: "I don't care what it sounds like, it sounds like it might work." I learned a lesson that others perhaps have learned too. There is enough journal space to accommodate anything any of us write worth publishing. There are enough organizational problems of radically different sorts impacting on enough different stakeholders to demand radically different ways of conception and research.

ON COMPLEMENTARITY

The commensurability of different research programs is far less interesting to me than other relations among research groups. I accept that we are all to some degree cultural strangers to each other. I am more interested in coaction than core agreement. I like our differences more than I fear them. In my view, productive conflicts are more important than unitary integrations. Perhaps that is why I am at ease with my 1996 suggestion that the normative, interpretive, critical, and dialogic perspectives (or any other scheme of contriving unity and difference) are moments of all complete research programs rather than exclusive projects. They are each present in every research project, though they rely on different reconstructed logics and although researchers differ in the extent to which they are and can be articulate about these different aspects. To say that a fundamental social constructionism lies before and after every neo-positivist study does not deny the value of doing them, but does take away the pretense of certain claims of truth and suggests that periodically we are wise to investigate the social origins and consequences of our preferred conceptions and methods. And to say that in many situations we have sufficient social consensus on concepts and methods (on ways of producing objects and our world) that we might like to model correlations and consider the predictive relations among these constructions takes nothing away from doing work that investigates the object production process and the various power dynamics therein. In some ways I found this approach easy 25 years ago and continue to do so in my own sanely schizoid everyday existence.

When I served as a department chair, I carefully counted the number of majors and determined predictive precursors to student success. But I also studied carefully how students came to be constituted as majors, how different departments were advantaged by the student-produced-as-major process, how different discourses sustain the divisions among disciplines, the difficulties of the historical division of departments, the competing types of outcomes and measures of success, and so on. One set of concerns without the other makes no sense. Institutional research answered some questions better, anthropology others better, and the cultural studies people kept us all honest.

As an organizational scholar, I hope to increase an organization's economic viability and positive social effects. But I understand the socially contrived nature and contestability of each of these goals, ranging from the historical processes by which current standard accounting practices arise, leading to contestable concepts of economic viability, and I know that social effects can be seen from the multiple interests of diverse stakeholders.

As a father with a daughter in the hospital (who is now doing fine), she and I defer to doctors and their science even with the typical discomfort of being out of control of one's destiny. But I would be remiss even as I defer if I did not also remember that Western medical science is based in specific conceptions of the human body and the nature of health, and many doctors have an ideological preference for specific forms of doctor-controlled interventions. To say that I hope someone is investigating these things (much to the doctors' and sometimes to my daughter's and my own chagrin) does not render Western medical science untrue, simply relativistic, or worthy of elimination. But to forget that it *is* relative and relevant to particular social desires and conceptions and not others would be a problem. As a sometime patient, I use medical science precisely because I share in many of those conceptions, not because I believe current medical researchers finally got nature right. *And* I, at the same time, believe that investigating those conceptions and considering alternative ones advances both our cultural understanding and often our medical science (see Mokros & Deetz, 1996).

Accepting the complementary nature of contradictory positions I find to be the core of our being rather than an occasional resolvable anomaly. How we live with our tensions rather than resolve them is key. But to me this is not to produce a world of separate but equal camps. Steve is correct in the Introduction in quoting my claim (Deetz, 1996) that Burrell and Morgan's concept of paradigm incommensurability provided a safe space in which alternatives to the tradition could grow. But he left out the second half of the statement, the lament that the primary outcome was to seal off mainstream work from the growing criticism of the impact of its fundamental unexamined assumptions. The recent Kramer and Miller (1999) response to criticisms of socialization research is a good example of how a pluralistic liberalism can lead us astray. Like many communities today that are multiethnic without being multicultural, the old mainstream is often multimethod without being multiepistemological. In many senses they just do not "get" what is being contested in their research programs. Historically, less dominant groups have had to be multilingual—they had to understand the dominant group in order to survive.

But we all need to be somewhat multilingual, we all need to understand and translate deep as well as superficial differences. Research programs should bump into those with different worldviews. Liberal openness just will not do by itself. Productive understanding is more challenging and leads more to complementarity than to unity. Acting as a critical theorist, I might show how systematically distorted communication reduces creativity and representation of diverse interests. In such a case, I think Kathy should rightfully ask which specific acts showed distortion, how many were there, and how one might measure creativity, though it is probably more her job to answer those questions than mine. And if Kathy studies the relations among communication processes and employee motivation, I might well ask that the "employee" not be treated as an object but as a historical discursive accomplishment and to look at the ways communication creates the employee with specific self-understandings and needs rather than just acts on the employee (see Jacques, 1996). But I will have to do that work, not her. Both of us help keep each other in contact with the flux of empirical activity that we might otherwise overlook in our particular way of being in touch with organizational life. Each research program can easily run astray without the check of the other. I am happy to keep rather than to resolve our differences. Dennis's essay does a good job of working in a similar view in much greater detail.

THE A PRIORI COMMUNICATION COMMUNITY

Clearly, stopping at simply identifying and accepting fundamental tensions is not sufficient in itself. I suspect that is why despite having rewritten that early essay about every five years for my entire career (most recently, as Deetz, in press), the answer has not resonated well outside of those who do work like mine. In fact others, like Steve, more often feel attacked. I suspect that some of this is conceptual slippage. For me to argue against "managerialism" in organizational research is not the same as saying that occasionally or often taking a management perspective is bad. Perhaps I have not been careful enough, or perhaps others have heard more what they expected to hear than what I actually said.

After reading the initial essays in this volume, I have come to feel that the major difficulty we have in understanding each other and living productively together rests not in the incommensurability of our theories of communication but in differences in our theory of communication among theorists. We can/could discuss and compare insights but we differ on the fundamental assumptions for, and processes of, that conversation. This difference boils down to whether social constructionism is treated as one perspective among many to be talked about or whether social construction through communication is treated as the metatheoretical background from which all perspectives arise (see Apel, 1979, for elaborate development).

If we accept the latter view, then normative, neo-positivist research is one among many social products and it, as well as any other, is well suited to answer only certain questions under certain conditions. With this view, the discussion among research orientations would be easy and productive. When we have irresolvable conflict, the appeal would be to the everyday language community out of which both social problems and perspectives arise (Apel, 1979). I sense, however, that most normative (neo-positivist) researchers are uncomfortable with this. They appear to prefer a common ontological ground ideally referenced to an assumed determinant rather than an indeterminant world. Triangulation remains for them an ecumenical goal, rather than as others see it as putting multiple methods in the service of one particular perspective (see Bullis, 1999; Clair, 1999; Miller & Kramer, 1999). In their view, if all the perspectives would join together, with enough studies we might yet get the elephant right. They see the metaphorical elephant as allusive but still to be found, rather than as an interesting produced artifact where more than elephants might be of interest. They appear yet to hope to overcome artifactual knowledge rather than investigate it.

We differ in our answers to core questions. Will our way of being together be based on the communication-based sciences that the end of the Enlightenment signals or in the physically grounded sciences of the Enlightenment? Are values to be added outside the research process, or are values intrinsic to our concepts and methods? Is the implicit hope for some degree of commensurability to lead to an understanding based on finding something in common or to aid our finding just how different we are. Steve and Kathy, it seems, have a hope for a humanist dialogue where we might find our agreement. Dennis and I (and perhaps George) hope for the productive interaction arising from confronting the radical otherness of positions—that which cannot be translated into one's own thus requires creative concept formation. Here, I cannot develop the full theory of communication processes based in difference rather than in sameness. My treatment is readily available (Deetz, 1990) but competing positions along similar lines are also useful (see, e.g., Hall, 1992; Pearce & Littlejohn, 1997).

Without reconsidering the model of communication to be assumed in our discussion, we will have continued unproductive misunderstandings. For example, in looking at researcher and research perspectives, I think Kathy misunderstood the intent of my 1996 essay partly because she does not understand the theory of language on which it was based. To me, words draw attention rather than name, they provide distinction rather than categorize.

In that essay, I tried to draw attention to two core questions a researcher implicitly answers in a project. First, to what extent should conceptions be brought in by the researcher and sponsoring groups versus being allowed to emerge in the study through participation with the subjects? And second, to what extent is the aim of the research to resolve issues and answer questions versus raise issues and initiate a more basic discussion?

It is no surprise to me that most good researchers cannot be placed in a category devised by using the poles of the questions to produce a 2×2 matrix—though Kathy seemed to think that it would be. I had no interest in making categories. Moreover, good researchers answer these questions differently at different times and different places. But while researchers do not fit into categories, the matrix does draw attention to idealized reconstructed logics that researchers use as shared resources to justify particular choices and claims.

I do not fit into any category either. In my own methodological reconstructions I readily recognize not only multiple methods but also multiple philosophies of science (Alvesson & Deetz, 2000). Similarly, philosophical positivism was not intended to be science but to offer an idealized reconstruction of the logic of scientific practice. Even neo-positivist researchers do not have to believe the logic. For example, positivism was grounded in theories of language most communication scholars would find problematic. Similarly, psychologists studying perception may find/believe that perception works far different from the theory of perception on which their empiricism is based. Much of the received history of the philosophy of natural science processed in social science textbooks fundamentally misrepresents the project, but is still used for justifications.

FOCUSING ON SOCIAL PROBLEMS

Ultimately, I think, being preoccupied with commensurability cuts a scholarly community off from the larger social community. Paraphasing J. L. Austin's famous contrast, the question "Is that a rat?" is a far different question from "What is the meaning of the word 'rat'?" The first question directs our attention out to the shared world constituting it in light of a particular interest. The attention is directed in the second, like with the commensurability issue, to competing definitions and nomenclature committees with the hope of applying an agreement to the world.

Focusing on commensurability is like a couple where each responds to every claim of the other with "What do you mean by that?" as if getting an answer would improve the relationship. Or better, it is like native speakers from different language communities worrying about the precision of translation. It is an interesting technical problem when you only get one chance to get it right. But the energies are directed differently if, when we are trying to solve a problem together, we worry less about getting it *right* than about getting it *done*. Different speakers teach each other bits of language, accepting the endless incompletion and loose edges. Meaningful misunderstandings will be discovered and worked out in time. I think it is less a question of whether we can all contribute to a body of literature on socialization or participation than of whether together do we engage the complexity of problems as they arise in organizational life?

My first-grade teacher posed questions poorly, I think. My favorite was the four boxes containing a cat, a dog, a tree, and a squirrel, respectively, where we had to circle the one that was "different." We did not yet have the word "hegemony" to account for the ease by which the "smart ones" circled the tree and believed they were following a plant/animal distinction preferred by nature. The teacher wanted the "correct" answer and we gave it. (This example is developed in detail in Deetz, 1992, Chap. 3.)

For me, it has become more interesting to see how different communities of people might have equally obviously circled something else. And I delight in working out the various costs and advantages of each preferred distinction. I now wish that advancement to second grade had been based more on how many sensible distinctions could be made rather than simply giving the socially preferred one. I wish all people might give up believing that their community's preferred methods of object constitution are preferred by nature. I would like more discussion of what is important than of what is there.

We are pulled together and make choices in solving real problems. Sometimes, following the analogy, the plant/animal distinction is more useful than others and we are wise to count how many of each there are and to suggest how each are likely to behave. But let us hope someone keeps that contestable. Counting carefully can lead us to overlook the choice of what we should be counting and systems of advantages unfairly embedded in our preferred means of object constitution and counting. These questions are not worked out in philosophy, controlled studies, metastudies of the literature, or comparing perspectives. They are worked out in the world that our perspectives are directed toward. Let us ground our studies in the world rather than in the literature. I think we should return to our communities to discuss problems and see the various ways a communication perspective can address them, to ask what kind of world we want as well as what kind of world we have (see my own attempt, Deetz, 1994). I am glad we can talk to each other in a civil fashion, but I wish we talked better with others in the civic arena.

NOTE

1. I think it is too bad that my children play in playgrounds where potential lawsuits are taken into account more than a child's fun.

CHAPTER 8

The Kindness of Strangers

Hospitality in Organizational Communication Scholarship

Eric M. Eisenberg

> Our common future depends upon our capacity to welcome
> the stranger, that is, our capacity for hospitality.
> —DARRELL FASCHING (1996)

PERSPECTIVE

In times past, religions, cultures, and individuals lived in relative isolation—there were many traditions but no single world tradition. Today, with the help of revolutionary communication technology, we are in the process of creating a global civilization. As such, we are challenged to design new ways of relating to one another that eschew simple agreement in favor of "unified diversity" (Eisenberg, 1984). Religious studies scholar Darrell Fasching (1996) characterizes these contemporary approaches as requiring a renewed hospitality toward strangers, one that includes an active willingness to temporarily "pass over" into another's world and see things through their eyes. When we do this, according to Fasching, we return to our own tradition enriched with new insight.

The primary authors of this collection are committed to some version of this ideal, the details of which are likely to be familiar to students of communication. In essence, Miller, Cheney, and Mumby each propose some sort of dialogue among perspectives, one that makes possible respectful communication among widely varying points of view (Arnett, 1986; Buber, 1965a, 1965b; cf. Eisenberg, Andrews, Laine-Timmerman, & Murphy, 1999). In this way, they call us to traverse the narrow ridge between self and other, simultaneously recognizing our own subjectivity and making room for people who are most unlike us. Dialogue holds promise not only for individual relationships but for the total research enterprise. Rather than regarding our scholarly perspectives as opposed, we can treat them as different but additive, each contributing a new way of seeing organizational communication. Cheney's metaphor is apt—in a dark cave, each new flashlight promises to illuminate a detail or passageway that was heretofore invisible.

It is no accident that our colleagues in the field of organizational behavior are engaged in a similar conversation concerning multiparadigm relations. Central to this exchange is the notion of *incommensurability*: the idea that different perspectives employ different languages, and hence are beyond reconciliation. Recently, however, there have been some positive signs. Responding to a journal forum on organizational theory, Karl Weick (1999) remarked that "reflexive conversation about organizational theory is possible" (p. 804), and recommended that, like smart firefighters, scholars "drop their heavy tools of paradigms and monologues" to communicate more effectively. In support of this idea, he offers the following quote from Czarniawski's (1998) essay, "Who Is Afraid of Incommensurability?":

> There are much more serious dangers in life than dissonance in organization theory. Crossing the street every day is one such instance. We may as well abandon this self-centered rhetoric [about incommensurability] and concentrate on a more practical issue: it seems that we would like to be able to talk to one another, and from time to time have an illusion of understanding what the other is saying. (p. 274)

Put differently, if there is anything like "common ground" to be explored here, it can only be found in dialogue (Anderson, Cissna, & Arnett, 1994; Eisenberg & Goodall, 1997; Senge, 1990). The focus of this dialogue, at least initially, should be on organizational practice, the micropolitics of everyday communication. No matter what our perspective, we share a desire to link our viewpoint to meaningful action. From personal narratives to performance management, the proof of any perspective's power is in the practice's pudding.

COMMENTS ON THE CHAPTERS

In her chapter, Kathy Miller argues persuasively that the interpretive turn in organizational communication created a caricature of positivism, one that no longer describes the vast majority of social scientific practitioners. Furthermore, she suggests that while communication researchers for the most part recognize the impossibility of value-free inquiry, this is not necessarily taken as sufficient reason to abandon objectivity as a goal. She calls for an end to the "vilification" of an outmoded positivism that no longer exists. This seems most sensible, and I look forward to conversing with those colleagues in search of important overlap in our work. At the same time, at least to me, there were some revealing slips in Miller's otherwise exemplary performance. For example, I had some anxious moments when she casually referenced "progress" as a goal of modified objectivists (one could ask, "Progress toward what?" "By what criteria?" "In whose interest?"), as well as when she tried to pry apart individuals' "lenses" from the "real world out there." With regard to this latter distinction, she quotes Phillips (1990), who in discussing Freudian concepts asserts that "believing in these things [like ego and id] does not make them real" (p. 43). I would beg to differ: it is precisely beliefs of this kind that are *most* real in their consequences, both for their adherents and for others (Jackson, 1989).

George Cheney is equally inspiring in his reflexive look at the many meanings of interpretation. While rejecting relativism, he argues convincingly for a multiparadigm approach to revealing the many different sides of any story, and for placing these versions in conversation with one another. For me, the best thing about his chapter was its light touch, which somehow manages to engage significant questions about communication while modeling the very openness he is advocating. Also helpful is Cheney's admonition that interpretive scholars must "come to terms with the material world," as well as his passing suggestion to look more closely at distributed cognition, which promises to provide a more useful operationalization of intersubjectivity than we have yet seen.

Finally, Dennis Mumby is on target in his interrogation of the binary oppositions that have perpetuated the functionalist–interpretivist debate for nearly two decades. Using a variety of examples, he affirms what for communication scholars is by now commonplace: that individual identity and social structure arise together through everyday communicative praxis. The push and pull inherent in this structurational process *is* power in action, neither purely objective nor purely subjective, neither fully cognitive nor behavioral. He further suggests that the proper object of communicative study is the communicative act, which in every case is a complex nexus of creativity and constraint (Eisenberg & Goodall, 1997; Martin, 1992). Finally, his four candidate "problematics"—voice, rationality, organization, and the organization–society relationship—seem to me fruitful avenues for future research with relevance across a range of disparate perspectives.

Along the way, Mumby references Habermas's (1984) description of three "quasi-transcendental" human interests: technical (toward prediction and control), practical (toward understanding and community), and emancipatory (toward autonomy and empowerment). These three capture nicely the various urges to study organizational communication, and one would be hard-pressed to find anyone in organizational studies who would chal-

lenge their importance. Moreover, these terms reflect the politics of epistemology that underlies the deployment of such terms as "functional," "interpretive," and "critical" to describe research programs. That we endorse
these goals as a collectivity does not, of course, mean that *each* of us foregrounds *each* one in his or her work! Instead, the set of interests are maintained through a kind of division of labor, through which individual members and groups carry certain commitments on behalf of the field. I wish to
discuss this process next.

PROJECTIVE IDENTIFICATION
IN ORGANIZATIONAL COMMUNICATION

Those familiar with family systems theory will recognize the notion that
while in theory each person has the capacity to display the total spectrum
of possible behaviors, in practice important characteristics are distributed
throughout the system, such that individual members "carry" certain key
attributes for the whole. For example, while everyone needs privacy, nurturing, and the ability to express anger, these behaviors may be "assigned"
or "taken on" by different family members, such that only dad can get an-
gry, only mom can withdraw, and only big sister gets nurtured (Hoffman,
1982). Members take on roles. At first, this distribution of qualities may
serve a useful organizing function both for the individual and for the group.
Over time, however, such divisions become caricatures as people get stuck
in a one-dimensional existence. Moreover, because the system needs the
whole set of qualities, it resists change on the part of any one member—the
quiet child is chastised for speaking up, the wild one for withdrawing, the
smart one for taking time out to rest or to play. While the preservation of
the *set* of capacities may sometimes be functional for the family, the
method by which they are distributed takes its toll on individuals and relationships.

The communicative process by which this uneven distribution of qualities occurs has been called "projective identification" (Scarf, 1987). By enacting a limited side of ourselves, we suppress qualities with which we are
uncomfortable, what Jung called the "shadow" self. Hence the "macho"
male disdains any signs of personal sensitivity, the "organized" woman all
evidence of chaos. Over time, we become lopsided in our orientation and
behavior.

What is more, we are both unconscious and ambivalent about our
shadow selves; we both consciously disdain that which we have aban-
doned, and unconsciously seek it so that we may recover balance. This is
why we tend to associate with others who are one-sided in ways that com-
plement our own tendencies, often without knowing why we do it. We project onto the other person those qualities we have repressed in ourselves,

and if we have chosen "well" they are all too happy to oblige. The nurturer pairs with someone in need of nurturing; the raging boss finds subordinates who are willing to be yelled at. In time, we revive our lifelong project of repressing our shadow side, only now with a more tangible target: the other person (or group). It is far easier to blame someone else (for being lazy, unmotivated, immoral, too sensitive, out of control) than it is to confront our internal conflicts over being unbalanced. War is declared, and given the right conditions everyone faults everyone else for expressing qualities they have repressed in themselves. Taken to an (il)logical extreme, the system disintegrates, and each individual is free to start again with a new cast of characters, chosen again because they are willing to express the shadow side. Learning and personal growth are impossible. *In fact, it is only when people become conscious of their tendency to attack in others what they most fear in themselves that this cycle may be interrupted.*

Arguments over research perspectives in organizational communication show many of the features of projective identification. By this I mean that researchers associated with various "camps" often display strong emotions and attachments to their perspectives, accompanied by an unwillingness to listen to other perspectives with anything resembling an open mind. It is as if they are afraid that allowing a multiplicity of approaches would somehow contaminate or pollute the field as a whole, and reflect badly on all of us. This is an especially ironic stance for a communication scholar to take, given our presumed understanding of the value and importance of dialogue across difference.

From this viewpoint, it is easier to see that certain groups and individuals have chosen to emphasize one or another of Habermas's interests, but taken together we have managed to retain them all. Along these lines, and with an appreciative and generous spirit, Miller, Cheney, and Mumby have made a breakthrough in thinking about our community of scholars. They have reconsidered our field as embodied by all three interests, then worked to show how different scholars have chosen to foreground different themes.

For example, the neo-positivists Miller describes help us to remember that, taken to unreasonable extremes, social constructionism becomes a naive sort of hubris, inasmuch as one rarely gets the reality one seeks to create (Ortner, 1984). Cheney's meditation on the multiplicity of meanings of interpretation recalls the many ways personal agency matters, and how patterns of interpretation have serious consequences. Finally, Mumby's recapitulation of the critical agenda provides a valuable reminder of how meaning and interpretation, knowledge and communication never exist apart from hierarchy, and that hierarchy always translates into an unequal distribution of power. Taken together, we could hardly ask for more; our collective memory is strengthened by the way, following Corman's lead, each scholar has framed their contribution not as oppositional, but as additive. But many readers will have a different response, which I address next.

SCHOLARSHIP AS ATTACHMENT

Some of you appreciate the idea of projective identification in principle, but are unwilling to see it working in this instance; instead, you insist on the incommensurability of perspectives and find distasteful the mixing of goals, metaphors, and epistemological and ontological assumptions. But where does this desire for perspectival purity come from? It is one thing to argue *from* a perspective, quite another to insist that one's view is superior to all others. Indeed, the sort of loyalty to a perspective that requires the denial or denigration of alternative perspectives is all too familiar in human relationships, visible in discussions of religion, ethnicity, and national origin. But why with regard to scholarship?

For most of us, our professional perspectives to a great degree serve as resources for our identities. As a result, the usual risks associated with ego development apply: we tend to take ourselves too seriously, to confuse our reality with "the" reality, and to become overly attached to our perspective or worldview. I have stated elsewhere that the history of this way of thinking about the world is deeply troubling, in that "every holocaust finds its reasons in certainty and in separation" (Eisenberg, 1998). Our quest for purity is as a rule motivated by fear of the "other," and by what an openness to difference might do to our sense of self, and to the integrity of our institutional "homes" (Calás & Smircich, 1999b). The worst-case scenario: Insecure in our own position, unconsciously recognizing our repressed tendencies in others, we caricature (and may seek to silence) opposing perspectives, in the hope of remaking the world in familiar imagery. When we succeed even partially (and, thankfully, we are rarely successful in silencing the other), the result is anticlimactic. Inasmuch as we rely on the "deviant" to prove our normalcy, once the other is gone we have nowhere to turn but inward, and what we find there is not comforting. New scapegoats must be found.

But there is another way. To me, a respectful dialogue among differences in perspective is the best choice we have for perpetuating both individuality and community, difference and cohesion. Philosopher Alan Watts (1972) described this process as playing "the game of black and white": We each form attachments and make distinctions only to return at some point to their source, to recognize the unity of all opposites, and the fundamentally relational quality of all human experience (Bateson, 1972). To wit: good is meaningless without bad; a table is only hard because flesh is soft; and there are no mountains without valleys. Seen like this, attachment and loyalty to egos, relationships, and schools of research is to be expected, even encouraged. Where we must improve, however, is in our tendency to hold on too tightly to what we believe. We should examine how an excess of certainty impacts negatively on our attitudes and behaviors toward others with differing worldviews. To regard one's own attachments as superior to others is more fetish than identity, and closes off the possibility of communication. But there is another way, where the strength of our commitments is rivaled only by the strength of our compassion, resulting in a more complete understanding of important organizational issues.

CONCLUSION: HOSPITALITY REDUX

In sum, the arguments I have presented here reflect my own peculiar aesthetic, through which I have always privileged beauty over truth, fragrance over formula, community over calculation. As I have become more confident as a scholar, I have become acutely aware of two paths through the academic forest, one narrow and steep, the other broad and level. While I have known many solo climbers, I have always sought the romance of the clearing, of handshakes and hugs and stories to tell and listen to. Perhaps this is also why I have a great affection for hotels, and for the very idea of hospitality, that we might extend kindness to persons we know nothing about, and whose personal commitments are irrelevant to our welcoming attitude. Others of you will see things differently, but I remain hopeful that at least some of the spirit of hospitality can take hold in the academic world. The answer may not be common ground, but rather a common orientation toward each other as fellow travelers in the world. If we are willing to risk it, the benefits will far outweigh whatever it is that we are afraid of losing.

CHAPTER 9

Paradigm Skirmishes in the Review Process[1]

Gail T. Fairhurst

In reading the essays by Miller, Mumby, Cheney, and others who have entered the "paradigm war" debates (see, e.g., Deetz, 1996; Gioia & Pitre, 1990; Pfeffer, 1993; Schultz & Hatch, 1996; Van Maanen, 1995a; Weaver & Gioia, 1994), I am reminded of the old Paul Simon song, "50 Ways to Leave Your Lover." Whether one alternates between paradigms in sequential efforts, unmasks caricature portraits of a paradigm to find a straw-man argument, blurs genres, appropriates concepts or questions from other paradigms, seeks metatheoretical bridges, or adopts both/and orientations to the management of tensions—all are suggestions offered in the spirit that paradigms are crossable even if one has a first love. Like many organizational communication researchers who have crossed back and forth between paradigms, I would agree, but would add one caveat: only if one respects their differences. While on the surface this recommendation appears painfully obvious, it always surprises me how much it is ignored in practice. If there are plenty of good debates about paradigm wars in print and at conferences (as Corman notes), as a veteran reviewer for journals in the organizational and communication sciences, I have observed increasing numbers of "paradigm skirmishes" in the review process as scholars attempt to cross paradigms in one or more ways that the reviewers or the editor finds objectionable. While one might reasonably argue that this is exactly what the review process is intended for, many of the decisions made in submitted essays result in their rejection or add substantially to the time it takes to get them into print. Authors can end up looking unreflective, amateurish, or sloppy. At the same time, reviewers and editors can appear overbearing, uninformed, or parochial. In this brief response, I would like to describe how these skirmishes might be avoided, or at least better managed.

I should begin by noting that I use the term *skirmishes* deliberately to describe small conflicts hidden from view from the rest of the field because the debate is restricted to the author(s), the editor, and the reviewers. As noted by others in this book, scholars cross paradigms because the world of organizations is far too complex for any single theoretical approach to fully grasp. In one worst-case scenario, scholars unreflectively appropriate concepts, methods, or approaches from other paradigms into their research programs. In another worst-case scenario, scholars are reflective about their choices, but reviewers find them problematic because of their own biases or lack of expertise. As scholars commit one or more perceived errors of paradigm use in their submitted work, the reviewers police the boundaries. Reviewers are often selected because they are the standard bearers of a paradigm. The editor adjudicates the conflict that marks the skirmish, and a particularly unique power dynamic is formed. The aim of this ritual is a noble one. As Cheney (Chapter 2, this volume) notes regarding interpretive scholarship, debate should be allowed to flourish because "we may never determine finally 'what ought to count as research,' but we can, perhaps, come to certain understandings about how to assess work within various communities of investigators" (p. 19).

The most egregious example of paradigm crossing—indeed, in this case we might call it "discipline crossing"—occurred when some interpersonal scholars earlier in our history treated organizational communication as little more than interpersonal communication with air conditioning. It was not uncommon to receive a manuscript for review that explored the relationship between two or more relational variables measured within a hypothetical organizational context such as students role-playing superiors and subordinates. The problem was not that these scholars were missing the subtleties of the organizational context: they missed the context altogether! Research with college sophomores operating solely from stereotypes of mixed-status roles lacked veridicality to the multilayered contexts of organizational settings.

Today's problems with paradigm crossing in organizational communication are somewhat more complex. The emergence of the interpretive, critical, and dialogic schools of thought; the acceptance of qualitative methods; and the spiraling use of language as data has had a profound effect on how we do research (Putnam & Fairhurst, 2000). Not the least of these is a recognition that communication in organizations is as much about the negotiation of meaning as it is about information transmission (Putnam, 1983) and a smorgasbord of discourse analytic approaches that focus upon the various ways in which meaning and structure are essential to human communication. In light of these choices, scholars *should* feel free to move about the conceptual and methodological landscape if the questions that they seek to answer send them there.

A PARADIGM-CROSSING EXAMPLE

My colleagues and I faced a paradigm crossroad when we first sought to study the relationship between perceptions of leader-member exchange (LMX) and the conversations that mark that relationship (Fairhurst, Rogers, & Sarr, 1987). In the LMX model, leaders exchange their personal and positional resources for a member's performance (Graen & Scandura, 1987). LMXs will vary in quality or maturity because members differ in their needs and contributions and because a leader's time and resources are limited (Graen, 1976; Graen & Uhl-Bien, 1991). Prior to this study, very little had been done to link LMX to discourse. Our initial approach was empiricist, or what Miller identifies as "post-positivist"; we used a relational control coding scheme to code the control aspects of leader–member interaction and then tested claims about recurring patterns against a baseline of randomness. We found a significant relationship between one measure of relational control and an unexpected combined measure of LMX and perceived decision-making involvement (Fairhurst et al., 1987).

However, I felt that the relational control coding scheme, which ignored interaction content, and the empiricist approach, which focused on the patterned regularity and frequency of social interaction, was missing the subtlety with which I needed to explore LMX processes. I realized that I had very little sense of how LMXs were "brought off" in social interaction. Thus, in another study I used a more interpretive or social constructionist approach to focus only on the conversations of six women leaders and their sixteen direct reports (Fairhurst, 1994). I traded in my "Why" and "How do you know" questions of post-positivism for the "How" and "Why do you talk that way" questions of social constructionism (Putnam, 1983; Shotter, 1993). I used a case comparison method to answer the question: "*How* are women leaders' LMXs accomplished and displayed in social interaction?" The approach was far more situated. I also intentionally cast a wider net vis-à-vis an approach to language analysis, but it was grounded in an iterative process of going back and forth between the data and the extant literature to generate new insight (Glaser & Strauss, 1967).

In the Fairhurst and colleagues (1987) study, we adopted standard empiricist concerns: an a priori coding scheme, large Ns, and testing claims about patterns against a baseline of randomness (Cappella, 1990). In my social constructionist study (Fairhurst, 1993), my concerns included fully specifying the interpretive basis of the study (a point to which I shall return), the use of argument by example (Cappella, 1990; Jacobs, 1986), and interpretation grounded in "structural corroboration" (Jacobs, 1988, 1990). With structural corroboration, convergent pieces of evidence are drawn from many different kinds of observation to corroborate claims such as the intelligibility of the discourse, how certain discursive forms appear in relief of other forms, and independent corroboration of the LMX relationship from members.

Interestingly, of the twelve distinct patterns that emerged in the interpretive study, only one was capable of being picked up by a relational control analysis. Was I wrong to adopt an empiricist, relational control approach in the first place? For the study of LMX at that moment, yes, because a more interpretive approach was clearly needed. I needed to know what forms LMX might take in social interaction, and that need required more sensitive data analytic tools than an a priori coding scheme developed for other interests and a subsequent search for frequencies. However, for the study of broad control patterns in manufacturing plants conceived as organic or mechanic systems, a relational control methodology was quite appropriate (Courtright, Fairhurst, & Rogers, 1989; Fairhurst, Green, & Courtright, 1995).

For me as a scholar, what was instructive about this experience was the need to recognize the integrity of the paradigm that I was crossing. To me this means that a paradigm should be treated as a grammar much the way Deetz (1996) identifies normative (empiricist), interpretive, critical, and dialogic studies as "discourses." Deetz persuasively argues that discursive paradigms are produced and reproduced in discursive practices of unity and separation. He notes: "Provisional ordering of discourses is not to police the lines, but to provide a view of the social resources from which researchers draw and an understanding of the stock arguments used by those who do police the lines" (p. 199). Deetz's "discourses" and my use of the term "grammars" are very similar except that the latter implies certain obligations one has to address the concerns of a paradigm when invoking its name—even if one ultimately rejects or modifies one or more concerns for an alternative position. Deetz is quite right to suggest that we do not want to reify paradigms to enforce a rigid policing of the lines. But, as he also notes, some crossovers matter more than others, and this may be difficult to see in the flow of research activity. Seen as "grammar," then, scholars must be cognizant of the *body* of knowledge and stock arguments of a paradigm and not treat it as a loose collection of pick-and-choose options.

I also learned that even if one recognizes the integrity of the paradigm that one is crossing, others will contest that knowledge based on alternative readings of the paradigm—some more nuanced than others. Going back to the LMX study again, one of the skirmishes that I faced as the article was reviewed was the need to pay very careful attention to the social constructionist claims that I was making and the discursive data that I had available to support those claims. As a discourse analyst, my primary concern was units of discourse, not people. Standards and concerns that relate to the measurement of people do not always apply to their discourse. For example, when I measured the LMX relationship, I measured a subjective interpretation of the relationship. Recall that part of the validity of the study was an independent corroboration of the LMX relationship from the *members themselves* based on their LMX scores. However, when I analyzed the discourse, I did not claim knowledge of subjective levels of interpretation nor anything about the cognitive basis of discourse production. Instead, I offered a conventional language interpretation based on examining the functions of particular discourse units that, in part, were determined by the way they were responded to with other discourse units and based on my standing as a member of the same language community. Following Folger (1991), I used journal space to make explicit the specific interpretive basis of the language portion of the study. I also avoided claims about frequency, typicality, or importance relative to other patterns.

Where was the skirmish? While *Communication Monographs* published this manuscript, and while it went on to win the NCA's 1994 Organizational Communication Division Article of the Year Award, it had been rejected previously by an organizational science journal because the editor at the time could not accept a conventional language interpretation of the discourse. His reading of the social constructionist paradigm and its concerns for subjectivism led him to the conclusion that *only* the actors could render interpretations of their discourse. My response, which was later described elsewhere (Fairhurst, 2000), was along the following lines:

> When the focus is on individuals' constructions of their communicative practices, it privileges the belief that individuals are freely in control of their experience and marginalizes how the practices themselves influence interpretation. Lannamann (1991) notes, "These practices are concrete; they are not determined solely by the subjective state of individuals but rather by the grounded practices of subjects in interaction with other subjects, symbol systems, and social objects" (p. 191).
>
> In the study of leader–constituent relationships, therefore, one must also ask, "What are the communication practices that shape interpretation of the relationship?" . . . To address this issue, one must acknowledge that interactional patterns are produced within relationships that draw upon private, restricted knowledge but also shared, cultural knowledge (societal and organizational), including that of language. By acknowledging the culturally recognized functions of language, individuals are seen as members of language communities rather than [as] distinct cognitive players (Baxter & Goldsmith, 1990; Hewes & Planalp, 1987; Sigman, 1987). . . . One level of inquiry is to ask how leaders and constituents use the culturally recognized function of language to enact a relationship that is culturally recognizable as a leader–member relationship. (p. 419)

We debated this issue to no avail because of (my reading) his narrow interpretive focus and general lack of familiarity with the multiple forms of discourse analysis. In fairness, if this was a skirmish I believe I should not have lost, there were certainly others in my research over the years that I deserved to lose. The point is to suggest again that the review process is the site at which paradigmatic knowledge becomes a contested activity on a playing field that is often uneven.

HOW TO MANAGE THE SKIRMISHES

An uneven playing field in the review process derives not just from different levels of expertise, but also from the widespread perception that the editor and the reviewers have all the power and the authors have none. After all, the editor chooses the reviewers who may or may not be sympathetic to the paradigm(s) one embraces. The reviewers have very little accountability for the blind reviews they write. They can write just about anything they want on point, with whatever tone they like, although they are urged to be constructive. Since editors have the final decision-making authority, they can choose to side with one negative review in a mixed field or with none of the reviews at all. In short, authors are at the mercy of the editors and their handpicked panels, or are they?

Certainly, it is generally acknowledged (though not usually discussed) that established scholars are sometimes recognizable even in a blind review (e.g., through choice of a research topic, familiar arguments, citation list, etc.), and this can marginally work in their favor. It can also work against them, but more often than not the former is true. However, I also believe that all authors have more power than they think they do if they know something concerning the triggers of cross-paradigm skirmishes, if they are willing to skirmish (i.e., make their case), and if they are willing to risk evolution of their product or practices.

For example, one of the most frequent triggers of cross-paradigm skirmishes that I have observed in the review process is what Cheney (Chapter 2, this volume) calls "methodological mystification." It concerns the belief on the part of some authors (e.g., empiricists new to interpretive scholarship) that the use of interpretive approaches (defined generally here) excuses the need for precision in research questions, descriptions of methodology, data representation, and/or data analysis. Neither Cheney nor I are the first to complain on this subject (see, e.g., Fitch, 1994; Tompkins, 1994), but it bears repeating. Specific problems include overly general research questions, vague descriptions of methodology, general impressionistic readings of the data, conclusions that appear from out of nowhere, too much or too little made of interpretive findings, or the use of certain forms of discursive data to answer frequency, typicality, or regularity questions. According to Cheney (Chapter 2, this volume),

> The burden of proof is sometimes dismissed as irrelevant ("I'm not doing *that* kind of research"), as unduly constraining ("I'm free to express my own subjectivity"), or on the basis of uniqueness ("No one could possibly

replicate what *I* did"). And, of course, there is the practical protest: "I would love to talk more about my methods but the editor didn't allow me sufficient space to explain them." (p. 24)

If such an essay is sent to one or more reviewers with interpretive backgrounds, as it most likely will be, these problems are red flags that result in major skirmishing over the acceptability of the study.

A second trigger of cross-paradigm skirmishing occurs when scholars working in different paradigms research the same topic and refuse to acknowledge research and conclusions from another paradigm. Conversation analysts, for example, are widely known for their "circle the wagons" mentality, with no acknowledgment of other cross-paradigm research, including other forms of discourse analysis that are highly relevant to what they do (see, e.g., Boden, 1994). However, I have also seen critical theorists and empiricists refuse acknowledgment of the other's work on a common topic such as resistance. Again, the selection of reviewers is critical here because this may not be an issue at all if a critical paradigm invoked in the essay is matched by a set of critical theorists as reviewers. If there is not a one-for-one match, expect a skirmish over the need to read and cite outside of one's paradigm.

A third cross-paradigm skirmish occurs when authors choose to submit a study that combines interpretive and empiricist orientations. Before the emergence of qualitative methods, interpretive "anecdotal" data always took a back seat to the quantitative findings (see, e.g., Courtright et al., 1989). This is no longer true, given the emergence of interpretive approaches in recent years and the sophistication of its methods. However, authors should consider separate research reports to deliver interpretive and empiricist findings because a combined study will likely elicit a mixed panel of reviewers, who may vie with one another for the positioning of the study. Alternatively, a combined study may be sent only to an empiricist panel who may not fully appreciate the interpretive effort (or vice versa).

Finally, there is the problem of cross-paradigm caricature that Mumby and Miller cogently write about in this volume (Chapters 4 and 3, respectively). Researchers who set up a straw man to argue for the superiority of their approach sometimes forget that the straw man has a family who, as reviewers, will lay bare the simplification that marks those arguments. Again, a skirmish will likely be avoided if the editor has selected like-minded reviewers, but a cross-paradigm panel will surely elicit one.

Assuming that some of the obvious triggers of cross-paradigm skirmishes can be avoided, authors have to be willing to skirmish. Most journal editors express amazement at the number of authors who receive a "revise and resubmit" decision, often a very promising "revise and resubmit," whom they never hear from again. I think it is safe to say that there is probably no single cause here, but ones that journal editors consistently report include an overly pessimistic view of the reviews, an unwillingness to do the work that is required, and/or an unwillingness to debate the reviewers and the editor. There is a tenacity that is required of authors that dictates that they go toe-to-toe with the reviewers and the editor if they disagree with them. After all, why does one enter academia if one is not willing to debate ideas in a scholarly forum? In many ways, the review process is a much safer forum than the academic conference or in print, where the devastating review is quite public. Most overlooked, perhaps, by authors is that either through the authors' response, the editor's decision, and/or the other reviews, the review process is an opportunity for cross-paradigm learning for reviewers as well. As the authors' mistakes are revealed, so too are the reviewers' assumptions, biases, and lack of knowledge made known.

Finally, if authors, reviewers, and editors can risk evolution of their ideas through cross-paradigm skirmishing in the review process, the research product and the research enterprise are the beneficiaries. I am not just talking here about skirmishes that produce a more careful reading of the data, but debate that results in novel applications of ideas/approaches from other paradigms, the discovery of new areas of overlap or bridges, stronger statements of contributions across paradigms, clarification and evolution of the stock arguments of a paradigm as applied to a research topic, or ways in which seemingly oppositional cross-paradigm tensions might be better managed. Mumby and Putnam's (1992) work on bounded emotionality, Schultz and Hatch's (1996) work on organizational culture, and Fairhurst's (2000) work on leadership communication are but a few illustrative examples.

In conclusion, I could continue with the theme of "50 Ways" to describe the skirmishing in the review process: challenging, perplexing, complicated, stressful, troublesome, contestable, complicated, difficult, tedious, frustrating, infuriating, ego deflating, ego enhancing, time-consuming, confusing, masochistic, disconcerting, uncaring, and much more. However, problems and challenges notwithstanding, skirmishing is not solely a means to an end. It is also an end in itself because of the learning that dialogue produces. The lesson of skirmishing is a simple one: if you cannot win the battle, at least win the war.

NOTE

1. I would like to thank Teresa Thompson and Patrice Buzzanell for their help in the preparation of this chapter.

CHAPTER 10

Disciplinary Controversies and Interdisciplinary Consequences

Michele H. Jackson

Positivism. Interpretivism. Critical. On the face of it, these terms provide as good a framework as any to organize or structure the variety of scholarship in the field of organizational communication. Of course, this tripartition is not unique to our discipline. Most social sciences have quite similar divides. Yet one motivation of this volume is the perception that these categories are particularly potent for us. Perhaps this is because ours is a relatively young field, so that many of our leading scholars have been witness to (and participants in) the debates surrounding the introduction and development of the challengers to hypothetico-deductivism: first the interpretive perspective and a few years later the critical perspective. By the time I completed my graduate training, however, the three perspectives had all been introduced, the territories largely marked, and the assumptions outlined. The controversies between them were more facts to be learned than they were dramas unfolding. What remained for the graduate student in organizational communication was the need to be able to articulate where within the schematic of *these particular* categories one fell, first to please one's defense committee and then to please various academic search committees looking for a candidate who would be a good "fit."

As the essays in this volume by Miller, Cheney, and Mumby show, however, contemporary research programs in organizational communication do not necessarily take simply one approach (noted also by Deetz, 1996, and Poole, 1997). Rather, the practice of research often tacks between various methods and approaches. To be sure, there remain those staunch adherents who will deny that such tacking is appropriate. Stray from positivism and one loses rigor, stray from interpretivism and one loses authenticity, stray from critical sensibilities and one loses morals. The merits or demerits of these positions aside, most scholars will find themselves, at some point, counting and/or interpreting and/or evaluating. Furthermore, while individual scholars may become known for adopting one or another of these perspectives or a particular combination thereof, the field of organizational communication is remarkably accommodating of multiple perspectives, at least in our public scholarly venues. For example, the support of a multimethodological approach to research was offered frequently and explicitly by a number of our senior scholars during the 1999 ICA doctoral consortium. While the metatheoretical fragmentation that worries Corman may indeed have negative consequences, it is unclear how the incivilities bandied about within the larger field of organizational studies are being enacted within our specialized discipline of communication.

My discussion so far could be taken as a trivialization of the issue of the incommensurability of the major perspectives within organizational communication. Admittedly, I do not consider the "incommensurability thesis" to be as crucial as Corman has set out. In fact, this essay first lays out briefly some reasons why we should be wary of a focus on incommensurability. However, I do agree with Corman that these perspectives set up *controversies*, and I agree that scholarly divides have important consequences. The substance of these agreements is peculiar, however, built from the vantage point of the philosophical and sociological studies of science and technology. First, deep intradisciplinary controversies are inevitable in the course of doing any science and I believe they may be responded to in such as way as to strengthen the discipline as a whole rather than to weaken it. Second, I further believe that the scholarly divides of most intellectual and practical consequence might not be those present within our ranks, but those we face when we seek to engage scholars and scholarship of other disciplines.

THE INCOMMENSURABILITY THESIS REDIRECTED

Corman's eloquent advance of the incommensurability thesis stands little chance against the picture of inclusive collegiality presented by Miller, Cheney, and (though he strains against it) Mumby. Incommensurability in these essays seems always to loom at the edges—assumed to be present but never wholeheartedly defended. Perhaps this is because the essays succeed in the task Corman has set for them: show possibilities of moving beyond the incommensurability thesis. Indeed, the extent of commonality among these perspectives seems significantly greater than that which separates them.

Within the history and philosophy of science, incommensurability is quite a significant charge. The conditions for incommensurability are such that positions cannot *choose* whether or not to be incommensurate (Eckberg & Hill, 1980; Kuhn, 1970). Incommensurate positions are definitionally incomparable. Though disciplinary matrices may place perspectives at odds with one another, the whole point of a matrix is to present a metatheoretical stance that makes comparison possible. In other words, though the perspectives outlined here might be considered by some to be apples and oranges, they are not incommensurate. Incommensurabilty is more like trying to compare apples with Buicks. Obviously, this does not represent the intellectual environment in organizational communication. And the point Corman is making is clearly that we act at times *as though* the perspectives are incommensurate, rather than looking for avenues of commonality and reconciliation. I do not want to dwell on incommensurability, but I do wish to suggest that an alternate way of characterizing this situation is to view the major perspectives as sites of disciplinary controversy.

ACCEPTING DISCIPLINARY CONTROVERSY

In their wonderfully titled book, *The Golem: What Everyone Should Know about Science*, Collins and Pinch (1993) use case studies to demonstrate the ways in which science is "done"—how what is known about the world comes to be regarded as facts (or comes to be contested) by scientific experts. They focus on scientific arenas in which claims to knowledge are at stake. In these arenas, controversy is unavoidable. The case studies are taken from the natural sciences, and so the emphasis is on experimental methodology, but the point is general and applies equally well to social sciences such as organizational study:

> The problem with experiments is that they tell you nothing unless they are competently done, but in controversial science no-one can agree on a criterion of competence. Thus, in controversies, it is invariably the case that scientists disagree not only about results, but also about the quality of each other's work. This is what stops experiments being decisive and gives rise to the regress. (p. 3)

The *experimenter's regress* is the potentially endless exchange between proponents and critics of a position. If an experiment is reported and the results support one's own position, then the claim is that the experiment was "good science." If an opponent's results contradict one's own position, this is explained away with charges that the experimenters did not follow proper procedures, were incompetent, or in some other way practiced "bad science." These are struggles that demonstrate deep commitment and involvement with one perspective at the expense of others, a resistance and even hostility to opposition and change, and decidedly human and subjective motives. As Collins and Pinch make clear, "What our case studies show is that there is no logic of scientific discovery. Or, rather, if there is such a logic, it is the logic of everyday life" (p. 142).

One of the insights of their work is that science in these conditions is not conciliatory, nor is there an objective position from which to arbitrate the controversies. They argue that all important science—that is, science that is important for the world in which we live—is controversial. None is decisive. Observations and claims are continuously contested and disputed. Thus, important science can never gather "all the facts" because likely there are none lying about simply to be gathered up. A second insight is that scientists are human and though they will have some well-developed skills and expertise, they are no different than other humans in possessing personal motives and interests, and having a limit to their abilities.

If the major perspectives of our science of organizational communication each serve as a vantage point from which to construct knowledge claims, then it is inevitable that they too will be sites for deep-set disciplinary controversies and the experimenter's regress. Sociological studies of science suggest that *consilience* (the coalescence of observations into a single, unified theory; see Butts, 1973, pp. 61–70) does not reflect the dominant practice of scholarship; a desire for such is romantic and perhaps unfair to scholars who—and this may surprise some graduate students—are only human. The move to common ground, while it may be important in many respects, *should* be difficult and should be done with some care. For if we agree to abandon controversy, what are we agreeing to? Setting aside for the moment the support we give to multimethodological research, the ability to move easily beyond controversy into common ground should be treated with caution. If the observations sociologists of science make are applicable to organizational communication as a science, then common ground easily attained is a signal that we are no longer contesting central claims about what it is that we know about the world. Nor are we contesting the modes of thinking that determine *how* we know what we know about the world and that give rise to fundamentally different insights (Chia, 1995). In their reflection on the paradigmatic debate in organization studies, Kaghan and Phillips (1998) conclude:

> The production of knowledge about organizations is a messy business and is used in a multiplicity of ways. Diversity and disorder are not necessarily weaknesses. . . . Mildly constrained paradigmatic pluralism and a thriving diversity of communities of practice—as it exists in organization studies today—is, rather, a source of strength as new methods, theories, and representational genres are invented, old methods, theories, and representation-

al genres are defended, rediscovered and modified and all are provisionally aligned in an ongoing process of knowledge production. This is the reality of a dynamic and active science. (p. 207)

THE PROBLEMS OF
INTERDISCIPLINARY INCOMMENSURABILITY

Despite a healthy regard and respect for disciplinary controversy, there is one controversy that I wish we could move beyond, or at least that we could keep within our ranks as we put on a unified face to other disciplines. That is, what *is* the study of organizational communication and how is it distinct from other disciplines? Graduate students, of course, experience this firsthand as they take courses in their cognate areas. I remember any number of occasions, sitting in that first day of class in a course offered in organizational theory, management and information sciences, sociology, and even English, as we each introduced ourselves. Most departments direct courses at the PhD level toward their own students, and so I was often the only student from an outside discipline. Upon learning a bit about my field, these good and smart people would be genuinely puzzled as to why there would be a *discipline* devoted to a study of what—it seemed to them—clearly fell within their own field.

It is difficult to maintain a straight and stern face against controversy in a discipline that is intrinsically interdisciplinary. In a sense, my confused and not always polite classmates were right. Communication does bridge multiple fields, perhaps at the expense of developing a clear sense of its own boundaries. The strong references in the Corman, Miller, Cheney, and Mumby essays to the state of the field of organization studies—as opposed to organizational communication—is something I take as a common indicator of the elasticity of our field. Our identity is in part tied to a related discipline. The debate over whether or not this elasticity is a virtue should be cast differently depending on what is at stake. For Corman, what is at stake is our own ability to work together, to move forward in a constructive way. An additional concern, one not raised by the three essays of this volume, is the effect of this elasticity on the conduct of interdisciplinary work.

It may be that collaboration with many other disciplines is little effected. In fact, our easy overlap with social or human science disciplines such as organization studies or sociology might even make such collaboration run more smoothly. My interest, on the other hand, is collaboration with technical disciplines. These fields, primarily the various engineering and computer sciences, have a very clear and definite sense of how to construct knowledge claims, and of what constitutes good science. Knowledge is attained through the process of design and through systematic methods of problem solving (Bucciarelli, 1994; Layton, 1976). Design becomes a worldview, a way of seeing that makes other perspectives—including ours—seem foreign (Heaton, 1998; Henderson, 1998; Kunda, 1992; Vincenti, 1990, 1997).

There are programs scattered across the academy that explicitly address the need to support and nurture conversation and integration of technical, social scientific, and humanistic perspectives (see Dutton, 1996, 1999).[1] And some communication departments do have remarkable relationships with engineering or computer science departments. But in general these are exceptions. On most campuses, a pretty good symbol for the intellectual distance between communication and engineering is the actual distance between the buildings in which they reside. True, technological issues have been explored for many years within organizational communication (see, e.g., Fulk & Steinfield, 1990). The point here is not *whether* we research technology. It is *with whom* we conduct this research. An important example is information and communication technologies (ICTs). There are signs that we are at a critical point for entering into collaborations with those who design and build ICTs. As an introduction to an analysis of the understandings of "human work" and "technology" across fields of study, Berg (1998) writes:

> Can social theory be of help in designing machines for human work practices? With only a few connections to the burgeoning field of constructivist science and technology studies (STS), authors on the crossroads between the social and computer sciences have started to explore how "better" technologies could be designed by drawing upon the theories from sociology, anthropology, and social philosophy. These constitute attempts to cross the "great divide" between social scientists and computer engineers—to traffic across and maybe even populate this border zone that seemed so inhospitable. (pp. 456–457)

Despite the notable but almost predictable absence of communication in the list of sources for social theory, the point is that there are cracks in the traditional wall that placed engineers on one side as designers, and social scientists/theorists on the other side as users, implementers, or critics. A good deal of work has been conducted in this regard within the interdisciplinary field of computer supported cooperative work (CSCW). From its inception, CSCW has called for the integration of social theory into design. Yet the field remains largely under the direction of computer scientists and engineers. How do organizational communication scholars enter into this project?

This question of disciplinary identity is not simply an intellectual exercise. Opportunities for social scientists to collaborate with technical scientists and engineers are likely to be found on many campuses. Often such collaborations arise within large-scale funded research projects, or are encouraged by campuswide "technology initiatives." They may also be more enduring, institutionalized in the form of interdisciplinary degree programs. For example, I serve on the faculty of a truly interdisciplinary degree program, composed of various kinds of engineers, a law professor, an economist, and me. These situations often introduce the organizational communication scholar to researchers and teachers who may have very little idea what the discipline of communication is about. In any of these situations, an organizational communication scholar could, no doubt, articulate his or her own *unique* contribution. Yet I think there are advantages to being able to articulate to these new colleagues what the discipline of organizational communication in general can contribute. And, even more plainly, we should be able to articulate to them the domain of organizational communication, including what is excluded, where the lines are drawn. I certainly find them able to articulate their fields in this way to me. And my guess is that, while opportunities for this sort of collaboration are increasing, most technically oriented researchers will evince far less patience than has been offered by my colleagues, for whom the field of organizational communication seems to be an ever-shifting shape. While I may agree on the merits of the inclusivity of my field, the absence of clear boundaries makes for rather exasperating discussions over lunch.

CONCLUSION

And this returns us to the aims of this volume. I think it is the case that the tensions and rivalries produced by the perspective debates and experienced by the established generation of organizational scholars will be much subdued in the next generation. True, other theoretical and methodological perspectives will arise, other demands will surface to challenge our commitment to inclusivity. These disciplinary controversies, within a supportive intellectual environment, are a sign of our vitality and richness. In my view, a critical challenge of the next generation will be to build a disciplinary identity from this richness, so as to demonstrate to other disciplines, as well as to the larger society, the distinct contributions of our field.

NOTE

1. At my institution, the University of Colorado, there are at least two sites nurturing cross-disciplinary conversation: the Interdisciplinary Telecommunications Program (of which I am a faculty member), and the Computer Science Department.

CHAPTER 11

A Case for a Different Kind of Dialogue

The After Action Review

Robert L. Krizek

I have decided to open my contribution to this project with a story. For unlike Professor Cheney, who claims to adopt a nonstory format for his essay in this volume,[1] I find that story affords the perfect venue for situating my commentary. It allows me to provide the reader with essential context for making sense of my attitudes regarding the "debate over metatheoretical commitments." My story takes form, as many stories do, with a few seemingly random turns of the cosmic tumblers. The first turn occurred earlier this fall when I participated in a course-related experience that prompted me to revisit, at least tangentially, certain aspects of this debate. Then, shortly thereafter, Steve Corman approached me about writing a commentary for this volume. He reminded me that we had talked numerous times throughout our ten-year friendship about our metatheoretical differences and similarities. He asked me to reflect on those talks as well as my research experiences as I contemplated a response. So as fate would have it, circumstances conspired to align the tumblers and I was left with a story to tell.

Oh, do I need to mention that I am an interpretivist?

MY STORY

During this current academic term I have been facilitating my department's gateway graduate seminar. As part of the course, I ask my students to keep a journal in which they, among other things, make a record of the communication phenomena, concepts, and theories as well as the ideas that, for whatever reasons, intrigue or excite them or both. I ask them, however, to do more than create a chronology of terms and ideas. I also encourage them to write about the "why," suggesting that they, if possible, connect the "why" to aspects of their personal biography. I want them to be able to revisit and reflect upon not only the issues that first captured their imaginations in graduate school, but also the reasons, personal and otherwise, for that interest. In the end, I want them to have produced something tangible on which they can reflect as they progress through their graduate education and beyond.

As my students shared excerpts from their journals during our weekly discussions, I decided to dust off a few of my personal journals as well and disclose to them some of my early fascinations from my graduate school experience. In retrospect it was a strange yet renewing experience to return to those days when everything seemed new and most struck me as interesting. I had forgotten how I thought about and became interested in organizational communication back then. From my journal scribblings it appeared that I was most enamored with the idea of organizations as communication cultures (Putnam & Pacanowsky, 1983; Trujillo, 1985). I also found intriguing the role of stories and storytelling in organizational socialization (Brown, 1985) and the notion that organized action may be achieved in the absence of shared meanings through a "socially shared repertoire of communication mechanisms" (Donnellon, Gray, & Bougon, 1986, p. 43). I was fascinated by the use of stories, metaphors, and fantasy themes in the creation of meaning in organizations. To this day I am interested in many of the same things for much the same reasons.

The most lasting impression from my early graduate education, however, took form when I read an essay by Michael Pacanowsky (1989). From my journal it was apparent that I believed him, or wanted to believe him, as he claimed that "different ways of doing research reflect exactly that, different ways, not superior and inferior ways, but different ways" (Pacanowsky, 1989, p. 253). The equality of it all impressed me. I felt confident, no, pleased that I had decided a few years earlier to reengage my education and noted in my journal my pleasure in being a part of such an egalitarian endeavor. Beyond his recognition of equality and difference, however, Pacanowsky also warned his readers that "using the logic or ideology of any one position will serve only to valorize that one position and demean all others" and "that each individual approach atrophies by itself and is nourished by all others" (p. 253). In response to his words I wrote such things as "our strengths can also be our weaknesses," "understanding thrives in the presence of multiple methods," and "at some level effective scholarship involves acceptance." I believed along with Pacanowsky that for scholarship to be effective it had to embrace the diversity of multiple perspectives. For me, Pacanowsky presented a "wonderful" vision of the academy in general and our discipline more specifically.

Pacanowsky ended his essay, rather ingeniously I thought, with a fiction about an evening filled with conversation among four individuals representing the somewhat disparate positions of the positivist empiricist, the classical conceptual theoretician, the particular humanist, and the critical theorist. Pacanowsky concluded his fiction by quoting the particular humanist as he explained the evening to his wife. "It was what a community of scholars is supposed to be. A scholarly quadrilogue straining, as it should, to be a conversation." And although he never mentioned the four of them physically sitting around a table as they openly discussed their positions, that is exactly the image I took away from his essay. In my journal I wrote: "The academy is the place where, metaphorically at least, we are able to pull a chair up to a table and express, at times with some strain or discomfort, our differences in a respectful manner."

A year or two later I pulled up a chair, in the literal sense, to a far different table than the one I imagined when reading Pacanowsky. I have detailed this experience elsewhere (see Krizek, 1998), but will recap it briefly here. As a graduate student, I witnessed an exchange between a job candidate and one of my department's senior faculty members. The job candidate, a highly regarded assistant professor trained in the ethnography of communication, had just completed summarizing his project understandings to an audience of faculty members and graduate students seated around a rather large rectangular conference table. Suddenly, the senior faculty member, seated to the left of the candidate, asked—actually, demanded—in a very loud and somewhat condescending tone, "Where's your falsification?" I said to myself, "So here's that strained conversation to which Pacanowsky alluded." I had not experienced it before in such a dramatic fashion. The candidate, after a long and, at least for me, tension-filled pause, tried to explain why falsification was "an inappropriate criterion for judging ethnographically derived understandings." And he did rather well, from what I knew as a graduate student, as he offered more appropriate criteria for evaluating his work. The vision of a table of equals invoked by Pacanowsky in his essay had been preserved, or so I thought. Surely, the ethnographer, this particular humanist, had satisfied the positivist empiricist's objection and order would be restored to "the table."

"Just tell me what I can do with data that can't be falsified? What damn good is it if it can't be falsified? This isn't research, it's anecdote! How do you expect to get tenure? No self-respecting journal editor will publish that!" With those words of the faculty member still hanging in the air, my vision of a table of respectful equals crumbled. This had been something far different than equals straining to engage in conversation. I experienced an epiphany. (I was into epiphanies back then.) I came to the stark realization that my literal experience of a table of scholars might be far more representative of the academy than the metaphoric one Pacanowsky had helped create in my mind.

And so it is against the backdrop of this story, recently revisited as part of my seminar facilitation, that I read the essays by Professors Corman, Cheney, Miller, and Mumby. It is also against the backdrop of this story, as well as a research experience I shared a few years back with two others (one with a post-positivist orientation, the other possessing decidedly post-modern critical urges), that I offer my comments.

MY COMMENTS

Since I opened this essay with a story, I suppose I should begin my comments by articulating the relevancy of my story for the overall project of satisfying the need for common ground in our discipline's metatheoretical commitments. But I will not do so now, although I will eventually. I will begin instead by congratulating Professor Mumby who questions the ideal of common ground. He asserts (in Chapter 4, this volume), quite convincingly for me, that since "we live in a polyglot community where multiple languages and dialects articulate many different (and often incommensurable) knowledge claims" (p. 68). that such a community might be best understood through a diversity of metatheoretical commitments. Although his use of a critical lens distinguishes his approach from Pacanowsky's, he reaches a conclusion not unlike Pacanowsky's. Both would have us embrace, as organizational communication researchers, as a community of scholars, the diversity and power of multiple methods of knowing. And although I strongly agree with this position, I would take Mumby's initial resistance to the ideal of common ground in yet another direction, one colored with a touch of sarcasm and a dash of irony. In response to a call for metatheoretical common ground, I would offer a question I seem to pose quite often in my academic life: "What problem are we trying to solve?" While I certainly agree that our conversations do have a tendency to degenerate into name-calling debates, as in the recent CRTNET exchange centering on the merits of communobiology, I see little compelling exigency, however, for a metatheoretical common ground other than to diminish these instances of name calling or, as Corman frames them, destructive conflict. By contrast, I view our subdiscipline's recent history of contrasting metatheoretical commitments as mostly a time of constructive conflict and intellectual prosperity punctuated occasionally by inevitable theoretical and methodological tantrums. I see some sort of scholarly "quadrilogues" straining to be conversations, as evidenced rather notably by this volume.

I am well aware, however, that an "everything is rosey" argument, especially one offered slightly tongue-in-cheek, may prove less than compelling for many. In addition, my regard for the fundamentals of various systems perspectives tells me that no matter how effective any process, system, or even discipline may appear, it can always be improved. Below I offer my suggestion for improving our discipline's current state. And even if my sarcasm has intimated otherwise, my intent is not to trivialize the common ground position, but rather to redirect our thinking and energies. My intent, instead, is to suggest a way of doing research that helps us "be" instead of "seem" (see Buber, 1965b) in our metatheoretical conversations.

In place of the ideal of a discipline characterized by metatheoretical common ground, I extend my vision of a table of equals conjured up during my reading of Pacanowsky's fictitious conversation. But unlike Pacanowsky, the naive graduate student of ten years ago, and perhaps some of the principal contributors to this volume, I do not believe that we can simply converse or dialogue our way into the actualizing of this table. Simply put, I feel that conversation, written or oral, is not enough. In support of this assertion I offer two reasons. First, the call for a dialogue of understanding has been made and seconded time and time again, only to be ignored, scorned, or rejected by some within our field. Although they are not the first to do so, many of the authors who wrote along with Pacanowsky in the volume edited by Dervin, Grossberg, O'Keefe, and Wartella (1989) essentially addressed over a decade ago many of the same issues covered in the opening essays of this project. Their efforts, as well as Pacanowsky's characterization of scholarship as productive conversation, certainly failed to deter one faculty member from acting as an inquisitor cross-examining a heretic disguised as a job candidate. At times talk might not be enough to influence a behavioral change. It appears to me that we, as a discipline, at least in regard to this issue, may be buying into one of the cultural myths that guide communication practices: more communication is better. If we just keep the conversation going, sooner or later we will achieve a satisfactory resolution.

Second, at times I believe we conflate dialogue with debate. For many of us, although we define dialogue in terms of judgment suspension and dialectical tensions, the practice of dialogue is no more than debate in disguise. But why? Tannen (1998) claims that we live in a debate culture where making or "carrying" our point is rewarded, while listening to and understanding the other's point are not. As an example of our "debate culture" mentality, I offer this recent experience. Not too long ago the local news reported that one of my state's high school students had won a national debate tournament and was being honored for his achievement. It occurred to me how indicative of our society that brief news bite was. As I watched I wondered what a culture would be like that orchestrated a national listening contest or sponsored an understanding tournament. I am not the only person with questions such as this. Questions concerning dialogue have attracted considerable attention both inside (see Anderson, Cissna, & Arnett, 1994; Bohm, 1996) and outside of the academy (see

Ellinor & Gerard, 1998; Flick, 1998), as well as in the liminal areas between the two (see, e.g., Tannen, 1998).

One outcome of this cultural proclivity for debate might be that we cannot help ourselves. While we might rationally adhere to the position that, in Pacanowsky's (1989) words, "different ways of doing research reflect exactly that, different ways, not superior and inferior ways, but different ways" (p. 253), most of us remain pious to our metatheoretical commitments. Why? Perhaps we actually believe our metatheoretical commitment is superior, at least superior for asking and answering the kinds of questions that interest us, and our debate mentality kicks in whenever the equality conversations diminish our perspective too much. Our emotional attachments may place our rational views in checkmate. Whatever the reasons, dialogue for many of us gets translated into restating our ontological, epistemological, and methodological positions a little slower, with fewer polysyllabic words, in the belief that sooner or later others will understand our point. So although we say "dialogue," we engage in *debate*.

MY SUGGESTION

In light of the fact that I have concerns regarding the need for a metatheoretical common ground, as well as doubts about the effectiveness of conversation as a means for achieving metatheoretical understanding, the question for me now becomes: "How do we achieve that vision of a table of equals?" Instead of common ground (or a common table) and in place of discussion heaped on top of discussion and/or of debate disguised as dialogue, I offer a different solution. I suggest joint action both preceded and followed by dialogue. Put another way, I suggest that we work with others of different metatheoretical commitments in meaningful ways on joint research projects of mutual interest. And before you counter with "what's new here?"—after all, Corman told us earlier in this volume (Chapter 1) of the existence of multiparadigm projects (Hassard, 1991; Schultz & Hatch, 1996) and we all have witnessed the mingling of methodologies within specific research projects—allow me to describe what my suggestion of "meaningful ways" entails, and what therefore is "new." I have not read these two multiparadigmatic studies so I cannot comment on them; however, my vision of a joint research project is quite different from much of the "team research" to which I have been exposed. It is also a vision born from experience not imagination.

A few years ago I was part of a triad of researchers, each of us interested in various aspects of the personal and social constructions of whiteness. Our interest in this concept brought us together, not the differences or similarities of our methodological or metatheoretical commitments. One of the other two members of this research team was Tom Nakayama, a critical rhetorical scholar and an active member of our discipline's postmodern circle, the other was Judith Martin, an intercultural researcher with an admirable history of excellent questionnaire/survey research. Finally there was me with my ethnographic sensibilities and a publishing record that paled (and still does) in comparison to those of the other two. Early in our preliminary conversations we noticed, each in our own time and way, that differences existed both in the questions we would ask and in the way we framed key issues. More unexpectedly, however, we discovered that, in some ways, we spoke different languages grounded in very different research paradigms. I do not know if Judith or Tom would agree, but it seemed to me that we each had a very distinct way of making sense of the world. We definitely organized knowledge differently. Yet, somewhere in all of this cross-paradigmatic chaos, we realized that if we were to comprehend whiteness as fully as possible, then each of us would be required to participate in all aspects of this project. This requirement, in turn, necessitated that each of us attempt to understand the sense-making processes of the others. Although we never explicitly set out to form a multitheoretical research team, in retrospect I can report that we did exactly that.

After our dual realization that a multitheoretical approach would enhance our overall understanding of whiteness and that optimal understanding demanded that we enter the sense-making worlds of one another, we also recognized that our involvements needed to be different from those of other joint projects we had experienced that utilized multiple methodogies. In these teams, researchers more often than not contributed to only a narrow portion of the project. One person might run the statistics, another conduct the open-ended interviews and direct content analysis, while still another connected the discussion of results to various issues with currency in the public realm. For example, many departments have one or two resident statisticians to whom others turn when their projects demand more than a *t*-test or basic descriptive statistics. This is *not* what I mean by working together in "meaningful ways" on research projects, and it is not what the three of us desired as a team. This more conventional form of participation in "team" research highlights individual skills at the expense of collective understanding. It simply utilizes the strengths of individuals operating primarily in isolation from one another.

While we did not envision this type of multimethods research team, we sensed that unless we did something dramatic there existed the real possibility that this more conventional form of interaction would emerge. Time constraints in the academy have a way of directing us to the path of least resistance, which, in this case would consist, at least partially, of individual contributions. So we made a decision: not only would each of us involve him-/herself in multiple aspects of the project, we also would sit down periodically and discuss our impressions, including the implications of our various methodologies/metatheoretical underpinnings. We decided we would discuss process and the arguments we constructed for our various contributions. As individuals we would engage literatures to which we had not been previously exposed. Even more, at some point we made the determination to audiotape these sessions and use them as an impetus for self-reflection to aid in our team's progress as well as our individual development as researchers. At least that is my impression of what we did and why we did it.

Although none of us knew this at the time, in essence we were following a design developed by the U.S. Army, adapted in recent years by various commercial and nonprofit organizations interested in organizational learning, called an "after action review" (Gulliver, 1987; Smith, 1994). In this process individuals address three primary foci: What did I expect to happen? What really happened? and What did I learn? As a group we focused on learning. By reflecting, first as an individual and then as a group, on what had transpired in a previous session, we were able to learn more about ourselves as researchers as well as more about each other as persons. We were able to see the strengths and weaknesses of each of our metatheoretical approaches when discussed in light of all three. And ultimately our after action reviews allowed us to take advantage of our team strengths by overcoming certain constraints inherent in each of our individual metatheoretical commitments. Eventually we became proficient enough in this process to comment to one another during our interactions regarding our differing ways of knowing and doing. For example, at times we would stop and reflect on one member's very linear approach to research design and conduct, perhaps even make a joke or two, but then discuss the strengths and weaknesses of such an approach. We became fairly adept at first recognizing and then considering what we could all gain and how our overall understandings could benefit from our colleague's linear, primarily rational, way of knowing.

I am in the process, and have been for some time, of documenting more of our experience. In retrospect, we unknowingly were striving to overcome the problems Pacanowsky (1989) foresaw when he stated that "using the logic or ideology of any one position will serve only to valorize that one position and demean all others" (p. 253). After working on such a multitheoretical research team I truly believe "that each individual approach . . . is nourished by all others" (Pacanowsky, 1989, p. 253) and highly recommend that others engage the process. In conclusion, it strikes me that more conventional team research utilizing the narrow contributions of individuals in more or less isolation from one another falls within Buber's notion of "seeming" (see Buber, 1965b). Anderson and colleagues (1994) tell us that the realm of "seeming" proceeds from how a person wishes to appear to the other. In this realm an individual produces a look or speaks in a manner calculated to position him-/herself as dominant, such as in a debate couched as discussion. By contrast, the learning after doing I am proposing aligns itself with Buber's notion of "being." Within the realm of "being," a person gives her-/himself spontaneously to the other without striving for some particular appearance or goal. This is what I experienced in my interactions with Judith and Tom during our research conversations.

Having revisited this issue through the fortuitous turns of the cosmic tumblers and having written this essay, I am left to wonder why I have not attempted to participate in other, similar research endeavors. At some point the question becomes what are the barriers that have kept me (or you) from forming or participating in a multitheoretical research team as described above. Perhaps it is the very nature of the academy or of the tenure process, which values single or first authorship much more than team projects. But that topic is best left for another volume and another story.

NOTE

1. Perhaps his nonstory approach is an attempt to dispel (or poke fun at) a stereotype often associated with "true" disciples of interpretive research—that we only write stories. And, although Professor Cheney is very explicit in his rejection of a story format for his contribution to this volume, I find interesting that he ends with "[M]y part of the story ends here. What is your conclusion?" Could this be a Freudian slip?

CHAPTER 12

Becoming Deeply Multiperspectival

Commentary on Finding Common Ground in Organizational Communication Research[1]

Kathleen J. Krone

I appreciate the invitation to participate in a discussion concerning the pursuit of common ground among organizational communication researchers. Like Steve, I find instances of paradigmatic sniping and cavalier dismissiveness disrespectful and disheartening. Unlike Steve, I worry less about the need to find common ground than I do about the need to become more deeply multiperspectival. I see this book as a continuation of the discussion initiated by Putnam and Pacanowsky (1983) concerning the need for alternative, nonfunctionalist approaches to the study of organizational communication. Over the years this discussion has taken the form of debates (see, e.g., Putnam, Bantz, Deetz, Mumby, & Van Maanen, 1993), which while helpful in clarifying key features of different research approaches and occasionally entertaining, tended to cultivate the appearance of incompatible positions and the need to choose one perspective over another. This discussion also has taken the form of calls to more firmly root our research within communication theory and to be more aware of what each theoretic perspective reveals and conceals about organizational communication (Krone, Jablin, & Putnam, 1987). More recently, the discussion of perspectives has been reframed as a collection of communication metaphors tracing the development of organizational communication research

(Putnam, Phillips, & Chapman, 1996). The format Steve and Scott have chosen for this book is yet another way to keep the discussion going.

I am organizing my remarks around the ways in which the subdiscipline of organizational communication studies has been and continues to be multiperspectival, reasons why we must become more deeply multiperspectival, and suggestions for ways in which we might go about doing so. Then, granting that the vitality of any community of scholars depends on its ability to attract new members (Crane, 1972), I also address how a small group of recent graduate students are experiencing the process of becoming multiperspectival.

As I read the opening chapters of this book, I was immediately struck by how the presentation of each perspective has evolved in recent years. For this reason, I find myself disagreeing with Steve when he says that postpositivists, critical theorists, and interpretivists have been operating entirely as closed systems. I believe growth is evident within each perspective, and that such growth has occurred as scholars remain relatively open to critiques both from within and beyond their respective perspectives. In Kathy's chapter we learn that post-positivist thinking now acknowledges that social reality can be understood as an intersubjective construction created through communicative interaction. In Dennis's chapter we learn that critical research has progressed beyond a view of social actors as powerless and hopelessly culturally programmed, to one in which actors are understood as discursively constructing identities that are both constraining and empowering. In George's chapter we learn that interpretivists are coming to grips with the need to acknowledge some material–economic basis of reality. These developments strike me as thoughtful expansions that have occurred at least in part because post-positivist, critical, and interpretive researchers continue to learn from each other. While there may have been earlier attempts by proponents of one perspective to discredit proponents of another, perhaps with the intention of ultimately replacing it, the result appears to have been a "revolution that didn't happen" (Weinberg, 1998, p. 1). Instead each perspective continues to grow and to guide interesting and important research. It may even be the growth within each perspective that is contributing to the increasing tendency for researchers to combine them in creative ways. While our discipline is sometimes "messy," I am grateful for membership in a discipline that for the most part respects and takes seriously such a broad range of research approaches.

Within organizational communication studies we indeed are operating from an enlarged frame of reference compared to our colleagues in other subdisciplines of communication and perhaps to our colleagues in management. If debates between perspectives are still raging among management scholars, perhaps it is because they finally are taking interpretive and critical studies more seriously. It does not hurt to revisit our paradigmatic wars, to assess our losses and our gains, but we do not want to get stuck in nonproductive battles. I believe that many of us in organizational communication studies have chosen to move on, learning as much as possible about each perspective and allowing the nature of our questions and our own set of skills to guide our choices of research approaches. It is not at all unusual for the top paper panels in organizational communication at our national conventions to include the best of post-positivist, critical, and interpretive scholarship. Similarly, convention preconferences often are organized to include multiple perspectives on important contemporary issues such as workplace democracy or the implications of a "new social contract" with American workers. Many of us routinely organize graduate seminars around specific topics (e.g., socialization, organizational structure, emotion) that we go on to explore through the use of research conducted from multiple perspectives. Organizational communication scholars of differing perspectives have been working side by side and occasionally collaboratively for quite some time now. Many organizational communication scholars can participate in civil, scholarly conversations with their post-positivist, interpretive, and critical colleagues. But we need to go further and deeper. And we need to do so for at least two reasons: (1) the vitality of our subject matter demands it and (2) our development as human beings and scholars demands it.

While many of us have long believed that organizational communication is sufficiently complex to require the use of multiple perspectives in order to understand it, an attitude of deep multiperspectivalism invites us into relationship with organizational communication as a subject—one that continually calls us deeper into its mysteries, some of which can *never* be fully named or understood (Palmer, 1998). As subject, organizational communication refuses to let us or our research perspectives reduce it to simple or final conclusions. Through deep multiperspectivalism we come to understand organizational communication as embodying what Rilke (cited in Palmer, 1998) refers to as "the grace of great things." Because it is both graceful and great, the subject of organizational communication will continually call us to gather around it, but it will actively resist our attempts to contain it within premature or partial explanations (Palmer, 1998). As subject, organizational communication demands to be approached through multiple perspectives, and even those will be inadequate to fully understand its mysteries. As subject, organizational communication continues to correct us in our sometimes clumsy attempts to understand it. As subject, organizational communication is capable of commanding our respect and inspiring a sense of humility when in its presence. Relating to organizational communication as subject requires that we make ourselves vulnerable to it as we remain open to yet unknown revelations.

Our continued development as human beings and as scholars also requires a deepening of multiperspectivalism. For some time, organizational communication researchers have been making choices among multiple research perspectives and doing so with an awareness of the general assumptions that each makes about people, communication, and the nature of knowledge. An attitude of deep multiperspectivalism goes further. We need to make enlightened choices about what we will choose to emphasize in our studies and ultimately what we will choose to ignore, for we know that the choices we make among perspectives are something more than power moves or professional posturing: they are expressions of who we are and how we must live to become and remain whole (Palmer, 1998). We are called to post-positivism, critical, and/or interpretive approaches because their use allows us to express some important part of our own identity. Any concerns we may have with possible epistemological incommensurabilities among research perspectives become secondary to the realization that who we are as people, at a given point in time, requires us to choose certain approaches and forgo the use of others. To choose in contradiction to who we are causes us to lose integrity and ultimately heart for the work that we do (Palmer, 1998).

Assuming, then, that the subdiscipline of organizational communication needs to become more deeply multiperspectival, how might we go about doing so? The suggestions Kathy, Dennis, and George offer all have potential for constructing a broader shared frame of reference among differing organizational communication researchers. Kathy invites us to reduce incommensurability by practicing new ways of talking with each other and by identifying and using metatheoretical bridges that operate across transition zones between perspectives. Dennis sensitizes us to the politics of finding common ground, reminding us of how power dynamics can motivate and distort any such search. As an alternative, he envisions how organizational communication research can find common ground by clustering around a set of shared problematics. In his interpretation of the interpretive approach, George demonstrates the creative research possibilities that can come from keeping the interpretive perspective in direct dialogue and productive confrontation with the post-positivist and critical perspectives. All of these strike me as viable ways to bridge the differences that sometimes divide us.

Making a decision to become more deeply multiperspectival also requires us to commit ourselves to making a sustained effort to continue learning about differing perspectives *and* about each other in relation to the research perspectives we choose. Being multiperspectival at this moment in time is more challenging than it was ten or fifteen years ago. New and more sophisticated methods of analysis, criticism, and interpretation are continually being developed, and it is impossible for most of us to become skilled in the use of them all. Still, at a minimum, we need to cultivate within ourselves and among our graduate students the ability to accept and to evaluate scholarship on its own terms rather than relying on standardized, cross-paradigmatic critiques. Learning about each other in relation to our research choices means understanding how our research, like all of our experience, is inevitably shaped by our location within concentric circles of power (Collins, 1991; Hartsock, 1983). Because of our diversity in life experience, our research approaches quite often choose us, rather than the other way around.

Choosing deep multiperspectivalism, then, can increase our feelings of vulnerability. Not only are we sometimes humbled by the great mystery of our subject, we also may feel fragmented and spread thin as we continue to learn about multiple approaches. Admitting that any one perspective (including our own) is not the only one requires an attitude of humility (Martin, 1992). We also can feel vulnerable when, because of our research choices, we are misunderstood or marginalized within our departments or the larger academic culture. For all of these reasons, deep multiperspectivalism is more likely to thrive when practiced within a supportive community. We might think of ourselves as a pluralistic community of truth (Palmer, 1998) in which the subject remains at the center of our attention, calling us in all of our diversity to gather around it, enlarging our collective frame of reference as we go. Truth, in this sense, is not the final word but "an eternal conversation about things that matter, conducted with passion and discipline" (Palmer, 1998, p. 104). Recognizing truth as an eternal conversation requires understanding, as George notes, that *all* research perspectives are interpretive frameworks. Recognizing truth as an eternal conversation should address Dennis's concern that we maintain a productive tension between consensus and dissensus. Diverse members truly engaged in pluralistic community cannot help but keep the conversation going. And these ongoing conversations among us need to be conducted in ways that continually define ourselves as a pluralistic community of truth. As Kathy suggests, this may require a commitment on our part to learn and practice non-argumentative forms of communication such as dialogue (Isaacs, 1993; Kofman & Senge, 1993). Hope and guidance for building a pluralistic scholarly community also may be found in the feminist principles of invitational rhetoric (Foss & Griffin, 1995). Proposed as an alternative to traditional forms of persuasion, *invitational rhetoric* requires us to forgo attempts to change or dominate others in favor of creating relationships rooted in equality, immanent value, and self-determination. As members of a pluralistic community, our relationships will be characterized by intimacy and mutuality rather than by domination (hooks, 1984). As members of pluralistic communities of truth we will understand the value of each other as a unique and necessary part of our community (Starhawk, 1987), and we will respect that each of us must ultimately make our own decisions for how we will live our lives (Johnson, 1991). Through the use of these alternative forms of communication, we may construct a truly pluralistic community. We may learn that all we have in common is our passion for this "great and graceful" subject: organizational communication. But perhaps that will be enough.

INCLUDING NEW MEMBERS

To get a sense for how the newest members of our scholarly community experience multiperspectivalism, I invited several recent doctoral students in organizational communication to reflect on their graduate school experience. How well are we doing in making ourselves and our students ready for deep multiperspectivalism and meaningful participation in a pluralistic community of truth? What are some of the practicalities associated with becoming multiperspectival?

There is something about organizational communication and its multiple perspectives that prepares students not only for greater participation in the subdiscipline, but in the field of communication studies and in the larger academic community as well. Several students seemed keenly aware of their location within layers of community, not all of which were equally multiperspectival. Learning about the assumptions and uses of multiple perspectives in organizational communication studies, though, appears to have served them well as they navigated their way through these intersecting and sometimes contending communities. Students tended to feel advantaged by their ability to think broadly and to locate course content within a broader range of metatheoretic approaches than other graduate students or even some of their professors. Understanding that there is something other than one right way to approach the study of communication left students feeling more scholarly, professional, and enthused about the creative possibilities of combining perspectives in interesting and unique ways. More than one student appreciated the climate of respect toward multiple perspectives in organizational communication studies, which in some cases contrasted with their experience in other courses either in their doctoral program or in their master's programs. In one form or another, all were aware of the need to select research approaches that would allow them to pursue their greatest passions. No one seemed to feel that their passion had to be contained within a single perspective, while at the same time they recognized how their various talents and life experiences were drawing them toward certain perspectives and away from others.

Becoming multiperspectival also appears to have a number of practical benefits. Many students felt that their knowledge of multiple perspectives increased their ability to secure jobs. Many felt advantaged by their ability to teach introductory quantitative, interpretive, and critical methods in undergraduate research methods courses. Perhaps more subtly, becoming multiperspectival also appears to have increased their ability as job applicants to hold conversations with potential colleagues whose own research is conducted from a different perspective. At least two doctoral students felt their awareness of mixed methods and their competency in more than one method contributed to their ability to conduct collaborative research with members of other disciplines. In both cases, even though students were drawing on their expertise in interpretive methods, their knowledge of positivist research methods contributed to their ability to participate meaningfully in mixed method research teams. One of these was an externally funded project designed to explore students' attitudes toward and experience with tobacco use in "tobacco-free zones" in high schools using a combination of traditional survey methods and interpretive methods.

Learning to become multiperspectival in graduate school is not without its challenges and risks. Entering a doctoral program without some background in the range of perspectives used to study organizational communication obviously was more distressing than entering the program with an already expanded frame of reference. And, while few in number, some students still recalled instances in which professors and some graduate students made belittling or dismissive comments about a perspective other than their own. These comments did not appear to dampen students' enthusiasm for multiperspectivalism, but it did heighten their awareness of the lack of consensus on the importance of multiperspectivalism within the discipline or the larger academic community. Comments such as this also construct an unsafe climate in which to publicly explore one's emerging identity as a researcher. Perhaps the greatest drawback, though, was the sense that even though they had exposure to multiple research perspectives, and were learning how to critique research on its own terms, the experience was sometimes frustrating. Initially, several students simply either had no interest in or were somewhat intimidated by at least one perspective. Almost everyone felt spread thin at times as they learned that it was impossible to become competent in the use of all perspectives. Many acknowledged that they would have to have taken many more hours of course work and/ or have had the opportunity to work on research projects with individual faculty operating from differing perspectives in order to feel more confident about their use of multiple perspectives and research methods. At a practical level, students sometimes had difficulty locating or scheduling the combination of methods courses they needed.

Clearly, becoming multiperspectival requires support. Several students commented on how they found this support in relation with other graduate students who may have been more knowledgeable about a particular perspective and were willing to share their expertise. Others recalled helpful conversations with faculty in which they finally were able to "see the light" about a particularly troublesome issue. One student even decided to pursue an emphasis in research methods as her minor area of study. A willingness to learn as much as we can about each approach, and learning that we can rely on each other for assistance, seem fundamental to constructing a pluralistic community of truth.

COMMUNITY BUILDING ACROSS
GENERATIONS OF SCHOLARS

We will be more likely to become deeply multiperpsectival and a pluralistic community of truth in organizational communication studies if our discussions occasionally transcend our differing perspectives, focusing instead on what brought us all here in the first place, and what continues to hold us here over the years. Because any conversation, including conversations about truth, are only as good as the questions they raise (Palmer, 1998), we might consider asking ourselves and others the following questions: What part of ourselves was and continues to be awakened by the study of organizational communication? How do our choices about how to study organizational communication express some important part of ourselves? How has our choice of perspectives evolved and why? How is our research evolving to do justice to organizational communication as a subject? Around questions such as these, we as a pluralistic community of researchers, can gather and renew ourselves, our commitment to one another, and our commitment to our study of organizational communication in all of its wonder.

NOTE

1. Many thanks to Debbie Dougherty, Linda Gallant, Lynn Harter, Erika Kirby, Jayne Morgan, and Diane Kay Sloan for sharing parts of how they experienced becoming multiperspectival throughout graduate school.

CHAPTER 13

"Paradigm" Critique

How to See Our Task as a Common One, and How to Work on It

Robert D. McPhee

In this chapter, I make two arguments that I think are relatively unique. The first isn't too surprising: I note that the three perspectives discussed in this book are not working on unrelated or scantily related tasks—instead, they share at least one important task, of generating valid explanations for social phenomena. That means they are unwise if they trash or even just ignore one another's work. Second, I argue that the three are different mainly because they prize different validity criteria for how to construct and ground a good explanation. That means that any single researcher will see work in the other perspectives as invalid—but they shouldn't! Why? Because all three sets of validity concerns make sense and have proven value. So, rather than criticize other perspectives, each of us should look for their relevant ideas. But more importantly, we should look to our own work and try to make it valid by all three sets of criteria—usually an impossible task. But at least we should consider the other criteria soundly, and try to dialogue with all within our own work.

In the Introduction and first three chapters of this volume, the focal question discussed is the relation among three . . . perspectives, paradigms, discourses—the choice of name is itself a possible stimulus to discord. While all join the quest for a "common ground," whatever that may be, the essays also reproduce a series of intellectual conflicts that has spanned generations and disciplines. The contemporary influence of the distinction among traditional, interpretive, and critical discourses can be traced to the work of Jürgen Habermas (1971, 1988), who refers in turn to a tradition in philosophy and social theory and most clearly to the critiques of Immanuel

Kant. This distinction recapitulates and reconfigures the *Methodenstreit* in nineteenth-century Germany between representatives of the *Naturwissensc-haften* and the *Geisteswissenschaften*, as well as an infamous series of disputes within the social sciences during the whole twentieth century. In our discipline the traditional/interpretive/critical distinction, with postmodern analysis added as a fourth pole, recapitulates the debates among laws, systems, and rules metatheories ("Alternative Theoretical Bases," 1977) and about evidence ("Symposium: What Criteria Should be Used," 1977; "The Dialogue of Evidence," 1994); about the validity of conversational analysis generalizations ("Chautauqua: On the Validity," 1990); and about theory ("Chautauqua: The Case," 1991; "The Future of the Field," 1993a, 1993b); as well as the exchanges in the paradigm dialogues volumes (Dervin, Grossberg, O'Keefe, & Wartella, 1989).[1]

The impression left by most of these debates is that the traditional, interpretive, and critical scholarly communities are united around distinct and discordant sets of ideas. While use of the Kuhnian term *rival paradigms* is probably not appropriate if any degree of rigor is sought, these perspectives (also usefully called "traditions" and "discourses") are divided by several of the characteristics encompassed by the term *paradigm*. The varying traditions do make mutually relevant, and sometimes at least seemingly opposed, claims. They do occasionally share vocabulary but not corresponding meanings. They do honor different exemplars and have different images of validity and quality in scientific work. Debates across their boundaries are often marked by disagreements about mutual comprehension and relevance of arguments. A relatively uncommitted scholar reading contributions on both sides of these debates might also be led to infer the moral that Kuhn articulated for clashes of paradigm candidates during scientific revolutions: there is no rule or piece of evidence that would be accepted by both sides as settling the question of which is superior, and there is no shared ground for compromise, so that any possible resolution of the dispute will not be peaceful or formulaic, but will be achieved, if at all, by a persuasive campaign involving methods that go beyond "neutral logic."

Some of the most notable scholarly treatments of the distinction of perspectives do seem to support this image of unremitting rivalry among the perspectives. For instance, Bochner (1985), in an interesting account that integrates Habermas's idea of cognitive interests with a Rortian pragmatism, presents the perspectives as distinct *vocabularies*. These vocabularies are optimally suited to variant goals: prediction and control for empirical–analytic theory, interpretation and understanding for interpretive theory, and criticism and social change for critical theory. Such different goals would seem to draw intellectual work in conflicting directions, but implicit in Bochner's account is the assumption that the perspectives are merely different pragmatic alternatives.

Mumby's (1997a) recent article is concerned more with the distinction of postmodernism from the other three perspectives, which he describes as sharing a commitment to modernism, but nonetheless "unpacks" work in these perspectives in a way that reveals substantial differences among all four of what he advocates calling "overlapping discourses." The differences involve such basic matters as the relation between knowing subject and known object (already a prejudicial description), the treatment of communication as conduit versus medium, and the treatment of social context. While Mumby (Chapter 4, this volume) argues that these perspectives share modernist commitments to Enlightenment goals, to a fundamental knowing and meaning subject, and to ways of achieving definitive authority for knowledge claims, in 1997 he interpreted them as rival "games of truth, articulating different 'disciplinary' practices and ways of constituting relationships among communication, identity, and forms of knowledge" (p. 3). Despite his willingness in the current essay to recognize their overlap, it is easy to find evidence of the differences he described earlier persisting in communication scholarship today.

Several main reactions to the division and debates have been most apparent in informal observation and conversation. One is boredom: we should deemphasize work that attacks or defends basic perspectives, and instead actually do research and theorizing. A second reaction involves what I would call "external integration": segments of a research or theorizing project are devoted to various perspectives, with each segment devoted to a different task or question (Martin & Meyerson, 1988; Morgan, 1986; Rosengren, 1989; I would say that this is the kind of array presented by Bochner, 1985, as well as assumed by many authors who use interview selections to illustrate quantitative findings). The third reaction possible is "internal integration"—fashioning or finding a perspective (structuration theory is often mentioned) that claims to include the most important parts of multiple perspectives. Based on arguments to follow, I would claim that integration can succeed only partly, and that if structuration theory is valuable, its value lies in its positive, novel formulations, not merely in a successful synthesis.[2] The fourth and final option, which involves participation in the debates, is one of "pure advocacy," where scholars choose their perspectives and monologically argue in favor of their own and against other perspectives. I do not want to denigrate such a stance, since it is practically demanded in the process of creating a new perspective, and insights of considerable value have flowed from it, as I argue below.

I would also agree, with "pure advocacy" and with Mumby and Bochner, that the perspectives *are* opposed in some basic ways. Efforts at integration too often fail to note the tradition of argument against rivals that each perspective has developed (cf. Polkinghorne, 1983). Often a perspective is inspired or at least has its development guided by its opposition to one or more of the others. Such argumentative and self-justifying work is part of the process of reflective evolution that leads to greater elaboration and rigor in the statement of a perspective. But it also means that coherent work within a perspective is well advised to avoid crossing boundaries, implied by a perspective's basic assumptions, which themselves were articulated in the process of differentiation from other perspectives.

Yet, while I think the description of the traditions as opposed and mutually inlooking alternatives is altogether consistent with the social and communication theory literature and is a valuable aid to understanding that literature, I want to suggest and argue for another reading of it. I will urge that we willfully attend to the perspectives as rival literatures, divided enough by assumptive commitments to communicate only with difficulty, yet united in a common scholarly argumentative enterprise. To summarize the two themes of my argument, I will illustrate the claims that (1) the perspectives are oriented to a common task, of developing valid theory-based explanations and explanatory resources; and (2) the debates between the perspectives should articulate, recognize, and appropriate the threats to validity evoked in the traditions of argument of rival perspectives. In the remainder of the chapter I argue for these claims.

CLAIM 1: THE PERSPECTIVES ADDRESS AND SHOULD ADDRESS THE COMMON TASK OF DEVELOPING VALID THEORY-BASED EXPLANATIONS AND EXPLANATORY RESOURCES

On the face of it, this would seem to be an easy thesis to support. The three essayists certainly embrace the concept of "common ground," but that is not quite the same thing as a common task of developing explanations.

All the traditions do seem to provide answers to questions like "How does communication work?" or "What factors lead to, or reduce the possibility of, the development of common understanding through communication?" Suppose an outsider raised the question of why workers in some organization were especially committed and devoted extraordinary effort to their jobs. A traditional scholar would identify general causes of commitment. An interpretive scholar might point to features of members' accounts of the organization's culture. A critical scholar might describe ideological processes leading workers to see the organization as legitimate, or might analyze the process of "the manufacture of consent" (Burawoy, 1979). In common parlance, all of these would qualify as explanations, rooted in distinct theories about the ways workers come to be committed. However, there are a number of problems that lead all but the traditional perspective to resist the idea of a common explanatory enterprise.

One problem is an empiricist commonplace, the "deductive" or "covering-law model" of explanation, which is tantamount to a definition of scientific explanation. In common with a number of philosophers of science (cf. Salmon, 1989), I think we should junk this model. It is misleading even about the minority of cases of explanation that it fits; its persistence is hard to understand. The idea of a common explanatory enterprise would be more widely accepted if we used a broader definition of explanation, such as: "A scientific explanation is an account that places an explanandum appropriately within a context of scientific knowledge and reasoning."

I would not claim that this definition is sufficiently strict or rigorous; it certainly employs, to clarify "explanation," the equally tricky terms "account," "appropriately," and "scientific knowledge and reasoning." It does have the virtue of pointing accurately at what scientific explanation is accomplishing, though: shifting from everyday discourse to a more-or-less discrepant scientific context involving technical usages and argument patterns as accounting resources, and, if successful, finding (or discovering) the proper context given the practices of the scientific discipline. But I would look hopefully on any revised definition that could fit, for instance, Philipsen's (1975) account for examples he gives in " 'Speaking like a Man' in Teamsterville."

Even this broadened definition, though, leaves us with difficulties when we try to use it to characterize the practices of scholars professing the other two perspectives. Four problems seem relevant when we turn to the interpretive perspective. First, the "cognitive interest" or "goal" typically ascribed to work within that perspective is not the development or application of knowledge abstract or general enough to be called "scientific," nor the satisfaction of (technically trained) curiosity through explanation, but the achievement of "interpretation and understanding" (Bochner, 1985, p. 41), or of "the preservation and expansion of the intersubjectivity of possible action-oriented mutual understanding" (Habermas, 1971, p. 310), especially during communication. Second, but in pursuit of such goals, interpretive accounts go outside or beyond the types of concepts usually classified as "scientific" by consisting of "translations," explications of meaning or significance in terms meaningful to an audience, rather than application of particularly "scientific" knowledge. The development or application of scientific theory seems tangential and unnecessary to this task. Third, interpretive inquiry often, perhaps even typically, involves accounts and arguments that go beyond science, to elucidate communicators' "ontological status as linguistic beings who engage dialogically with an 'other' (person, text, community, etc.)" or, in the case of organizations, "the ontology of organizing as a collective communicative act" (Mumby, 1977a, pp. 6, 7). In other words, interpretive (and, to foreshadow, critical) inquiry is partly philosophical. Finally, various philosophers and social theorists have argued that explanation and interpretive understanding are distinct and irreducible enterprises (Taylor, 1985; von Wright, 1971) because understanding depends on interpretive processes that are reflexive, self-defining, and potentially interminable—that is, unfixed and value-dependent in a way that explanations typically are not.

The first two problems, of a distinction of goal and content between interpretive analysis and scientific explanation, depend, I claim, on a partial misdescription of interpretive social science. Elucidation of meanings can be pursued as a shallowly practical endeavor aimed at development of narrow skills or circumscribed understandings, or it can be pursued in a reflexively aware way that leads to abstract conceptualizations of the process and findings of interpretation. If we examine exemplary cases of interpretive research, we find accounts involving theoretical concepts that provide explanatory context for the communication practices at issue. Thus, Philipsen (1975, one of the examples of interpretive social science mentioned in Mumby, 1997a) generated a general account of "speaking like a man" in terms that are assimilable to communication rules theory (Cushman & Pearce, 1977) and later formulated a more abstract conceptualization in terms of a code of honor that distinguishes "Teamsterville" from other subcultures using other codes. Similarly, Basso's (1970) account of silence in Apache culture sums up disparate interpretations in a "hypothesis" about the kind of situation in which Apaches choose silence. As another example, conversational analysis (widely though debatably classified as "interpretive" scholarship [Heritage, 1984]) describes interactive procedures using such theoretical categories as adjacency pairs and preference. In these cases interpretation leads to improved capacity for common understanding only by enhancing conscious, theory-based insight—by generating scientific explanation. And Habermas (1971) argues that the commitment of historical–hermeneutic sciences to a practical interest should not imply a disconnection from theory.

The other two problems posed by the interpretive perspective, of the philosophical content and of the interminability of interpretive scholarship, I see as demanding that we widen once again our sense of the meaning of *explanation*. The traditional perspective leads us to think of scientific knowledge as contingent and likely to involve variation, while philosophy explores the universal conditions of, for example, human existence. But at least since early work by Toulmin (1953), mainstream philosophers of science have accepted that testable scientific theory overlaps indivisibly with philosophical conceptual analysis. Outside of the traditional camp, this insight has an even longer history. Similarly, while the Hempel–Oppenheim model of explanation posits formally complete explanations, no other reason exists to deny it the same openness and provisionality that we allow for interpretations (Gadamer, 1960). Roy Bhaskar (1979) even reconceptualizes "cause" to allow for the inclusion of reasons subject to interpretation. In particular, "placing in context" makes the interpretive nature of explanation more apparent.

One of the same problems reemerges when we turn to critical theory.

The goals cited by Habermas and Bochner include "criticism and social change" (Bochner, 1985, p. 45), critique of "ideologically frozen relations of dependence," and emancipation through self-reflection (Habermas, 1971, p. 310). Once again the question arises: Are these goals best pursued by valid explanations, as opposed to "useful fictions," or by mere rejection of ideological explanations? In the case of critical theory, I think the answer is even clearer than for the case of the interpretive perspective: their commitment to the assumption of totality leads critical theorists to oppose merely local answers or temporarily useful claims in favor of accounts rooted in an overall theory or theoretical stance, and this tendency is apparent in the most pessimistic (Horkheimer & Adorno, 1972) as well as in the most constructive (Habermas, 1984, 1987) work from that perspective. One need only look at examples of critical research on organizational communication (Burawoy, 1979; Clair, 1993; Mumby, 1987) to note the prevalence of (1) explanation of workplace domination through application and extension of theoretical concepts such as consent, hegemony, power and domination, and ideology; and (2) the choice or development of theoretical concepts based on grounding in and evocation of aspects of observations, rather than choice of concepts purely with an eye to emancipatory potential.

It is useful to emphasize one caveat: I do not believe that the common explanatory enterprise means that the researchers adhering to the different perspectives will ask or can answer exactly the same questions. Perspectives have at least an elective affinity for different sets of central questions. On the other hand, I think that Bochner (1985) and Deetz (1996) have vastly overstated the extent to which different perspectives are constrained to ask and answer different questions. For instance, take an ostensibly empiricist question: What social interactive patterns (if any) lead to the most effective group activity? This topic is a mainstay of empiricist contingency theoretic research, but each of the other traditions has its own grounds for interest in that same question, with important modifications. Interpretive researchers have explored the issue of how cooperation in such groups is achieved at all, and have a definite interest in misunderstandings. Critical theorists have an interest both in the question of whether participative/democratic groups are generally as effective as others and in issues of dominance and distorted communication and their results.

Recognition that we are engaged in a common enterprise of explanation can itself have some useful effects on the perspective debates. It ought, for instance, to deter presumptive isolationism, the tendency to presume that work from other perspectives is just irrelevant and that debates involving them are fruitless. The discipline of communication suffers too much from inattention by other disciplines such as psychology, and has too much experience of the results of warfare both within such other disciplines as sociology and within its own history in the strife between social science and rhetoric, to reenact such patterns of barrier raising within communication. I do not anticipate that conclusions or practices will converge; if anything, I see the biggest change potentially occurring in the conduct and utility of debates.

CLAIM 2: RESEARCH WITHIN THE PERSPECTIVES SHOULD ARTICULATE, RECOGNIZE, AND SEEK TO RESPOND TO THREATS TO VALIDITY EXPOSED BY RIVAL PERSPECTIVES

I mean for this second claim to have a Gadamerian tone to it. Perspectival debates are in a number of ways like the meetings of distinct traditions Gadamer (1975) treats. Like him, I regard genuine dialogue as enacting a "fusion" of horizons, with no presumption that "fusion" implies acceptance or convergence, or any other single determinate outcome. I regard convergence as especially difficult because all of the perspectives have achieved their identity partly through a process of critical argument against, and development of alternatives to, prior perspectives. Specific arguments against the validity of prior belief systems, and even whole modes of social theorizing and research, inspired, gave direction to, and justified the development of each of the four perspectives. This means that each perspective has more at stake in any debate than simple adoption or avoidance of a specific tenet or procedure. They do not simply disagree, *they are designed to disagree,* and get much of their motivating energy from challenges to the validity of the other social scientific practices. Although I cannot, for various reasons, develop in depth the history or tradition of argument of each of these perspectives, I can mention some of the distinctive validity challenges (which I will call "validity concerns" below) and some of the background ideas for each (summarized in Table 13.1).

The *traditional or empiricist perspective* gets its distinctive origin during the Enlightenment, with the rise of natural science and the revolt against traditions (seen as biases) of common sense, religious thought, and the then-current philosophical tradition against Bacon's "Idols"; and the revolt in favor of the decentralization of political power and rights. This drive to root out unnoticed bias and error due to presumption in knowledge, supported by the natural-scientific sense that general patterns can be found by persistence and breadth of data collection, leads to an emphasis on maximally mechanical observation of as wide as possible a range of instances, and upon the design of research to avoid or test for presumptions and biases that have been found to condition our results and conclusions without our awareness. So the threats to validity that traditional empiricism would alert us to are unwanted biases and limitations to our ability to uncover those, usually due to a biased or inadequate sample of observa-

TABLE 13.1. Validity Concerns of the Three Perspectives

Perspective	Validity concerns
Traditional/ empiricist	• Unwanted researcher biases and limits to our ability to uncover them
	• Biases introduced by an inadequate sample of observations
	• Inability to test claims against observations
Interpretive	• Ignoring the human capacity to mean, understand, act, and relate
	• Overlooking processes that construct reality
	• Using research practices that distort life practices of the group being studied
Critical	• Unspoken commitments to individualism, scientism, and capitalism
	• Unexamined support of institutions, power imbalances, and language systems
	• De facto acceptance of constraints of the status quo

tions, but secondarily due to a conceptual formation that will not allow for testing against diverse observations.

The *interpretive perspective* arose in the tradition of opposition to empiricism, which over the years took many forms and involved many axes of difference between natural and human sciences (Polkinghorne, 1983). The difference that has endured is that between natural events and objects that have no symbol systems of their own, and human activities that involve specific socially and individually developed reflexive frames of reference and powers of control. The threats to validity focused on from the interpretive perspective are those that ignore or eliminate aspects or consequences of the human capacity to mean, understand, act, relate, and construct social reality. Typically, validity concern about empirical social science research develops because empiricists do not formulate variables that capture important shades and distinctions of meaning or sociality in the group being studied, or use research procedures that distort life practices of the group, or develop theories that advance causal explanations while ignoring meaning-based explanatory options (Polkinghorne, 1983; Taylor, 1985).

The *critical perspective* emerged in the aftermath of the French Revolution and in the left-wing reaction to the German idealism of Kant and Hegel. Marx formulated in an especially compact way the style of dialectical historical critique in philosophy, the science of political economy, and the will to merge theory and political practice. In the wake of the limited success and impure (to put it mildly) translation of critical theory into communist politics, the enduring dynamic of critical theory is now to trace the sources of repression and stagnation in all spheres, including the intellectual, and to seek ways of liberating us from these dominating constraints and forces. "Traditional theory" is especially subject to critique because it encodes reified, alienated, and/or ideological commitments to individualism, scientism, and capitalism. The threats to validity emphasized in critical theory are the assumptions, innocent in the eyes of other perspectives, that involve unexamined commitment to the institutions (including those of language and everyday communication), power imbalances, and unreasoned constraints of the status quo.

These validity concerns are relevant to both research processes and theoretical formulations (if we assume we can separate them). They spring from deep-seated reactions to inadequacies in past work that have motivated the positive intellectual developments within each perspective. It is, of course, possible to formulate them as positive maxims or rules, but to understand them we optimally should trace them back, as broadly and adaptively as possible, to their originary concerns. I want to claim that any one perspective can do this with the threats articulated by any others. The concerns each focuses on, while less basic and innocent as seen by proponents of the others, do (or can often) make sense as concerns to those proponents. Nothing about the critical perspective, for instance (except perhaps for agonistic avoidance of its opponents' ideas), stops critical researchers from recognizing concerns regarding bias and insensitivity, reformulating them as fully and faithfully as possible given the critical research interest, and carrying out research that "Pareto-optimizes" the validity of research along the three dimensions identified by the perspectives. The other perspectives can do the same, even while giving primacy to their own concerns and goals. The result of trying to phrase our arguments more dialogically—in terms that are designed to appeal to audiences from all perspectives—almost certainly will not be agreement, but each perspective can find in the others new ideas and/or bases for reformulating its own procedures and arguments that will strengthen its own internal performance as well as external appeal.

ON MILLER, CHENEY, AND MUMBY

The three essays in this volume agree in some ways with the prescriptions of this commentary, but they are incomplete mainly in reflecting on validity claims and their implications. Katherine Miller is very clear and thorough in drawing out the assumptions and implications of post-positivism. She emphasizes in particular the fact that the post-positivist perspective assumes that science is itself a social and interpretive process, that observational criteria and procedures are theory-dependent and changeable rather than rock-sure knowledge foundations, and that objectivity itself is a similarly evolving ideal rather than a palpable virtue of today's science. Her essay documents considerable responsiveness to interpretive and critical arguments by the more enlightened of empirical researchers.

However, it is not clear from Miller's essay what changes in validity concerns and practices accompany the change from "positivistic" to "post-positivist" assumptions. Of course, her (perfectly appropriate) chosen mission is to outline the new assumptive perspective of post-positivism, but still no specific changes in theory building or methodological strategies to register or cope with study-level complaints by interpretivists and critical scholars are mentioned. Moreover, there is at least some evidence that, based on post-positivist assumptions, completely traditional theory and research might proceed without modification.

Consider the quotation of Barbara Wilson cited by Miller (Chapter 3, this volume, p. 59). It mentions the rich individualism of children's interpretations, but then promises to focus on "common patterns" characterizing a majority of the children. It seems reasonable to fear that the variables used to seek common patterns will overlook unique meanings and shades or complexities of meaning, no matter how important to the specific interpretation being studied, and will fail to search out distortions in interpretations that might be traced to arbitrary constraints and power systems. My inference is that post-positivist assumptions do not directly lead to procedures that respect or address the validity concerns of other perspectives at the level of actual research. Such procedures might lead directly to more substantial bases for perspectives to "talk to each other," in Miller's first prescription for change.

The essay by George Cheney pays more attention to the clash of validity claims, especially in the section where he discusses research on participation. His essay demonstrates, most clearly of the three, the common interest in explanation and the most common trajectory of discord about specific research foci. He also articulates very clearly the validity concerns of interpretive scholars, in response both to empirical research and to critical arguments and research; most strikingly for the purposes of this article, he develops the critical challenge to interpretive procedures.

However, based on claims in this commentary, I would urge him to make two changes in his presentation. First, I would urge paying more direct attention to empiricist validity concerns, which are neglected partly because Cheney follows the usual order of exposition of the perspectives. Moreover, Cheney's actual development of the critical view of his research example, while demonstrating thorough understanding, does not emphasize ways that interpretive researchers, at an abstract level or in conjunction with specific research, might positively recognize and respond to the validity concerns of critical scholars. Instead, he argues for "limitations" of the critical stance itself that would discourage us from taking it (Chapter 2, this volume, p. 35). His emphasis is appropriate for an exposition of the interpretive view, but the prescriptive force of my position is that an interpretive scholar should ask him-/herself "How can I avoid ignoring the power-imposed parameters and myths that constrain my understanding of the research situation?"

Mumby's article does a fine job of articulating and arguing for the validity concerns at the heart of critical theory, and is, I believe, properly suspicious of the homogenizing dangers of a call for "common ground." If recognition of the common relevance of problems brought the disappearance of diverse concerns in theory construction and research, I believe that our level of insight into communication would decline in quality, interest, utility, and on every value dimension except placidity. But Mumby does not discuss possible recognition of and adaptation to the validity concerns of other positions by critical researchers. In its newer "radical humanist" variants, critical theory developed by drawing from and modifying interpretive insights, so it is relatively easy for Mumby to take account of the interpretive emphasis on meaning in his own conceptualization of good research. His discussion of concerns like "reductionism" and the "subject–object polarity" fails to recognize, and even seems designed to deny, the range of legitimate concerns that led empiricists to objectivity, as opposed to bias, in stance and methods. My argument is that critical theorists (and everyone else) should *also* do the exact opposite of this sort of antagonistic critique— which does have value. They should also construe the concerns and insights of other perspectives in the most responsive and relevant way possible, and try to find all possible ways, consistent with their own methods and validity concerns, of meeting them.

Working on a common explanatory task, as described above, does not necessarily mean ever finding "common ground," whether as common problems or common or complementary solutions. It will make work within each perspective better by reducing the blindness of practitioners of each to the concerns (and consequently other ideas) of other perspectives. An interpretive study, for instance, will be stronger, in some sort of general sense, in utility and persuasiveness for other perspectives, if it is responsive to concerns about generality, power dependence, and difference. But that increase in strength does not necessarily involve full-fledged conformity to the prescriptions of those other perspectives. An interpretive study that pays as much attention as possible to threats of bias and undetected sources of variance will still be an interpretive study. Moreover, such a study may still not speak to empirical, or critical, or postmodern researchers, either because of topic, central method, or nature of research outcome. But the chances of mutual relevance, of finding utility in critiques by others, and definitely of respect for one another's work, will almost certainly increase, and that's the goal that should be embraced by this book.

NOTES

1. I will not discuss postmodernism further in this chapter; however, as I have argued else-where (1998), postmodern research does seem committed, in an especially self-critical and pluralistic fashion, to the ideal of a common explanatory enterprise, and its research would be improved by appropriate attention to the validity challenges developed by other tradi-tions.

2. I feel it important to mention that I disagree in limited ways with the treatment of the the-ory of structuration in the essays by Miller and Mumby. Miller follows Weaver and Gioia (1994) in regarding structuration theory as a "metatheoretical bridge" leading easily to synthetic formulations that overcome "bracketing" by other "paradigms." While Giddens was certainly eclectic in formulating his position, he also took clear stands in opposition to "the wrong train station" of empiricism, the claim that hermeneutic "thick description" is always necessary, and most of the substantive claims of Marxism and postmodernism (cf. 1976, p. 13; 1981, passim; 1984, p. 285; 1990, passim). So the "metatheoretical bridge" is often blocked, and the benefits of structurational advances over other metatheoretical posi-tions come with their own constraints. I also disagree with some of Mumby's comments about the "systems appropriation of structuration theory," which seems to include my own work. I certainly do agree that work on small groups often (but not always—cf. Poole, Seibold, & McPhee, 1985, pp. 287ff.) neglects macrosocial power concerns, but, I would say, by bracketing them rather than denying their legitimacy or importance. The trouble is that Giddens's thought goes far beyond his admittedly insightful analysis of ideology, and even his general views on power as domination, to focus on issues of social organization, space and time, agency, macrosocial change, and modernity as an institutional and experi-ential order. His whole span of thought has even appeared to a number of critics to neglect or underdevelop the "critical edge" to an unfortunate degree, especially in discussing fea-tures of "modernity" without considering their discriminatory impact—and I myself think the critical edge of structuration theory needs lengthening. But the theory per se is more like a Swiss Army knife, and if we act as though the "critical edge" is the whole knife, we ignore other tools, the blade metal, the handle, and most importantly the design of the whole, so as to do bad service in the common explanatory enterprise.

CHAPTER 14

Challenges for the Professional Newcomer in Doing Common Ground Research

Craig R. Scott
Laurie K. Lewis

In considering our commentary for this book, both of us realized that these metatheoretical perspectives and especially the idea of "paradigms" had been a source of confusion and trouble since our first days of graduate school. In the master's program, the focus was on figuring out what your paradigm was—and exactly how the word was pronounced (Craig used to doodle two shovels to poke fun at those who mistakenly said "pair-a-dig-ems"). In our doctoral programs, we created jokes about how many (inter-pretive/functional/critical—pick your favorite target) scholars it took to screw in a lightbulb (the answers to which would not be in keeping with the spirit of this book). In a job interview meeting with a group of graduate students with a "critical" orientation, Laurie was asked with the same sympathetic tone one would use in inquiring about a serious disease or tragic circumstance, "What is it like to be a functionalist?"

Now, after being (collectively) in seven research institutions since we began our graduate educations, we doubt that the incommensurability between paradigms that so characterized our socialization into the discipline has been especially valuable. We too believe there is a need to move away from the doodles, jokes, suspicion, and the far more serious problems discussed by Corman in the Introduction to this book, and to now seek more common ground. Without question, the chapters by Miller, Mumby, and Cheney—as well as the other commentaries in this book—all offer valuable suggestions for finding that common ground. We echo their calls for greater understanding, more interplay, bridging theories, connecting the micro to the macro, use of dialogue, multistage research projects, guarding against the dominance of a single paradigm, and so forth, as important steps for building common ground.

Although we argue that identifying ways of bridging metatheoretical perspectives is necessary, it is not sufficient for actually conducting scholarship within this common ground. There are pragmatic considerations that must be addressed as well. Our reactions to the visions articulated in this book reminded us of the appealing comments made by Buddy Goodall at the ICA doctoral consortium we both attended as graduate students. In response to a query about tenure criteria, he thoughtfully explained that we could write anything we wanted because tenure decisions are based on whether the candidate has "led a scholarly life." At the time, his remark resonated with what many of us felt *should* be the standard for measuring the worth of a scholar. However, the realities of "publish or perish" faced by most of us entering research universities in the following years brought an awareness of a far different set of standards communicated in terms of expectations regarding minimum numbers of publications per year, definitions of "good outlets" for placement of work, a sense that joint authorships were viewed rather suspiciously, and a knowledge that "expert" was a desired label to be acquired before tenure. Similarly, if the common ground vision in this book is to be realized as something more than an optimistic, but unrealistic, ideal, we need to address a number of structural and cultural barriers to cross- and multiparadigmatic research and theory-building—barriers that, in our view, are embodied in many of the institutional practices of our departments, our universities, and our whole scholarly community.

Furthermore, we believe that these challenges are felt most acutely by relative newcomers to the profession. Indeed, hearing the call for finding common ground, developing metatheoretical approaches, and engaging in complex dialogue with counterassumptional positions gives rise to a salient identity for both of us (and likely many others who will read this volume): being untenured newcomers in the discipline. The average, young, untenured scholars who face real pressures to publish, build national reputations, define an intellectual focus, and ultimately produce a new generation of scholars, may hear this call with more anxiety than well-established, senior, and tenured scholars like Goodall, Cheney, Mumby, and Miller— whose own intellectual commitments may be one of the only hindrances to creativity in scholarship. Although some concerns of the newcomer to the profession may be viewed by others as pedestrian, overly exaggerated, or easily resolved, we wish to give voice to them as legitimate issues that have to be addressed.

So, our goal here is not to revisit the many useful and important suggestions for how we build metatheoretical bridges that illustrate the compatibility between paradigmatic views. Rather, we examine and offer solutions to the structural and cultural barriers that may prevent the newcomers to our profession from embracing these suggestions. We argue that our ability to work in this common ground is not something most of us can do in isolation, nor something that can happen simply by wishing it so. That means that tenure and promotion committees, editors and reviewers, senior faculty in positions to mentor, and others must also begin to realize the value of scholarship that works in this common ground. For us, this specifically means addressing issues related to defining ourselves intellectually, doing collaborative research, manuscript review, and graduate education. We devote our remaining presentation to discussing each of these areas by identifying what we see as the general barrier and offering potential solutions for addressing these concerns, so that the visions of this book might better be realized in our scholarly practices.

DEFINING ONESELF INTELLECTUALLY

Perhaps one of the greatest struggles for many graduate students and most assistant professors is carving out their own niche and adequately answering the question "What is it that I do?" The advice many of us receive in graduate school—and continue to get from mentors even afterward—has to do with developing a national reputation and being identified as an expert in one's area. This is, oftentimes, strongly tied to calls to be "programmatic" in one's research.

Although we believe this is generally good advice intended to promote an admirable goal, that expertise oftentimes becomes associated with a singular metatheoretical view accompanied with its own favored methodologies. In fact, those who cannot be easily pigeonholed into a familiar paradigmatic box are instead dismissively described as "all over the board," "lacking depth," or "without direction." The suggestions made elsewhere in this book to bridge metatheoretical perspectives, to seek interplay between them, and to engage in research efforts that span paradigms all run the risk of creating (usually falsely) these rather unflattering assessments of our work. For some, any confusion (from their perspective) about intellectual (especially paradigmatic) commitments can spell disaster when tenure decisions are made.

Thus, finding the common ground in our metatheoretical perspectives also requires us to rethink how we define ourselves intellectually and how our scholarly identities should be evaluated. Individually, we think scholars should emphasize their *content* area rather than their metatheoretical or methodological leanings. "Interpretevist" or "quantoid," for example, should not be our primary form of self-definition as a scholar, and are not labels we should accept from others attempting to define us. Rather, by emphasizing the phenomena of interest to us, we remain open to a variety of metatheoretical and methodological views and can more readily be accepted as moving among those perspectives and seeking other forms of common ground between them. Relatedly, we as individuals must clearly articulate who we are as scholars to mentors, tenure committees, and even ourselves. It is not enough for us just to adopt the many useful strategies for finding common ground suggested in this volume—indeed, we must frame those choices positively and persuasively to other stakeholders in the research process.

At a more structural level, senior and likely more influential scholars need to encourage those other stakeholders (e.g., tenure committees, mentors, deans) to be supportive of the type of scholarship and the type of scholar who seeks to conduct research in this common ground. We must make efforts to educate these stakeholders and to provide professional guidelines (through conferences, scholarly discussion, letters of reference used in pretenure reviews, and books such as this) that redefine and reframe notions of programmatic research and expertise. These sorts of changes are necessary if scholarly research that bridges or moves between paradigms is to be seen not as unfocused and without direction, but as another creative way to accomplish discovery.

INDIVIDUAL VERSUS COLLABORATIVE RESEARCH

One of the questions frequently asked by both graduate students and untenured faculty pertains to the desirability of collaborative research. Again, the advice we often receive suggests that truly defining oneself intellectually means proving our ability to independently conduct research. The doctoral dissertation symbolizes the great independent scholarly accomplishment, and all too often launches us toward a path of solo-authored research on our way to tenure. Collaborative research, at least in our subdiscipline, is often viewed as something to do after tenure because coauthored work does not "count" as much in the review process.

Although we agree that being capable of conducting independent scholarly endeavors is vital, we think this emphasis too often produces an anxiety that discourages collaborative research. Yet several of the suggestions made in this text and elsewhere (see Poole, Putnam, & Seibold, 1997) for finding common ground may be best accomplished by collaborative research—because it is through such collaboration that common ground is really uncovered and examined. Unfortunately, when the impression/reality exists that young faculty are not supposed to involve themselves in collaborative research (especially with senior scholars who are presumed to be "doing all the thinking") as much as they are to produce solo-authored work, there is a huge disincentive to enter into cross-paradigmatic projects (which, by their nature, are likely to be greater in scope and more difficult for a single researcher to manage). Ironically, just at a time when we as scholars might be best positioned to learn more about other metatheoretical perspectives that inform our work (but were not part of own graduate training), there is a barrier to seeking such experiences.

Thus, doing research that capitalizes on the common ground among these metatheoretical perspectives demands that we change our views about the value of collaborative research. As individual scholars we can begin by articulating the value and importance of collaborative research to those previously mentioned stakeholders. More importantly, we must seek opportunities to engage in collaborative research with other scholars who provide unique contributions that begin to unfold our paradigmatic boxes. To counter concerns about what "counts," the junior scholar might more often take the lead author position on projects. Collaborating in research with more senior scholars who work in the same content area, but whose approaches are different, provides excellent opportunities to learn and to contribute sound scholarship—while still retaining lead author status.

At a collective level, we need to foster a research climate in our departments, our discipline, and our professional associations that rewards and values this sort of cross-paradigmatic collaborative research. Promotion and tenure committees need to be convinced that these collaborative approaches have value—especially when they involve opportunities for the faculty member to learn new ways of combining perspectives from senior scholars in their area. Influential senior scholars can help make this argument through their own participation in the tenure review process in their own departments and as external reviewers of tenure cases. Senior scholars with experience in combining paradigmatic approaches also need to serve as mentors for junior colleagues with less experience in conducting this type of research. Our own professional organizations and divisions within those can encourage this type of research by setting up voluntary junior faculty mentoring programs and databases to help match scholars suited to these sorts of endeavors. Special recognition for collaborative research that finds common ground between paradigms may also be needed. Such efforts can then be promoted to other divisions in our associations and ultimately be used to reinforce positive evaluation of these research approaches in departments where promotion and tenure decisions are made.

THE MANUSCRIPT REVIEW PROCESS

Newcomers to the profession are under the greatest pressure to have their best research presented at conferences and printed in journals or books so as to disseminate that work to others. In most cases, our research manuscripts are competitively selected by peer reviewers at conferences and publication outlets. Given the high stakes of this process, we sometimes experience fears that someone "outside our area" will review and critique our manuscript. In our experience, a common complaint about "bad reviews" is the apparent bias of the reviewer against our own methodological or metatheoretical orientation. Such concerns have led to a level of paranoia that encourages authors to submit work only to those journals, or to those editors, where they will likely not experience such problems. This tendency to search for a "paradigmatic-friendly" review, to reject the critiques of those who appear to challenge our paradigmatic views, as well as the associated reluctance of scholars to review manuscripts "outside of their area," has led to an increasing paradigmatic segregation that discourages both dialogue among paradigms and the benefits of assumption contrasting (i.e., comparing rather than competing paradigmatic views of phenomena).

Although we are among the many guilty of having such concerns and being thankful for the review process that generally prevents them from materializing, we also recognize that these current practices do not lend themselves well to fostering the sort of common ground described in this book. Essentially, we see two main problems in the review process as it relates to the goal of this volume. First, research that truly finds an interplay between paradigms or intricately mixes what have often appeared to be incommensurable assumptions will be difficult to evaluate. It may not fit with a journal's—or more accurately, an editor's—identity; it may present real difficulties in terms of locating qualified individuals to review it; and even if such individuals are identified, they may have a difficult time evaluating such work. Our journals and review boards are not always as multiparadigmatic as we might expect, and there are difficulties in presenting/publishing research that bridges basic assumptions about research. Second, as we noted above, the current review process has encouraged a great deal of paradigmatic isolation in general. We are used to writing only for those who share our own metatheoretical assumptions, which fosters a type of complacency in terms of "translating" our work for others whose metatheoretical assumptions are different. The current process also promotes an atmosphere in which it is easy to ignore the input of other perspectives.

To realize the common ground ideal within the context of peer-reviewed publications and conference presentations that are so key to both the research process and tenure decisions, aspects of the review process must be changed. Our suggestions here are almost certain to be perceived as the most controversial ones we make. But if we do not make the review process one that not only can evaluate "common ground" research but also encourage greater cross-paradigmatic thinking in all of our research, then many of our efforts to build that common ground will go unrealized. Like the proverbial tree in the forest, scholarship that is never heard or never read makes no sound.

Individually, we recognize that we as researchers have to take a few risks in creating common ground scholarship. Those risks can pay off in producing more sophisticated research by considering diverse metatheoretical positions or finding valuable paradigmatic bridges. Although taking risks with all one's publication submissions—especially before tenure—may be a recipe for ulcers, a balanced diet of truly cross-paradigmatic and more uniparadigmatic (though still informed by other metatheoretical views) research can appropriately fill one's scholarly plate. Following our earlier suggestions to pursue research opportunities with senior scholars who may hold different views may help to produce a return on these seemingly risky investments. Second, we as individual reviewers should take the opportunity to review work that comes from different paradigms. Although we may often turn down such requests because we feel unqualified, such behavior simply reinforces this felt lack of qualification and maintains ignorance about research generated within other paradigms. Further, it fails to challenge submitting authors to consider what may be valuable concerns generated from different paradigms.

Of course, if we are to take such risks in submitting our research and if we are to agree to be reviewers for research that stretches our paradigmatic thinking, we must make several more structural changes to the review process. We think it is vital to emphasize that the changes suggested here can be done without extending the already lengthy review process—which is an important concern especially for untenured faculty racing a tenure clock. First, we call for greater tolerance from our journal editors. They must not only show a tolerance and appreciation for cross-paradigmatic research that finds the common ground discussed in this book, but they must also be willing not to edit out Future Directions and Implications sections that often suggest where work in other metatheoretical traditions relates. Closely tied to this, we think all publications should include a section on "translation," where the primary goal is to show how this work connects to various audiences—including scholars who embrace different paradigmatic views. Selecting the type of editor who will display this tolerance and promote this sort of structure demands that individuals with those qualities be encouraged to seek out editorships and that influence be exerted on the publications boards of our professional association to select such editors.

Perhaps more radically, we propose adding one more reviewer for each manuscript who will address cross-paradigmatic issues. For example, a "feminist" scholar might be asked to review a piece on leadership by a "post-positivist" author. Even if this cross-paradigm review was not considered as heavily in the overall assessment of the research, it would force a dialogue between the scholars (through the review process). Furthermore, it would set up a structure that necessitates reading more of one another's work. Most importantly, it would provide an opportunity to suggest some avenues by which work might embrace more diverse perspectives while that work is still under development. In even more fully realizing the last goal, the review process in our professional conferences could benefit greatly from such an approach. Rather than accepting all volunteer reviewers and then randomly assigning them manuscripts, we might seek to more strategically provide a set of reviewers who could both speak to the primary metatheoretical views in any piece of work and provide a useful "out-of-paradigm" perspective on the research.

We are fully aware that the solutions we suggest in this section could serve to build paradigmatic fences (rather than bridges) if not properly implemented. For those reasons, we suggest that such strategies begin with a single journal and with a single conference review process on an experimental basis. As a community of scholars, we could then assess the degree to which such practices were encouraging the sort of scholarship advocated in this volume. Ultimately, we believe the solutions suggested here can succeed and provide the necessary changes in the review process that would facilitate the realization of more common ground research.

TRAINING GRADUATE STUDENTS

A vitally important aspect of our jobs as newcomer scholars is our teaching. Focusing on graduate education, it is the role of the faculty, among other tasks, to teach seminars, to direct dissertations, and to serve as mentors for the next generation of scholars in our field. Part of that training involves providing guidance in the areas we have addressed in this commentary: How exactly should one define his/her intellectual commitments? How should one go about conducting research? What risks should one take in pursuing publications? Arguably, the training graduate students receive at this crucial time will be the single largest initial influence in how they conduct their scholarly lives.

Ironically, that ever-valuable training is one of the largest barriers to achieving the common ground discussed in this text. We all are the "victim" of our own training, in that most of us were probably trained predominantly, if not exclusively, in one paradigm. It is difficult, even if one is willing, to train graduate students to appreciate and embrace diverse perspectives when we have such difficulties doing so ourselves. Thus, the cycle usually continues, as we generally teach others in the same manner as we learned. But, as we begin to break that cycle, we find that the familiar areas of guidance are shifted: How do we develop scholars who have both the necessary respect and the broad knowledge of multiparadigmatic approaches to scholarship, but still have adequate depth of skill and understanding in an area of expertise? How does one employ collaborative research to explore cross-paradigmatic research projects? How does one ensure that this research based on common ground perspectives makes its way through the review process? We hope the previous sections have begun to suggest some answers; but, if graduate training is truly the formative time we believe it is, a few solutions specific to this context deserve discussion.

Individually, as instructors, we have to approach our classes with a commitment to looking for common ground among paradigmatic views. Our discussions of paradigms should not be focused solely on the differences and helping students to develop singular paradigmatic stances. Rather, our emphasis should be on each view's potential contributions to both knowledge and the research process in general. This sort of orientation inevitably leaves our graduate students with a greater respect for different paradigmatic assumptions, which is essential in fostering not only tolerance and respect, but also motivation to seek this common metatheoretical ground. These goals may be challenging given the lack of preparation many faculty have had in this area, but we do see solutions. As seminar leaders, we should choose readings that illustrate this sort of research (Cheney, in Chapter 2, this volume, offers some examples in this vein). These seem especially important in our general survey and introductory courses to the field. Furthermore, we advocate truly cross-paradigmatic seminars that actively embrace the blending of approaches. These might need to be team taught, or taught by scholars who have already had some success with research of this type, but they have the potential to begin breaking the unfortunate cycle of graduate education described earlier.

If we are to make these sorts of changes in our graduate teaching, we will need help from our colleagues and professional associations. We believe the scholarly community might benefit from regular workshops at conferences for both faculty and graduate students seeking to find this common ground and then teach others how to conduct research in this way. As Miller, Mumby, and Cheney each illustrate in this volume, we have scholars who are capable of doing this, and have such insights. However, mentoring from such individuals is needed to better train the discipline at large. Books, such as this one, and other printed resources that address the issue and provide guidelines are also needed to assist us in properly training graduate students. Perhaps even encouraging students to put together examination and dissertation committees that span and/or integrate these perspectives can begin to alert them to the opportunities this common ground presents.

CLOSING

In summary, we applaud the efforts of this book and its goals. It greatly extends Burrell's (1999) claim that multiple metatheoretical views represents "normal science" by suggesting that the common ground found between these views may actually provide for "exceptional scholarship." If we were to update the joke about how many scholars are needed to screw in a lightbulb, our improved answer would be this: A few turns of the same bulb by each perspective might result in the most illumination—but, if the necessary ladder to reach that bulb and the electrical wiring to energize it are not also put in place, there will be no light. Thus, our contribution here is a simple, but important, one: finding that metatheoretical common ground is necessary, but not sufficient, for actually conducting research this way. To realize the common ground ideal, several structural and cultural barriers must also be assessed and addressed. We have highlighted four such issues that are of special salience for newcomers to the profession: defining oneself intellectually, doing collaborative research, manuscript review, and graduate education. It is our hope that the suggestions offered can begin to reshape the research practice in ways that make room for the exceptional scholarship that may emerge from this blending and crossing of paradigmatic views.

CHAPTER 15

Potential "Sites" for Building Common Ground across Metatheoretical Perspectives on Organizational Communication

David R. Seibold
Andrew J. Flanagin

Perhaps like other essayists in this book (see, e.g., Mumby, Chapter 4, this volume) and many among its readers, we initially experienced a mixed reaction to both the premise and the prospective hope of this project: finding common ground across the perspectives that undergird scholarship on organizational communication. To be sure, the potential practical and intellectual merits of finding common ground in organizational communication studies are enormous. The "stridency" surrounding paradigmatic divisiveness noted by Corman in the Introduction to this volume has become tiresome at best, and deeply troubling at worst. Far from strengthening approaches to understanding organizational communication, such diatribes have engendered second-order conflicts that have diverted attention from the subject of our work. From a pragmatic standpoint, it would be less onerous to labor in consort with a "community" of scholars tilling the common ground concerning organizational communication scholarship. From an intellectual standpoint, common ground surrounding shared assumptions, conceptual language, tests of knowledge claims, and a corpus of research findings could be foundational for theory development and communication among scholars in the area.

At the same time, the search for common ground carries with it the deleterious potential for homogenization, mediocrity, and even wrong-headedness. When common ground becomes *the* (only) ground into which all intellectual footings are sunk, the loss of creativity and critique inherent in the diversity associated with perspectivism is virtually assured. In turn, the potential for an intellectual analog to a "regression to the mean" is highly likely. Thus, we should not take as a given that common ground is preferable or desirable (Mumby, Chapter 4, this volume). In fact, the abandonment or blending of well-developed and defensible—but different—ways of knowing is a possible consequence of the search for such common ground.

Notwithstanding these reservations, the many benefits that might accrue to our research and to our field from "building common ground" noted by the three essayists in this volume encouraged us to respond to the editors' invitation to offer this commentary. It would be easy and delightful to elaborate upon what we take to be especially useful points raised by the essayists (e.g., Miller's response to "straw-person" critiques of functionalism and her effort to reframe post-positivist research in ways that make common ground with interpretivism seem possible; Cheney's heteroglossic analysis of employee participation processes in ways that reveal common ground among perspectives while maintaining the integrity of each; and Mumby's attempt to surmount the problems inhering in oppositional typologies of organizational communication research by situating four "discourses of knowledge" about organizational communication as increasingly transgressive points on a continuum). Similarly, it would be enticing to debate some of what we view to be questionable arguments advanced by these essayists (e.g., Miller's attempt to blend realist and social constructionist ontologies within a post-positivist position; Cheney's well-intended but limited application of the empirical–analytic perspective in his hypothetical investigation of employee participation; and Mumby's tendency to make communication overly problematic and structure underly problematic in his analysis of "organization" and its fundamentally political character).

However, consistent with the editors' charge of moving beyond individual essayists while also focusing with them "on ways we can accomplish or develop the common ground" described by Miller, Cheney, and Mumby, we identify below four "building sites" for integrating the post-positivist, interpretivist, and critical theory perspectives: integration across micro- and macro*levels of analysis, (meta)theoretical* integration, integration in *applications* of organizational communication research, and the *pragmatics* of integration. We treat each as a "site" for forging integration, a space in which common ground might be "built." By doing so, we hope to highlight the potential for synthesis across perspectives, while keeping sight of the unique utility offered by each.

MICRO-/MACROLEVEL INTEGRATION

One of the fault lines underlying the surface of the social sciences has been the constant tension surrounding the *level of analysis* at which explanation and understanding are to be found. In simplest form this has been reflected in the opposition of perspectives that privilege individual agency and those that emphasize collectives. Indeed, Alexander and Giesen (1987) read the history of sociological theory through the lens of this micro/macro debate. Social theories can be contrasted in terms of the emphasis they place on whether societies emerge from the unfettered interactions of individuals, or whether fully "socialized" actors map social structures into their interactions.

In many respects this micro/macro tension underlies prominent differences associated with post-positivist, interpretivist, and critical theory approaches to organizational communication. Flowing from positivists' atomistic explanations for natural phenomena, organizational scholars steeped in that tradition have most often fostered microlevel accounts of organizational communication "variables" and their relationships. On the other hand, organizational communication scholars working from a critical theory perspective have drawn on the work of Marx, among the most important macroperspectives in the social sciences, for the ascendancy it accords to collective material conditions in the instantiation of individual action.

Of course, there have been notable exceptions in each approach to the study of organizational communication, as with "macro" researchers working within the empirical–analytic tradition and focusing on interorganizational communication phenomena (see, e.g., Monge et al., 1998) or critical theorists' more microlevel depictions of patterns of power reflected in organizational meetings and narratives (Mumby, 1987). And while scholars working in the interpretivist perspective have produced microlevel ethnographically oriented research for the most part, others have integrated micro- and macroperspectives (e.g., critical feminist research by Buzzanell, 1994, and Clair, 1993, among others). Still, the general effect of these micro/macro predispositions has been to create differences in the level of analysis at which scholars in the respective perspectives work.

One site for building common ground, therefore, is enhanced micro/ macro integration in organizational communication scholarship. Several strategies are available. First, when possible and when appropriate, design and conduct studies in ways that self-consciously integrate all three perspectives (as with Cheney's illustration involving analysis of employee participation processes; Chapter 2, this volume). This would not only foster broader and more penetrating insights into the foci of investigation, but would begin to reduce the distances among these perspectives.

Second, and relatedly, perform mesolevel analyses (Rousseau & House, 1994) in ways that examine interactions within and across micro- and macrolevels that bear on the phenomena of interest. For example, Waldeck and Seibold (1998) utilized a mesolevel analysis to examine individual, work group, and organizational needs that affect socialization dynamics, as well as contingent factors that moderate the relationship between these needs and a variety of traditionally studied outcomes of socialization. The mesolevel analysis required broadening what began as a review of post-positivist research to include studies borne of the interpretivist and critical theory perspectives that addressed contingencies at more complex levels of analysis.

Third, frame research "agendas" for organizational communication scholars in ways that link micro to macro. Mumby and Stohl's (1996) "problematics" of voice, rationality, organization, and the organization–environment relationship frame key issues ranging from the micro- to the macrolevel. This serves to emphasize the interrelatedness of organizational members' actions, researchers' agendas, and environmental pressures and invites the application of multiple perspectives in order to address the key issues raised.

Fourth, focus research attention on "mediating structures" in organizational communication—the effect of which would be to require more broad-based analyses. For example, some scholars (Poole, 1998; Seibold, 1998; Weick, 1979) have called for greater attention to organizational groups (e.g., work groups, cross-functional teams, short-term project groups, task forces, executive/administrative groups, committees, and the like) as action/structures that mediate individuals and larger collectives. Groups are at the nexus of individual interaction and organizational structure. They have pervasive effects that channel individual agency, yet mediate larger organizational (even societal) structures in processes that constrain individual members. Parallel claims have been made for the salience of examining "discursive fields" that not only are manifested within organizations but that extend beyond the site of organization, such as Cheney's (1998) analysis of how marketing metaphors not only inform the discourses of business practice but pervade intraorganizational life at multiple levels. Not only do such analyses enjoin both micro- and macroanalyses, but they can conjoin the three perspectives in organizational communication when those approaches proffer the best understandings at different levels of analysis.

(META)THEORETICAL INTEGRATION

Another "site" for building common ground across diverse approaches to organizational communication is the development of theories and metatheories that have the potential to integrate scholars from different perspectives. Much as the theories of Weber and Parsons in sociology formed a basis for some connection between adherents to macrostructure (theorists such as Durkheim and Marx) and proponents of microexperiences (theorists such as Mead and Cooley), perspectives that foster (meta)theoretical integration in organizational communication are possible. Such metatheoretical integration might form the basis for paradigm-crossing techniques (see Cheney, Chapter 2, this volume).

One such perspective, as Miller (Chapter 3, this volume) emphasizes, is Giddens's (1984) structuration theory. Giddens locates both the daily "systems" of individuals we observe and the "structures" of society we theorize as emerging from the interpretations of those engaged in interaction. Even as interactants retrospectively assign meaning to the practices in which they are immersed, they produce patterns of larger institutional forms. Society is not only produced and reproduced in this way, but structures of power are developed, meanings are legitimated, and norms are sanctioned. At the same time structuration theory has found application in the work of organizational communication scholars identified with the post-positivist perspective (see, e.g., Poole & DeSanctis, 1992; Poole, Seibold, & McPhee, 1996; Scott, Corman, & Cheney, 1998), it has its roots in some of the same phenomenological and structuralism soils that gave rise to interpretivism (see Taylor, Flanagin, Cheney, & Seibold, 2000). This perhaps helps to explain its widespread appeal to communication scholars and its continued potential for building common ground between perspectives.

There are other (meta)theoretical perspectives with the potential to integrate organizational communication scholars. For example, Taylor and Van Every (2000) draw upon developments in artificial intelligence, especially "subsymbolic knowledge" (a property of the network of interaction rather than of any node within it), to develop a perspective on organizational "distributed cognition" that is at once consistent with the work of some conversation analysts who work within the interpretivist perspective and with the work of "semantic network" analysts associated with the post-positivist approach. Alternately, drawing on activity theory, Engeström (1990; Engeström & Middleton, 1996) has highlighted how the material bases of communication in organizational tasks, contexts, and as mediated by technologies are discursively manifested in members' interactions in ways that presage organizational change—a perspective readily relevant for scholars from all three perspectives. Furthermore, Cooren (1999) uses Greimas' sociosemiotic model to self-consciously and explicitly "bridge the gap that traditionally separates functionalism and interpretivism by concentrating on the organizing properties of communication" (p. 294).

Finally, we should neither ignore nor underestimate the potential for work emanating from self-organizing systems theory (Contractor, 1994, 1999; Hawes, 1999; Houston, 1999; Krippendorff, 1999) to forge common ground among organizational communication scholars. Research on the "self-organizing processes" and generative mechanisms of various social systems can be enriched by invoking multiple metatheoretical perspectives. For example, computational modeling techniques (Carley & Prietula, 1994; Hyatt, Contractor, & Jones, 1997), employed to simulate multiple, nonlinear generative mechanisms in organizations, must be validated against additional data and observations. In this pursuit, and in order to ensure that the researcher is not too far removed from his or her subjects (see Cheney, Chapter 2, this volume), interpretive perspectives may prove valuable in assessing the reasonableness of simulated models by comparing interactants' experiences to proposed patterns of interaction. Moreover, a critical view can be employed to contextualize the wider implications of modeled behavior. Thus, multiple perspectives can profitably be engaged to probe the boundary conditions that serve to define and maintain generative mechanisms in self-organizing processes.

INTEGRATION IN APPLICATION

Perhaps one of the most pervasive and appropriate "sites" for building common ground across organizational communication perspectives is the "world" in which we find ourselves. We are partners and parents, neighbors and citizens, volunteers and voters, community activists and consultants—even as we are academic researchers. In these myriad roles we encounter multiple opportunities for seeding, conducting, or applying "research." As Cheney (Chapter 2, this volume) notes, "research is understood to be part of the larger stream or *durée* of life. What becomes research is not always known at the outset of what might later be termed 'a project.' And what may be identified as a research project ought to flow naturally back into other life activities" (p. 20).

The blurring of boundaries concerning potential foci and contexts for research are dynamics central to the interpretivist and critical theory perspectives. Moreover, this notion is not inconsistent with post-positivism, especially as the assumption of value-free inquiry has been rejected and as objectivity has come to be seen as a "regulatory ideal" rather than as an absolute and attainable requirement (Miller, Chapter 3, this volume). The organizational communication research literature is replete with empirical–analytical studies rooted in contract-driven applied research projects, needs assessments, formative evaluations, policy analyses, and summative research, among others. In most cases, these were not "basic" research but investigations that employed organizational theory and research methods as means toward applied ends, and whose theoretical implications were realized and reported upon in the process of serving those applied ends.

To draw upon a personal example, in an article published in the *Amer-*

ican Journal of Hospice Care, Seibold, Rossi, Berteotti, Soprych, and McQuillan (1987) reported an evaluation of a hospice volunteer program. While we necessarily and inevitably drew upon major research constructs and findings as ways of framing the context and the problem (volunteer turnover), we did not begin with the goal of addressing or advancing this literature. Rather, this research served as a basis for interpreting why the volunteer program succeeded in retaining some volunteers while losing what hospice administrators regarded as too many others. We did not set out to test postulates about the effects of "role conflict" on organizational turnover, for instance, but simply drew upon what insights organizational theory afforded us (which we later reported elsewhere; see Berteotti & Seibold, 1994) as a means to answer a specific question about a specific problem in a specific setting.

As the recursivity of *theoria* and *praxis*, of research ends and means, and even of one's life and one's research become more apparent, the opportunities increase for building common ground across perspectives in organizational communication. As researcher-citizens investigate and seek to ameliorate problems of participation and voice, efficacy and influence, inequity and marginalization, productivity and performance, oppression and powerlessness, intergroup conflict, misunderstandings, and quality of work life, among many others, the axiological, ontological, and epistemological assumptions of each perspective offer alternative frames of understanding. In turn, the research methods attendant to alternative perspectives afford different means for attaining insights. Where appropriate, multimethodism borne of each perspective can offer further explanatory traction. If Cheney's (Chapter 2, this volume) depiction of each perspective's approach to studying employee participation processes is not viewed as separate and sequential, but as simultaneous and seamless, the potential for another "building site" of common ground is apparent in the "application" of all three perspectives.

PRAGMATICS OF INTEGRATION

In the final analysis, building common ground across perspectives in organizational communication will require not only collective determination concerning how we enact our field but also individual integrity related to how we enact our roles as scholars. In the first area, the field, the very fora in which divisiveness, claims of incommensurability, and even name calling are heard, can just as readily be converted to venues for establishing common ground. Each academic year there are myriad opportunities to build "institutional sites" explicitly devoted to integration across perspectives: entire volumes like this one; integrative sections, chapters, or commentaries in edited volumes; special issues of journals or colloquy sections on a routine basis; preconferences, seminars, and panels at our professional society meetings; exchanges on CRTNET; visiting lecture series at host universities (with subsequent publication of proceedings); and collaborative research ventures—among others. The more that such "sites" are routinely and ritualistically used for addressing prospects and problems attendant to building common ground, the less guarded we all may become about the need for the same.

But individual agency must play a crucial role if there is to be common ground for all. As Cheney (Chapter 2, this volume) notes concerning the foundations of incommensurability, "in some cases researchers do not even reach the point of articulating a principle such as incommensurability because either (1) they are not fully aware of competing perspectives (by holding caricatures of them) or (2) they simply do not recognize the competing claims that originate from outside their own strongly held ideology as valid" (p. 38). However, as Miller (Chapter 3, this volume) notes, actions as simple as *talking* to each other might reduce perceived incommensurability across perspectives. Disciplining ourselves to read research literature from other perspectives, to integrate that literature into our syllabi, and to ponder differences fairly (and to refrain from using the caricatures that obscure them) are crucial acts within each scholar's prerogative.

In essence, we must think of ourselves as "individual sites" for potential integration. By doing so, we might "abandon the binary" contrasts set up to validate perspectives, thereby transcending false oppositions and halting their reification (see Mumby, Chapter 4, this volume). Furthermore, we may also begin to "rescue from vilification" each individual perspective and avoid caricaturing one another's primary metatheoretical emphases (Miller, Chapter 3, this volume). Ultimately, then, finding whatever common ground is available in organizational communication across the postpositivist, interpretivist, and critical theory perspectives requires *each* of us to perform simple, everyday acts of courage.

CHAPTER 16

Pedagogy and Paradigms
The Search for Common Ground[1]

Cynthia Stohl

The Babel fish, said The Hitchhiker's Guide to the Galaxy
quietly, "is small, yellow, leechlike and probably the oddest
thing in the Universe. It feeds on brainwave energy received
not from its own carrier but from those around it. It absorbs
all unconscious mental frequencies from this brainwave energy
to nourish itself with. It then excretes into the mind of its
carrier a telepathic matrix formed by combining the conscious
thought frequencies with nerve signals picked up from the
speech centers of the brain which has supplied them. The
practical upshot of all this is that if you stick a Babel fish in
your ear you can instantly understand anything said to you in
any form of language. The speech patterns you actually hear
decode the brainwave matrix which has been fed into your ear
by the Babel fish. . . ."

Meanwhile, the poor Babel fish, by effectively removing
all barriers to communication between different races and
cultures, has caused more and bloodier wars than anything
else in the history of creation.
—DOUGLAS ADAMS (1979, pp. 59–61)

On a first reading the quotation above presents a rather negative and pessimistic view of the entire premise of this book: the need for common
ground. Indeed, the plea by Corman (Chapter 1, this volume, p. 8) for organizational communication scholars to "construct some common system
of reference that could allow explanations from different points of view to
be compared or integrated," seems, paradoxically, to portend precisely
what he wants to avoid: more and bloodier science wars. However, rather
than being seen as a refutation of the fine intentions Corman explicates in
his Introduction, in this brief commentary I propose that the goals are wor-

thy and important but the means, that is, establishing common ground, a common reference system, a common language, is problematic.

I suggest that it is not necessary (and perhaps even undesirable) for proponents of radically different paradigms to speak the same language. I am using the term *language* here to encompass the vocabulary and syntax of a paradigm including "the phraseology or terms of a science, art, profession, etc." (*The Oxford Universal Dictionary,* 1955, p. 1104), which "serves as a creative mental and intellectual tool" (The Linguasphere Observatory, 2000).

Like Miller, Mumby, and Cheney who each, although for very different reasons, challenge the incommensurability thesis, I, too, propose that resolving incommensurability is not the answer to our problem. Miller (Chapter 3, this volume, p. 63) succinctly captures the essence and the problematic nature of the conclusions drawn from the incommensurability thesis: "like the allegory of the Tower of Babel, it is a 'single, shared language that allows work to proceed and its absence halts all joint efforts' (Kaghan & Phillips, 1998, p. 192)." We should not try to reconcile theoretical paradigms nor speak only one shared language. Rather, to address the destructive and discordant trend that Corman aptly describes, I believe that each of us needs to develop at least rudimentary fluency in research languages other than our own. By learning others' languages we can converse, share, and build upon one anothers' ideas, as well as begin to understand those seemingly untranslatable words, phrases, terms, and concepts that are so commonplace and frustrating to capture when one works in only one language. The human and structural connections, so obvious from one perspective, yet veiled or missing from others, become clearer as we converse in other tongues and dialects. As Victor (1992) notes, "No two languages carry the same associations. Each language, in turn, determines the likely associations of one thought to the next" (p. 19).

The underlying premise of my commentary, then, is that "multilingualism" in research perspectives will give us a far richer and more complex sense of the world we study and the academic community in which we reside. Despite the pervasive myths of this century regarding the problems of multilingualism (see Altmann, 1999) and the cautionary biblical tale of the Tower of Babel, evidence now indicates that multilingualism has no negative effect on competence and performance and indeed enhances verbal fluency (Romaine, 1995). Likewise, I suggest that learning the vocabulary and grammar of multiple research paradigms will facilitate respect, enable us to do our research better, and provide a context in which dialogue and difference can exist simultaneously. The ability to switch and mix codes enables imaginative inventions and creative collaborations that could not be developed within one paradigmatic language.

Clearly, expert fluency in multiple research languages (although a desirable condition) is unrealistic; typically we will remain most comfortable and most competent speaking one language over another. Nonetheless, the process of learning other languages has unintended but significant consequences. The certainty that one form of language is superior and always best suited for the study of human communication processes becomes a difficult position to maintain as one learns to operate within new linguistic models that comprise new ways of talking, thinking, and making knowledge claims. Furthermore, learning new languages cannot be approached individually, in the isolation of a library carrel or alone in one's study. It requires, minimally, some interaction with speakers of the language (preferably speakers whose first language is the one we are trying to learn) and, maximally, immersion in the new language community. Thus, I am not suggesting that disarmament in the science wars occurs solely at the individual level; we must engage one another, on each other's territory, enacting structural changes that can help quell the stridency of our debates and make it less likely that academic skirmishes and differences turn into war.

But before we address systemic responses to the challenge posed by Corman, let's return to the initial argument. The need for researchers to move among discourses and engage in "bridging discourses" (Miller), "paradigm dialogues" (Cheney), and "overlapping discourses" (Mumby) is a theme that runs throughout the analyses and suggestions made by the three primary authors. Miller writes: "As a discipline, we can deal with the incommensurability problem both through dialogue and through the use of metatheoretical frameworks that allow for productive work within several paradigmatic assumptive bases" (Chapter 3, this volume, p. 66). Cheney (Chapter 2, this volume) proposes paradigm dialogues among researchers, and explores the potentially positive outcomes when paradigms speak to one another, appropriate one another, and become one another. Mumby strives to provide a framework that "generates a set of research issues that facilitate common ground without sacrificing the kinds of difference and multivocality that make our field so rich and diverse" (Chapter 4, this volume, p. 81). In other words, each author attempts to resolve the tensions that lead to war by presenting possibilities and openings for us as members of the research community.

I would like to suggest, however, that it is not simply our roles as practicing research scholars—the identity specifically addressed by Cheney, Mumby, and Miller—that is relevant to this discussion. Rather, it is in our roles as educators, as professors, as members of institutions of higher learning that we can make the largest difference and work toward establishing the type of scholarly community Corman envisions. I am not suggesting in any way that these eminent scholars do not think teaching is important; indeed, each of them is also an outstanding and committed teacher. Rather, my point is that the bifurcation and reification of our roles as scholars/teachers often keep us from considering what we can do together in our multiple overlapping roles as members of the academic community. But, as

Mumby and I have suggested elsewhere, our work "must be contextualized in terms of our understanding of the educational role played by organizational communication scholars" (Mumby & Stohl, 1996, p. 54).

In other words, what I am suggesting is that for us as a community to develop the skills, knowledge, and sensitivities needed to enact the new and productive forms of communication across paradigms that most of us seem to agree is desirable, we need to address graduate education and find ways to help our students become multilingual. It is, after all, not only far easier to learn a second language at an earlier age but once a person is bilingual it becomes easier to learn other languages (Altmann, 1999). Moreover, it is the new generation of scholars who will determine the future of our field. We, who are already entrenched within one perspective or striving to transcend those boundaries and cross the borders to other paradigms, can perpetuate the conditions for the continuation of the destructive conflict or lay the groundwork for productive engagement. Our roles as teachers/scholars give us great responsibility and enormous opportunity.

To foster multilingualism within graduate education does not mean that students (1) need not develop a particular theoretical area of expertise; (2) become dilettantes, knowing very little about a lot and a lot about very little; nor (3) must they develop balanced, nativelike command of all the languages in the theoretical repertoire of organizational communication. Rather I use the term *multilingual* in the sense discussed by the linguist Kamal Sridhar: "Multilinguals develop competence in each of the codes to the extent that they need it and for the contexts in which each of the languages is used" (1996, p. 50).

As an example of one faculty's pedagogical attempt to address the very issues confronted in this volume, I will detail a new two-semester course sequence recently developed at Purdue as a requirement for PhD students. I know that other universities are attempting the same thing (indeed, our department spent a great deal of time looking at the courses other departments have developed). I use Purdue's model because it is the one I am most familiar with and because we are extraordinarily lucky to have a faculty who, although very capable of enacting the science wars described in the literature and experienced by some of us, is committed to a broader vision: a form of graduate education that prepares our future colleagues to formulate and articulate a particular approach while having respect, knowledge, and familiarity with others' positions.

It is important to note that the course was developed because graduate students wanted to experience a cohesive overview of issues relating to theory development/appraisal and major theoretical approaches in the field. As future scholars, they recognized the need to learn the languages of multiple traditions not isolated from one another (as in taking separate courses) but in tandem, interacting with and engaging in direct dialogue and productive confrontation with major theoretic paradigms. Over two semesters, more than a dozen faculty members, in the areas of rhetoric, public affairs, and issue management, and organizational, interpersonal, and mass communication, representing historical, interpretive, post-positivist, and critical approaches to the study of human communication, met weekly with graduate students to discuss the goals of the course, the format, the curriculum, the types of assignments, and so on. In many ways, these open meetings and the energized discussions that took place became a model for what we all hoped the course would be.

The two-course sequence, team-taught by scholars whose own work is strongly entrenched in two distinct paradigms, is designed to introduce doctoral students to major and emerging approaches to understanding human communication and provide them with the theoretical background and analytic skills needed to navigate the tensions among these approaches. The courses review the intellectual history of communication inquiry, overview traditional and innovative questions about human communication, examine the ways in which these questions can be addressed from different perspectives, address some of the varied forms that knowledge about human communication can take, and explore how different research traditions go about making and warranting knowledge claims.

The course objectives are explicated to foster multilingualism (a term not used by the faculty/student group during the yearlong development of these courses but one I have appropriated for this commentary). These objectives, once developed in the open working group, were discussed, modified, and accepted by the faculty as a whole:

1. To develop students' understanding of the fundamental assumptions underlying different approaches to the study of communication and how these assumptions inform research on communication.
2. To develop students' capacity to describe, and to compare and contrast, several prominent approaches informing the study of human communication.
3. To promote among students and faculty dialogue, conversation, and debate about the strengths and limitations of different approaches to the study of human communication.
4. To encourage students to evaluate critically the different approaches to the study of human communication and the appropriateness of these approaches for finding answers to questions of practical and academic concern.
5. To assist students in elaborating their own responses to foundational questions concerning the nature of human communication and approaches to its study.

6. To introduce students to a broad range of faculty research interests represented in the Department of Communication through presentations by a broad range of individual members of its faculty.

As graduate students and faculty from these different perspectives are asked to articulate knowledge claims, explore what comprises a knowledge claim, and investigate what it is that makes good scholarship and not only good conversation within each paradigm, we hope to begin to develop the foundation for multilingualism. By reading across perspectives, engaging proponents of these perspectives, and comparing and contrasting positions, the budding interpretivist learns how to recognize good quantitative studies from bad, the nascent critical theorist to recognize quality ethnography from poor ethnography, the promising post-positivist to understand and appreciate critique and praxis. Moreover, participants will need to grapple with the possible ways in which ethnographic accounts can inform a survey, network analyses can unmask the many faces of power, and so on. They can begin building within one paradigm using the insights from the others. The goal is not to develop one common reference system, but a common understanding and respect for many reference systems. Each perspective speaks in terms that can be understood by the other, because the one understands the language of the other. Finally, through this dialogic process, we hope that students are able to utilize a variety of perspectives to generate knowledge and be comfortable working in the collaborative teams that are essential for the multiperspectival, multilingual, interdisciplinary studies needed to understand today's global, multicultural environment.

In sum, the purpose of these two courses is to provide beginning PhD students with an understanding of the major and emerging paradigms, perspectives, theories, and bodies of research that constitute the field/discipline of communication. Students will become conversant with the major epistemological, ontological, and axiological issues that underpin this work. Because of its place in the curriculum, the course is designed to provide all PhD students, regardless of area of specialty, with a grounding in the various debates and dialogues that characterize the field so that they themselves can become meaningfully involved in those debates and dialogues.

In summary, I believe this type of course and these types of dialogues among students and faculty will help us face the challenges posed by Corman. It is through our pedagogy that we can produce the type of multilingual environment that will allow our field to go forward in constructive and creative ways. Contrary to the view in the United States that monolingualism is the norm, linguists have been saying for a long time that bilingualism is far more common globally (Reich, 1986). It is time for our field to "globalize" in all senses of the word. By having students and ourselves engage with others who speak differently, by putting a human face to these multiple perspectives, by struggling to understand and be understood by others, then perhaps like the legendary soldiers of World War I who met and conversed in the trenches and no longer could fight against one another, we will have found our common ground.

NOTE

1. I would like to thank Felicia Roberts and Michael Stohl for their helpful and always enjoyable conversations.

CHAPTER 17

A Common Ground, Common Grounds, or Footbridges?

James R. Taylor

I was intrigued by Kathy Miller's small experiment in which she canvassed three of her colleagues to find how each of them would situate themselves on Burrell and Morgan's (1979) famous two-by-two map of the social science territory. Not one of the organizational communication scholars in her department, you will recall, was ready to identify unambiguously with any of the four quadrants that define Burrell and Morgan's typology. I reacted to her story in part because I had had a similar experience not long before: my reaction to Bob Craig's somewhat different carving up of the field, in the May 1999 issue of *Communication Theory,* where he argues for the continuing dominance of seven traditions in communication research:

- The rhetorical: communication as the practical art of discourse.
- The semiotic: communication as intersubjective mediation by signs.
- The phenomenological: communication as dialogue, or the experience of others.
- The cybernetic: communication as information processing.
- The sociopsychological: communication as a process of expression, interaction, and influence.
- The sociocultural: communication as a symbolic process that produces and reproduces shared social and cultural patterns.
- The critical: communication as a discursive reflection that moves toward transcendence that can never be fully and finally achieved—but the reflective process itself is essentially emancipatory.

Okay, I said to myself when I had finished reading Craig's analysis, where do you fit, Taylor? And I discovered that I felt more or less comfortable slotting myself into all of the traditions. I realized that in my own writing I regularly incorporate elements from all seven camps. And I would have had as much trouble as Kathy's colleagues in identifying my place on Burrell and Morgan's map.

It was hard not to notice that each of the essayists is careful to keep their distance from the hard-and-fast positions of an earlier generation: Miller's "post-positivism" sounds suspiciously interpretive; Mumby's critical stance merges into a rather different perspective, that of dialogism; and Cheney's interpretivism could be read, without too much of a stretch of the imagination, as tinged with criticalism. And, of course, all are experienced practical researchers, so that when push comes to shove, they share a common bond of professional skill and mutual respect. At first glance, at least, the gulf between the perspectives does not seem to be as large as all that.

So what is going on here? Are the debates over communication theory just another whited sepulchre, "beautiful outward," but "within full of dead men's bones" (Matthew, 21.27)? Is part of the problem, outlined so well in Steve Corman's Introduction, that we have been caught behind the lines, defending positions that no longer have much strategic value (to continue the war imagery he introduced in setting up this whole discussion)? Has the quarreling he documents in his Introduction degenerated into futile name calling, at exactly the moment when the names no longer mean what they once did?

In my contribution to this search for a common ground I would like to offer a few observations that are stimulated by the perception that, if we are to establish common ground, then one thing we may need to accomplish is to find a new language for maintaining a constructive dialogue, even if it means abandoning the security of the semantic shelters that we have been occupying so comfortably in the past. But will this be enough? Are there deeper issues of substance that we have to take account of than just problems of terminology? I suggest the concept of a common ground— a single meeting place—may be overly optimistic. Perhaps there is more than one common ground we should be concerned about. I am going to propose three areas where we might look for common ground (not to question that there may be others as well): a common ground of theory, a common ground of evidence, and a common ground of object of research. And then I will conclude by suggesting another metaphor, that of the footbridge.

A COMMON GROUND OF THEORY?

Let me begin with a first observation: the essence of science is the building of theories. Miller, in her essay, cites as one of the motivating factors in the turn to positivism that characterized the early development of the communication field something she calls "physics envy." But the thing about physics, as a science, is that it is far and away the most theoretical of all the sciences. Many of Einstein's hypotheses could not be verified for decades. The theory was so elegant, and so persuasive, that it just had to be true. Physicists in today's generation regularly find themselves in the situation where they never directly see the objects they speculate about, either because they are too small, or because they are too large (and too far away), or because the very act of observing the object they are interested in transforms it. Physics is shot through and through with theory.

The life sciences are in their own way confronted with the same issue. Atlan (1979), in his "essay on the organization of the living," begins his book with an account of biologist D. Mazia trying to isolate the structure of the cell: by the time he had succeeded in determining its structure, the cell was dead. There was no way to discover the organization of the cell until the being it structured had ceased to exist in its natural living form. The living being escapes definitive analysis in the end precisely because it is living. The biologist, like the physicist, has to rely on theory.

Communication science, it seems to me, confronts a similar dilemma. We can never capture the reality of communication by simple observation and measurement. What we can do is construct better theory. And it is here that the shoe begins to pinch. As Mumby observes in Chapter 4, "I have always been surprised by the degree to which the *act* of communication (as opposed to the antecedents or derivatives of this act) is ignored as an object of study in our field." "We tend," he goes on, "to draw heavily on definitions and explanatory constructs of human behavior that have been generated by other fields such as sociology and psychology. As such, we have problems developing common ground when we overlook the phenomenon that binds us together, and instead allow other fields to dictate our self-definition" (p. 78).

Craig (1999) is even more categorical: "I argue that communication theory as an identifiable field of study does not yet exist" (p. 119). As he remarks, the result is that "communication theorists neither agree nor disagree about much of anything. There is no canon of general theory to which they all refer" (p. 119).

Miller (Chapter 3, this volume) believes that structuration theory may offer the possibility of a unifying framework. I am sympathetic to that suggestion, although it is fair to observe that communication had a very small role to play in Giddens's original formulation, and it has not always been clear that the adaptations different communication scholars have made of the original, including my own, have resolved the incommensurability problem that Corman signals as central. Structuration theory may well be the tree on which all of us could begin to hang our hat, except that I am not certain that everyone is reading the theory in the same interpretive mode. Mumby is unsure, for example, whether some of the interpretations of structuration theory may not have softened the critical edge of the original.

Banks and Riley (1993) are even more skeptical: they refer to what they call "the en passant problem," where structurational terms and concepts become a vocabulary that is grafted onto some set of problems to provide an after-the-fact account of an already established categorization of experience, based on a quite different set of theoretical assumptions.

This again raises the thorny problem of when a theory stops being the same theory and starts to evolve into a quite different theory. As we know from the literature, some of the most passionate polemics are not those that pit one theory against another, but one interpretation of theory against another of the same theory. This may be the problem of structuration theory, that it is not yet clear that it is authentically a communication theory, as opposed to a refit, borrowed from sociology, with some added new features and a good paint job.

On this score, that of theory development, I perceive a growing awareness that, until we do develop a common body of theory, it is hard to foresee a common body of scientific discourse. I received my own training in the positivist mold of the 1960s, when behaviorism in psychology and functionalism in sociology reigned supreme (there was no corresponding "ism" in communication—unless you could count eclecticism). I can still recall the pathetic cripples that passed for "theory" when the only admissible theoretical statements were those that could be immediately "operationalized" by the measurement of "subject" or "respondent" responses in the context of some experiment or survey. That is not what I think any of the authors in this book, or Craig, is talking about.

Both behaviorism and functionalism, I began to realize, achieved their scientific rigor by actively eliminating the possibility of genuine communication. The stimulus–response (S–R) format of the experiment guaranteed that the sequences of communication being studied were chopped up into such small segments that communication could not be carried on normally. Survey research records the results of communication but it studiously avoids the contamination of actual situated human communication. So it seems to me that our first challenge is to address the issue of what communication is, and how to theorize it. From this may come, as a crucial by-product, a common language, in which we all feel fairly comfortable.

A COMMON GROUND OF EVIDENCE?

A second place we might look for common ground is in what counts as evidence to support some theoretically based hypothesis or question. I have nothing but admiration for the eighteenth-century empiricists John Locke and David Hume, who between them blew away whole fogbanks of idealistic vapor and created a basis for contemporary social scientific research. But I doubt whether anyone in communication studies today, and certainly not the three lead authors in this book, really believes that knowledge is constructed synthetically out of the sensory experiences we have of the world. We do not have to be disciples of Immanuel Kant to understand that we actively structure our experience, as much as our experience structures us. Still, it is not so very long ago that notions of "reflex arc" and "operant conditioning" and "S–R learning curves" were accepted dogma: even as late as the 1950s Skinner was prepared to claim that language could be explained as an effect of conditioning, in the S–R sense of that term (Skinner, 1957). Chomsky (1959) demolished his argument beyond possible repair, but the ideas on which it was based were still very much in evidence when I entered graduate school in 1966. Methods meant experimentation, and the experimental model was inspired by S–R.

The problem with this, as I have said, is that the S–R model is such an impoverished representation of communication. It so restricts our field of view that it seriously reduces the issues of research we can even consider— especially where the object is organizational communication.

I have a sense that a more likely candidate for a common ground on which contemporary researchers in communication might assemble is the essentially pragmatic perspective bequeathed to us by Karl Popper (and before him by C. S. Peirce) that if the business of science is the development of theory, then the contribution of empirical research is the correction of theoretical statements that cannot be substantiated. I cannot imagine any of the three principal authors who have established the parameters of our discussion disagreeing on this principle.

The issue becomes what counts as admissible evidence in supporting or contradicting some hypothetical assertion. Here I am less sure where we are likely to find common ground. My own experience as a teacher suggests that students who wrestle with terms such as "positivist" or "interpretivist" immediately become more comfortable when they can think of these same approaches as, alternatively, *quantitative* and *qualitative*. I am not intimating that these are really synonyms: certainly, I would think, not all post-positivists would feel uncomfortable relying on qualitative methods, where they thought it was appropriate, nor do I believe all interpretivists shy away from quantitative analysis, where it illuminates the topic being investigated.

Nevertheless, it is fair to say that the quantitative–qualitative divide does define fault lines in our profession, and does enter into decisions such as whether or not to publish some article, or to award a distinction at some conference.

Part of the problem is that the term *qualitative* is itself ambiguous. It covers a whole spectrum of means to collect evidence, from (1) the ethnographic, which John Van Maanen (see Taylor & Gurd, 1996) thinks of as a prolonged bath of experience in some previously unknown community to produce a convincing chronicle of the experience; to (2) the ethnomethodological, which in its recent manifestation as conversation analysis, subjects recorded protocols of exchange to intensive analysis in order to reveal hidden rules of procedure; to (3) the hermeneutic, which as content or discourse analysis takes as its corpus some extensive body of writings or otherwise recorded material, in order to get to the heart of a culture through an understanding of its communications; to (4) forms of naturalistic inquiry, in the spirit of developing a "grounded theory" by methods that may differ from quantitative analysis, but still aim to uncover patterns of cause and effect. And, of course, the term *discourse analysis* itself is a catchall expression for some quite different approaches to assembling evidence. And, too, sometimes more than one method is in play, in the course of a single study.

My own sense is that we have to consider the collecting and analysis of evidence as being itself an exemplar of organizational communication. My own preferred reading of the practice of science is a chapter written by Humberto Maturana in Fred Steier's (1991) collection of essays called *Research and Reflexivity.* As Maturana sees it, science is one domain of experience, among many, that is defined by habits of what he calls "languaging" (I think the influence of Wittgenstein is evident here). As a domain, its preoccupation is with explaining (explaining is, of course, one genre of languaging). The issue is why some forms of explaining are, and some others are not, acceptable to the community of discourse to which the explainer belongs. Maturana lists his criteria for what it takes to produce a scientifically acceptable explanation: (1) presenting one's own experience in a way that is recognizable to others, whom he idealizes as "standard observers"; (2) showing that the experience is in conformity with general rules governing how observers are supposed to approach their object of research; (3) generalizing from one's particular experience to other experiences that could be explained by it; and (4) reporting on what was actually experienced.

What attracts me to this way of looking at the activity of doing science is that it is fundamentally a communicational explanation of how to generate and evaluate explanations. The notion of languaging is at the heart of it, and it sets up a basic tension between the activities of some individual researcher and the discourse community to which he/she belongs. The issue, as Maturana sees it, is "the consensual participation in the domain of scientific explanations" (1991, p. 33). What counts in evaluating any piece of evidence is not its truth, because, as he says, science is not a gateway to "reality." Reality, to use Weick's term, is *enacted,* in science as much as anywhere else. What counts are the enactive, or communicative, practices of the observer, evidence of which must be visible in the account of research that is subsequently rendered to the larger community. We exist, Maturana says, in language: an experiential domain that in many respects is characterized by closure.

Corman, in his Introduction to this book, alluded to the issue of the review process. I have a feeling this may be where we should start to look for common ground. It is here, in the everyday review process, that the essential encounter between researcher and research community takes place, and where the rules of languaging are established. The principle of anonymous peer review has been enshrined as the law of Moses, but perhaps it needs looking at. I, too, like Steve Corman (and I imagine most people who submit articles would say the same), have felt the sting of some sniper's bullet, and the bile rose in my throat, as it clearly did in Steve's. But to be honest, my experience with both editors and reviewers has been on the whole overwhelmingly positive, and I have benefited greatly from the criticism, which was mostly fair and usually helpful. Nevertheless, I think we might want to start here in our search for a common ground, simply because it is here that the large intellectual battles get fought out, on the ground, by the slogging foot soldiers: the authors and their overworked reviewers.

A COMMON GROUND OF OBJECT OF STUDY?

Ruth Smith (1993), in an oft-cited but never published paper, conducted an analysis of the organizational communication literature dating back to 1960 and found evidence there for three "root metaphors": a container metaphor (communication in organization), a production metaphor (either communication produces organization, or organization produces communication, or both produce each other), and an equivalence metaphor (communication and organization are synonymous, since they are merely alternative ways of referring to the same reality). We (Taylor & Van Every, 2000) recently added a twist on the first of her metaphors: organization that emerges in communication. The boundaries separating the different approaches are undoubtedly porous, since for most people the difference in perspective that the system of classification attempts to capture is context-sensitive. There is no necessary contradiction, for example, in someone's believing that organization produces communication (or even that communication produces organization) and that communication is contained by organization. Which aspect gets emphasized depends on the circumstance of the discussion. Nevertheless, Smith's classification does index real differences of focus and attention that characterize the organizational communication literature.

The tendency to treat communication as going on in, or within, organization (the container metaphor) highlights one aspect of communication—interpersonal dynamics—and backlights organization as an institutional phenomenon. It also, as Smith observes, risks reifying organization since the genesis and continued existence of the latter is treated as nonproblematical. This metaphorical basis of research is illustrated by studies of supervisory practices and relationships, the socialization and acculturation of new members, conflict and conflict resolution, gender relationships, storytelling and rhetorical strategies, and group dynamics.

The production metaphor, in contrast, tends to emphasize the structurational dynamics inherent in forms of communication that generate, and are generated by, organizational forms that transcend the bounds of the local interaction. Here, both organization and communication are treated as active agencies (unlike the container metaphor, where organization is merely a fixed environment of communication). But the location of agency may be attributed in very different ways. The literature on organizational culture offers a fair illustration. It is a very different thing to say that an organization *has* a culture versus that an organization *is* a culture. The first of these interpretations has a certain affinity with the container metaphor, in that culture is seen to be one of the properties of organization that both environs and forms members' habits and expectations. The second interpretation of organizational culture focuses our attention instead on the properties of member beliefs and interactional patterns, on the basis of which we can infer underlying tendencies and norms. The first of these interpretations is illustrated by management vogues of the 1980s; the second is more like an ethnographic view.

Structuration theory attempts to bridge the gap, in that it assumes a duality: both organization produces communication and communication produces organization. The result is, in principle, a rather more complex explanatory construction in which attention is drawn away from either organization or communication and instead directed to an intermediate domain of investigation that Giddens (1984) called "modality." The difficulty I see in this displacement of the organization/communication dialectic is that it remains unclear how to study modality. In Giddens's own treatment, communication is relegated to a minor role in structuration, as one facet of system dynamics, or interaction. But, as we attempt to show in our book (Taylor & Van Every, 2000), modality is already present in the instrumentality of communication, namely, language (e.g., norms—to take one of Giddens's modalities). Unless the issue of modality is resolved, then the natural tendency in putting structurational theory to work is to simplify, either by putting the emphasis on system dynamics (namely, the role of interaction in interpreting organizational structure) or on social structure: in effect dropping back to either the communication-produces-organization or the organization-produces-communication metaphor—both alternatives that Giddens hoped to supersede.

Smith's organization–communication equivalence metaphor seems to have been introduced in the interest of logical coherence, since there does not seem to be much of a literature inspired by this trope. The difficulty in finding common ground at the level of what is the appropriate object of study of organizational communication is not the disparity of perspective that these alternative metaphors encourage; after all, each is a legitimate way to approach research in our field. The problem is that the absence of a unifying theory of communication within which each of the perspectives becomes just that: a perspective. So, in the end, we come back to the issue of communication theory.

CONCLUSION

At the beginning of this chapter I raised the question of whether our differences are more semantic than real, and whether, if they are not, we should not abandon the idea of a single common ground in favor of a more modest goal of creating avenues of exchange and dialogue. The central issue remains one of communication theory. I have tried in my own work to formulate an explanatory system that would simultaneously reconcile what appears to me to be the undoubted reality of organization as an actor in its own right with the very different domain of individual experience of self and others, in the ongoing interaction of human conversation and collaborative work. But is such a reconciliation possible? Bob Craig was kind enough to review a couple of my recent efforts to square the circle, and, although he expressed his admiration for the scope of the initiative, he remains unconvinced that I have succeeded. In one of his critiques he comments that I "skip too lightly across the ontological divide between functionalist and phenomenological analysis of mind and meaning" (personal communication, September 26, 1999). I had cited Luhmann at one point in a paper, who argues that consciousness and communication are coupled but autonomous systems. Craig, citing Searle, would argue instead that intentionality and meaning are not logically reducible to functional relationships, and that

> we rightly put things that have conscious experiences in a completely different category than entities that do not. The former have rights and responsibilities intrinsically, the latter if at all, only as useful fictions based on metaphorical extension (e.g., the corporate person in law). I think what basically bothers me about your mixture of cybernetics and discourse theory is that it skates across this distinction without seeming to notice the bumps. (personal communication, September 26, 1999)

My own take on this exchange is slightly different. I prefer to remain an agnostic on the issue of whether, as Searle argues, there is a fundamental ontological difference between the human intelligence lodged in some sentient being and more distributed forms of intelligence that characterize collectivities of working people, whose activities are mediated by tools of various kinds, as some analysts, including Bateson (1972), Hutchins (1995), and Weick and Roberts (1993), believe exists. The ontological issue of experiential being is certainly part of our philosophical inheritance in the Western world, but I have a feeling it distracts us from looking at what is specific to communication—its "value-added," in a way. So I would like to bracket the ontological question and instead look at how communication instantiates both individual and organizational identity through the mediation of language—structurational thinking. But is this a legitimate response to Bob Craig's concerns? Is this really a possible "common ground" for communication scholars to meet on? I really do not know.

For the moment, then, it seems to me as if the most productive course of action we might take is to keep the channels of dialogue open. In French, we prefer a different expression to the notion of common ground: what is called in French a *passerelle*. A passerelle, literally, is a footbridge, but I think it is worthwhile citing a longer definition, furnished by the *Petit Larousse*. According to the latter authority (I am translating freely) a passerelle is a very narrow little bridge, reserved for pedestrians. It is also a gangplank, or light bridge joining a moored ship to its landing.

What I like about this image is that it poses no threat to anyone's autonomy as independent researchers (one of Mumby's concerns), while at the same time it suggests a way for ideas to circulate, because there are little bridges to carry them from one community to another—another instance of the strength of weak ties. I have a feeling this is about what we can realistically hope to accomplish in the present state of communication studies.

CHAPTER 18

The Shifting Common Ground

Feminism(s), Organizational Communication, and Productive Paradigmatic Tensions

Angela Trethewey

When Steve Corman first approached me about contributing a short commentary on the "common ground" essays for this volume, I must admit that my first response was perhaps less than enthusiastic. I felt ambivalent about the project of establishing a shared, cross-paradigmatic vision for our discipline. In many ways, I am quite comfortable with the field's, some would say, increasingly fragmented and contested status (Corman, Chapter 1, this volume; see also Ellis, 1996; Martin & Frost, 1996; McKelvey, 1997; Reed, 1999). After reading Cheney's, Corman's, Miller's, and Mumby's contributions to this text, however, I am excited by the possibilities that a "collaborative coexistence" might engender (Miller, Chapter 3, this volume). While I do not hope or wish for a discipline devoid of theoretical tensions and contradictions, I am eager for the opportunity to engage in useful, instructive, and potentially transformative dialogues with my esteemed colleagues. This volume might enable me to do that in exciting ways I cannot yet predict.

As a feminist (yet another "F word"), I am often called upon to live with contradictions, both mundane (e.g., If I shave my armpits, am I supporting the beauty industry that undermines women's self-esteem?) and profound (e.g., How can I "give voice" to my research participants without adopting, however unintentionally, a paternalistic stance toward them?). In short, I have yet to find feminist ground that is not riddled with ontological and epistemological fissures. Yet, I, and other feminists who often occupy disciplinary borderlands, am still able to stake claims that advance our understandings of organizational life, however situated and contextual they may be (Calás & Smircich, 1999a; Trethewey, 1997, 1999a, 1999b). Indeed, I argue that feminist scholars provide a paradigm case for organizational communication researchers who are interested in the problem of "common ground."

In the pages that follow, I suggest that feminist scholarship provides a model of research that evidences "unified diversity" (Eisenberg, 1984), that moves forward while critiquing and undermining its very foundations, and that offers solutions, albeit provisional and partial, to "real life" problems. In short, the common ground for feminists is shifting but still propels us forward toward emancipation. Conceiving of common ground in organizational communication similarly may be a useful way for us not to reconcile, but to hold in productive tension, paradigmatic differences in our own field. More specifically, I first address some of the paradigmatic, epistemological conflicts among feminists. Second, I articulate the benefits that have accrued to feminists through conceiving of common ground as a perpetually shifting and contradictory foundation. Third, I suggest that organizational communication scholars follow (some) feminists by living productively with contradictions, ambiguities, and ironies. In fact, doing so may be a useful lesson in survival in an increasingly chaotic and turbulent postmodern world (see Trethewey, 1999a). Finally, I provide an example of how we might engage in multiparadigmatic analyses that do not erase differences, but explicitly point to and articulate the tensions that undergird our differences while still providing (provisional) knowledge and solutions (Mumby, Chapter 4, this volume). In so doing, such projects—like this volume—build bridges not by developing synthetic (and necessarily simplistic) models, but by mapping, clearly and honestly the " 'lay of the land'—the assumptive bases and practices of post-positivist, interpretive, and critical theorists" (Miller, Chapter 3, this volume, p. 67).

FEMINIST THEORIZING: A HISTORY OF CONFLICTS, TENSIONS, AND PROGRESS

Like organizational communication theorists, feminists have been grappling for decades with exactly what constitutes feminist theory and method (Tong, 1989), and have yet to come to any consensus. Perhaps the only common ground feminists can claim is that "there is something rotten in the state of the relationship between the sexes/genders," but precisely what that something is "the bone of fierce contention" among them (Stanley, 1997, p. 8). Additionally, feminists disagree about the nature of gender and gender relations and the appropriate agenda for social change and emancipation. Over the course of the past several decades, feminist theorizing has taken a variety of epistemological twists and turns as feminists from the margins have challenged dominant articulations of feminism. The end result has been the development of a number of "brands" of feminism, including liberal, radical, psychoanalytic, Marxist, socialist, poststructuralist, womanist, postcolonial, and others. Each offers a different articulation of problems and solutions for contemporary organizational life (Buzzanell, 1994). For example, positivist liberal feminists are concerned about inequities between males and females (fixed biological categories of persons) and believe that those inequities may be remedied by reforming extant institutional arrangements. Poststructuralist feminists, who challenge the very idea of the biologically determined self, believe that the "good society" requires perpetual deconstruction and localized responses to particular forms of disciplinary power (Calás & Smircich, 1999a; Trethewey, 1997). Not only do the various brands of feminist offer different solutions based on different ontological and epistemological positions, they often offer competing ones. What, then, is a feminist to do? How is she/he to decide among those competing knowledge claims and choose a "winner?"

Rather than falling back on pesky binary thinking (either/or, winners/ losers) (Mumby, Chapter 4, this volume), feminists often adopt a "both/ and" approach to theory, method, and praxis. For example, Ferguson (1993) maintains that feminists must often grapple with at least two seemingly contradictory, but equally important, goals simultaneously: articulating women's voices (or interpretation) and deconstructing gender as a conceptual category (or geneaology). On the one hand, interpretation is a strategy that seeks to name and act on women's experiences and voices. On the other hand, genealogy attempts to move us away from the male/female dualism that constrains our lives. Interpretive endeavors reveal underlying truths that hold liberating potential and are often subject-centered. Genealogical projects deny that there is a truth to be discovered and problematize the very notion of the subject. Where interpretation critiques the status quo in light of a different and more enabling order, genealogy attempts to shake up the "orderedness" of things and warns that what is held up as liberating will also be constraining in some ways.

Despite the seemingly vast divide between these two projects, Ferguson (1993) argues that they are not necessarily mutually exclusive; rather, they are contrasting themes that are both often present within a particular feminist argument. The fact that feminists are not absolutely theoretically consistent need not be troublesome because the interpretive and the genealogical moves are both necessary to a larger feminist agenda. Singly, neither project is sufficient, and each contains problems to which the other responds. Feminist theorizing requires adopting an ironic stance to hold together needed incompatibles, a constant ability to keep "oneself within a situation that resists resolution in order to act politically without pretending that resolution has come" (Ferguson, 1993, p. 35).

Adopting such an "ironic" stance has enabled feminists to make real and material strides without imposing an artificial unity on feminism's disparate adherents. Of course, there are those who claim that the irreconcilable debates among the various strands of feminism have "left a hole at the center" (Hutchings, 1992), a center that I believe never really existed, except in an exclusionary, false consensus sort of way. Others argue, more persuasively, that the differences among feminists only serve to enhance feminist scholarship (Buzzanell, 1994; Fitzgerald et al., 1995; Spitzack & Carter, 1988). Feminists of color, lesbian feminists, and other historically marginalized feminists "offer the tools and impetus to look critically at the [white, heterosexual, middle-class] core, to ask meaningful questions, and to obtain valuable insights" (Fitzgerald et al., 1995, p. 496). Patricia Hill Collins, an African American sociologist, challenged much of the either/or thinking that characterized earlier scholarship in her groundbreaking volume *Black Feminist Thought* (1991). She and others demonstrate that identity cannot be conceived in terms of either race or gender. Gender and race (along with issues of class, sexuality, age, etc.) are two of the many discourses that intersect to construct particular "both/and" identities for women of color (Allen, 1995; Collins, 1991; hooks, 1984; Houston, 1992). Moreover, Collins forced white, middle-class feminists to consider how black women's "outsider within" identities or standpoints are alternative sites of knowledge production.

Similarly, feminist have debated the relative merits of particular methods, including ethnography (Stacey, 1988; Wheatley, 1994) and interviewing (Finch, 1984; Kauffman, 1992; Oakley, 1981), and have forced feminists of all stripes to be much more careful about the assumptions they make about their own positions as researchers, the nature of the relationship between researchers and participants, and the emancipatory qualities of research. These debates have not resulted in a common or essentially feminist vision of theory or methods; indeed, quite the opposite is true. Yet, these "partially" feminist projects are those in which the researcher honestly and explicitly faces up to the dilemmas and ironies inherent in her work, while articulating a provisional but important body of knowledge, the knowledge of historically oppressed and silenced groups. Feminist research constructs knowledge that helps fill these gaps and holes in our understanding (Kauffman, 1992). This is precisely the reason feminist research, however contradictory, is so vital.

Feminists do not occupy common ground regarding theory or methods. Yet what they do share is a willingness to turn the lens of critique on themselves, and, in so doing, to build new, dynamic frameworks for understanding the politics of knowledge production. Thus, the seeming feminist "identity crisis" is precisely its strength. Stanley (1997) argues:

> "Contested feminisms" indicate not only the disagreements and sometimes conflicts that exist but also the preoccupation of different "schools" or

styles of feminism with each other, with their internal definitional, knowl-edge-producing and claims-making activities. Paradoxically, in the very "moment" at which feminisms appear most to disagree they are also the most intimately involved, with their gaze settled firmly upon each other. (p. 11)

This mutually involved gaze takes itself and other feminisms as a topic of analytic discourse, as a "a prism through which the world is seen" (Stanley, 1997, p. 12). This reflexive gaze enables feminists to simultaneously look outwardly upon the world and inwardly upon themselves and their knowl-edge-production practices.

ORGANIZATIONAL COMMUNICATION SCHOLARSHIP: LIVING WITH CONTRADICTIONS

It appears that those of us in organizational communication are now strug-gling to do the very same thing. We have just begun to critique each other and ourselves in productive and useful ways. This book project has asked us all to make explicit our own assumptions; to listen attentively to the as-sumptions, goals, and hopes of others; and to open ourselves to the very real possibility that we have much to learn from one another if we let our-selves become "intimately involved" (Stanley, 1997). Indeed, George Cheney has asked us to continue to do so in his chapter, "Interpreting Inter-pretive Research: Toward Perspectivism without Relativism" (Chapter 2, this volume). He asks us to consider our own, paradigmatically bound, taken-for-granted, knowledge-producing practices and to consider how they both enable and constrain what we have to say and how we are able to say it. If we continue to do so, we may, in fact, learn to live with disciplin-ary tensions, contradictions, and ambiguities, to adopt an "ironic stance," as many feminists have done.

Organizational communication scholarship that is concerned with not only "what is 'out there' but also what is 'in here' can illuminate the boundaries, the contested areas, the shifting centers of power and control, and become the motor force of changes over time" (Stanley, 1997, p. 9). Additionally, from a purely pragmatic position, there are good reasons for us to live with and learn from our differences. It would appear that in to-day's social landscape an ability to recognize and respect multiple articula-tions of organizational communication as "right" and "true," even if con-tradictory, is an important and timely skill. As I have argued elsewhere (Trethewey, 1999a), organizational environments, including our own, are becoming increasingly complex and turbulent, and organizations and their members are being pulled or are purposefully moving in several different directions at once, balancing "creativity and constraint" (Eisenberg &

Goodall, 1997). For example, Deetz (1998) argues that organizations are laying off employees in record numbers and are simultaneously expecting and often receiving enhanced loyalty and commitment from their members. Others have argued that organizational contradictions, paradoxes, and ambiguities are the stuff of organizing, and that analyses of these contradictions can lead to more enriched understandings of organizational processes (Eisenberg, 1984; Hatch, 1997; Meyers & Garrett, 1993; Trethewey, 1997, 1999a; Weick, 1979) and theory development (Poole & Van de Ven, 1989). If we are willing to examine the contradictions and tensions of contemporary organizational life, we should be equally willing to learn from the contradictory truths of our own knowledge-making practices

Moreover, when we take seriously the notion that there is no longer one truth, but several, perhaps contradictory, truths at work simultaneously, then we must examine how particular discourses come to be legitimated while others are marginalized in organizations. We must examine how some knowledge claims come to assume the mantle of the "real," the "scientific," or the "scholarly," while others are reduced to "biased" or "political" claims. Kathy Miller's essay in this volume (Chapter 3) does that, I think, by effectively tracing the contours of the ascendancy and subsequent problematization and transformation of positivism into its current post-positivist incarnation. In short, I argue that, like feminists, we cannot afford to erase our differences because to do so would result in the loss of important voices and resources. Our paradigmatic differences need not be viewed as fixed boundaries or walls. Our differences are "borderlands," spaces between where we are able to gain insight from multiple truths simultaneously because all those truths are necessary, if not unified (Bordo, 1992).

AFFINITY, NOT IDENTITY: (PROVISIONAL) COMMON GROUND IN ORGANIZATIONAL COMMUNICATION SCHOLARSHIP

Recognizing our differences and using those differences to push our own and others' understanding does not mean that we must reject the notion of a common ground for organizational theorizing; instead, it suggests that any common ground we do develop will be provisional, partial, and subject to continual critique. Again, I turn to feminist scholars as models of those who are able to create shifting and inclusive common ground. Feminists are able to form meaningful connections based on "affinity" rather than some essentialized notion of a feminist (or even a female) identity. A politics of affinity recognizes that there is "nothing about being 'female' that naturally binds women"; rather, identities are conceived as the result of "contradictory social realities of patriarchy, colonialism, racism, and capitalism"

(Haraway, 1990, p. 197). The traditional basis of political action, namely, a normalized, totalized, and essentialized identity, gives way to a politics of "conscious coalition, of affinity, of political kinship" (p. 198). Feminists interested in creating knowledge for social change are left with the responsibility of building unities rather than naturalizing them (Haraway, 1990).

Likewise, organizational communication scholars would do well to adopt a politics of affinity as a way of developing (an always destabilized) common ground. More specifically, I am hopeful that as organizational communication scholars "we" (recognizing that my own construction of an "us" is potentially essentializing) may be able to come together in the name of political kinship. In other words, our common bond need not be our paradigmatic leanings or our identities as quintessential positivists, critical theorists, or interpretivists, but our interest in a specific cause or finding solutions to very real problems. Organizational communication researchers may come together, locally and temporarily, to study a specific issue or problem from a variety of perspectives, resulting in several possible solutions or different kinds of knowledge claims, all of which may enrich our understanding and provide directions for praxis. I envision us developing research "adhocracies" or temporary, problem-centered, flexible research teams that will investigate pressing issues in contemporary organizational life (Morgan, 1997), including, but certainly not limited to, the following: the impact of downsizing on members, both those who are laid off and those who remain; the implications of the temporary workforce; privacy; identity construction and negotiation; technology; the relationship between democracy and participation; the myriad ways members' bodies are produced and controlled by organizational communication; work/family balance; entrepreneurialism; organizational knowledge production; discrimination and normalization; globalization and the effects of multinational corporations—and the list continues.

All of the aforementioned problematics can be informed by post-positivist, interpretive, and critical approaches simultaneously, and indeed there is some evidence to suggest that problem solving is enhanced in such diverse work groups (Cox & Blake, 1991; Larkey, 1996). These temporary, issue-oriented research "adhocracies" will allow us to work on "real" problems (read: objective in a post-positivist sense, socially constructed or experienced as "real," and/or an effect of a power/knowledge regime), despite, or perhaps because of, our differences. Like Deetz (1996), I believe that "complementary of forms of research questions and procedures is probably better" than conceiving of cross-paradigmatic research in synthetic or additive terms (p. 203).

By adopting "parallel" research strategies (Cheney, Chapter 2, this volume) or an "ironic stance" (Ferguson, 1993; Trethewey, 1999a), we may be able to offer other disciplines, practitioners, organizational members, and ourselves appropriately complex and perhaps even contradictory solutions to increasingly complex organizational problems, recognizing all the while that those solutions are open to continual critique and revision. Again, taking our cue from feminist researchers, we must work together to find (provisional) solutions to common organizational problems, but "be strong enough to challenge and change the dominant and colonizing *discourse*, over and over again" (Calás & Smircich, 1999a, p. 9), even if that discourse is our very own.

PART IV

AFTERWORD

CHAPTER 19

Reflections on Finding Common Ground

Marshall Scott Poole
Owen Hanley Lynch

> Alice said to the Cheshire-Cat, "Would you tell me, please, which way I ought to go from here?" "That depends a good deal on where you want to get to," said the Cat.
> —LEWIS CARROLL, *Alice's Adventures in Wonderland* (1992)

At this point we are confronted with the choice of which path to take. The essays in this book attempt to send the reader in either of two directions, projecting our discipline as one that should embrace a common ground or, alternatively, as one that should embrace productive dialogue yet maintain the tensions between different perspectives. Of course, a third path is also available: to select one perspective, work within it, and argue against all others. In this concluding comment, we will attempt to pull together some common themes and pose some critical issues that must be addressed when we confront different perspectives on organizational communication.

To help understand the distinction between the suggested future that Miller as post-positivist, Cheney as interpretivist, and Mumby as critical scholar offer, perhaps it is best to understand their pasts. Miller advocates a future of consensus in our core understanding of the disciple, a true common ground in which each perspective branches off from a central commensurable understanding and dialogue. Mumby advocates the opposite, suggesting that it is the debate across and within perspectives that contains the grounds for future development and research. Cheney is comfortable riding the fence between these perspectives, directing attention to the incongruity of the current position and implying that though there may be a common ground perhaps reaching it is not as important or as revealing as the experiences and insights we gain along the way.

When these contributors put on their perspective's "hat," they tackle the question of common ground consistently with their paradigmatic assumptions. Positivists search for commonality, critical theorists search for conflict, and interpretivists are interested in diversity and the process of social construction. This is reflected, too, in Corman's Introduction, which spells out the rationale for this book. Corman is a post-positivist searching for a common ground and is disturbed by the lack of common goals and the increased stridency within our field. The object–subject distinction retained in post-positivist thought underlies the idea of a common field on which to compare and join perspectives. So, as Mumby and several others observe, the entire project of this book may be tinged with post-positive assumptions, which may explain the number of responses that expressed discomfort or disagreement with the premise of the book. Even the commentators' positions are somewhat predictable according to the perspective from which they operate. It must be recognized, however, that the reviewers are not always easily pigeonholed. The following excerpts reflect the differential predilections of each perspective.

The post-positivist's search for a common goal informs several comments. For example, Scott and Lewis note: "Finding that metatheoretical common ground is necessary, but not sufficient, for actually conducting research this way. To realize the common ground ideal, several structural and cultural barriers must also be assessed and addressed."

The critical scholar's desire to capitalize on interperspectival conflict characterizes others:

- Deetz: "Dennis and I (and perhaps George) hope for the productive interaction arising from confronting the radical otherness of positions."
- Trethewey: "If we are willing to examine the contradiction and the tensions of the contemporary organizational life, we should be equally willing to learn from the contradictory truths of our own knowledge-making practices."

Interpretivists see the value of both positions and stress that diversity and not necessarily conflict is what is important for scholarship:

- Fairhurst: "I would agree but add one caveat: only if we are respectful of difference." Later she agrees with Cheney as she quotes him: "We may never determine fully what ought to count as scholarship."
- Taylor believes that neither common ground nor separation is productive and suggests that "the most productive course of action might be to keep the channels of dialogue open." This channel he likens to a *passerelle,* a narrow bridge.

- Krizek is not denying the common ground as a possibility, but instead is questioning the rationale for attempting to reach it.

And those whose work does not sit squarely in any camp, curiously, respond rather like interpretivists:

- Jackson: "I do not consider the incommensurability thesis to be as crucial as Corman has set out." She argues that how we deal with conflict is important because conflict is inevitable.
- Krone: "As subject, organizational communication demands to be approached through multiple perspectives, and even those will be inadequate to fully understand its mysteries." She argues that a metatheoretical theory is possible but would be so abstract as to offer little benefit. It would also dilute the expertise a researcher has in his/her methodology by creating the "jack-of-all trades."
- Conrad: "The strength of organizational communication is the eclecticism that allows the avoidance of serious conflicts like those in other disciplines."

We began this review by pointing out the irony that even when the research question is the search for a common ground most of us slip into the basic frame in which we study. As reviewers of the book, we have to be conscious that we are likely to do this too. Perhaps we can avoid this trap because we have different research orientations, one of us being primarily an interpretivist and the other an eclectic post-positivist. To do this we begin by examining the three main essays. Following this, we examine trends within the commentaries. Finally we consider some suggestions for bringing perspectives into dialogue.

QUESTIONS

In response to Miller's post-positivism, we ask, "Can the leopard really change its spots?" As Miller observes, classical positivism, with its assumptions of truly objective observers and an ambiguity-free descriptive language, has been discredited since the 1930s. So, many arguments lodged against positivism in communication missed the mark because they did not clash with the version of positivism that informed quantitative inquiry, a version that recognized the constructional nature of social science and focused on solving problems and reaching plausible explanations rather than arriving at timeless, objective knowledge. This version, as Diesing (1991) notes, has its roots in John Dewey and not in Carnap.[1]

But the post-positivist position faces an important challenge. In the end critical realism depends on having an unchallenged, real (objective?)

referential world that contains the phenomena being studied. Part of this real world are the social constructions that actors develop and employ, which can themselves be studied to identify regularities and patterns that are really there. This study can be pursued using objectivity as a "regulatory ideal," which we all recognize really isn't attained, but which we strive to realize through continuous criticism of our methodology and results. This is an attractive and commonly expressed line of thinking. It still suffers, however, from a key problem associated with earlier "positivist" approaches: post-positivism continues to operate under the same bias toward submitting theories and contested claims to the court of "reality."

Underlying post-positivism is the assumption that we can adjudicate conflicting claims against what is "out there" to establish one common ground of belief. But how do we submit our cases to this court? Reality (which isn't fully accessible to us or understandable by us) can be approached only by employing the proper methodological tools correctly (and even these give us only partial access, so that "we see through a glass darkly"). Arguments about results or the meaning of results rest on the methods used to obtain them. Hence contested claims ultimately rest on arguments about proper methods and how to use them correctly. Whether a method is "proper" is judged based on critical realist standards such as whether the method provides a means to determine the degree to which we have conducted our study or analysis in an objective manner (methods that provide such means would be judged superior to those that do not).

This move shifts the argument about how to judge social scientific claims onto the conceptual turf of critical realism itself, thereby disadvantaging methods that do not conform to its canons. A social scientist who justified his methods on the grounds that they provide better empathy with the subject, for example, would be unlikely to prevail before a jury of critical realists over one who employed classical test theory to design and validate her measures. This recourse to evaluation of knowledge claims in terms of the methods used to develop and support them ultimately favors explanations in line with the post-positivist approach and disqualifies other explanations. This brings us back to the same problem that led to the interpretive–critical rebellion in organizational communication research: there is a tendency in post-positivism to favor objectivizing, variabilizing approaches over other modes of inquiry and to evaluate the claims advanced through other modes by post-positivist standards.

Does the post-positivist researcher inevitably have to fall prey to this tendency? No. One who maintains a thoroughly critical stance could avoid such blanket rejections of other positions, provided a level playing field were provided. One step in this direction is to recognize that each form of inquiry has its own criteria for judging accounts and to enlarge the post-positivist stance to include such criteria as well. That post-positivist research operates mainly from a single paradigm—what Mohr (1982) called "the variance approach"—has contributed to its difficulties in recognizing the validity of other models. The variance model relies on establishing causal and correlational relationships among variables, employing classical test theory as a measurement model, and using the general linear model as the preferred statistical method. Today, more diverse methodological approaches to conducting post-positivist research are being developed and diffused, and this can contribute to a loosening up of post-positivist inquiry. New developments, including dynamic systems analysis (Barnett & Thayer, 1997) and the appropriation of historical and quantitative methods in narrative positivism (Abbott, 1990) and process research (Poole, Van de Ven, Dooley, & Holmes, 2000), may give post-positivist inquiry models in addition to its traditional variance-based approaches.

An apt question for Cheney's interpretivism is "Can the leopard have too many spots?" As Cheney's essay indicates, the hallmark of interpretive research is to consider a number of different readings and layers of meaning. It is easy to enjoy this multiplicity, but much more difficult to work out how the different readings relate to each other. As each new reading is developed, all the others are potentially qualified. There is, in principle, an endless process of expanding readings that illuminate the object from many points of view. But as they multiply, these illuminations can eventually constitute a blinding prism that shows us so many fractured bits of the phenomenon that the whole becomes incoherent. It is certainly true that some interpretive scholars emphasize the fragmented nature of social life. But many, if not most, interpretivists strive to produce coherent pictures of organizational communication. The multiplicity of readings that emerge as the study proceeds has the potential to undermine this coherency on a continuous basis. Coherency can be reestablished by emphasizing some readings and overlooking others, but this involves denying or downplaying plausible views.

When confronting conflicting claims, the interpretivists cannot resort to reality or the regulative norm of objectivity, as the post-positivists do. Standards of interpretation and methods of interpretive research have developed over the past 250 years, and they have attained a high level of sophistication, equal to that of quantitative methodologies. These standards can tell us which interpretations are suspect or bad ones, but they offer little help in judging which of several good interpretations is best. Indeed, the issue of which interpretation is "best" is not particularly meaningful to the interpretivist. Each careful interpretation is simply another side of the story. We then proceed to try to reconcile the various stories, insofar as this is possible. There is no final recourse, and we are often left in a state of "interpretive satiety," whereby we are stuffed with insights and understandings, but doze off, not doing much with them and waiting until, hungry again, we enjoy yet another reading. And it is not clear where all this leads.

Need interpretivism be so passive an occupation? Good qualitative studies, as William F. Whyte's classic studies of work motivation and the Hawthorne studies illustrate, have led to firm conclusions and sound insights. However, as Cheney recounts, further readings of the Hawthorne studies have challenged many of their conclusions and the implications drawn from them. Again, this is an instance of interpretation without end, as apologists for the Hawthorne studies could find new readings that reconcile the Hawthorne studies with Gillespie's results. Cheney offers some excellent recommendations for how interpretivism can be more directed—though, as Conrad notes, they shift it in a critical direction.

Of the critical perspective we ask, "Can the leopard stop biting?" Negation is the first, and most stirring, moment of any critique. Critical insights sweep away alternative perspectives and shift attention to the hidden operation of power and structural determination. This is quite satisfying, because it gives us an epiphany, a feeling of insight. A fully developed critical theory is remarkable in that it not only presents an analysis that cuts through appearances, it also advances a solution that can change the situation so as to eliminate the inequality. It is hard to see how anything could stand against that.

However, this exhilaration, like many others, is enabled by a subtle, hidden maldistribution of power that favors the critical theorist. It is unclear due to the critical stance of negation and the mission to initiate empowerment whether any other perspective can have a mutual dialogue with a critical theorist. There are two options in a discussion with a critical scholar. On the one hand, one must admit the possibility of the operation of deeper power circuits and of ideological control that runs counter to the best interests of subjects. On the other hand, one can go on the offensive by denying that the deeper power exists or by suggesting that the critical theorists themselves are a hegemonic force denying their subjects the free will/vision to see the chains that bind them.

If the operation of power circuits is admitted, the dialogue has shifted to turf where the critical researcher is most comfortable, and so this dialogue can no longer be mutual. Moreover, it exempts the critical theorist from having to test the counterfactual (the negation), that there is no oppression at work, or of admitting to themselves that they are colonizing those they have attempted to set free.

If the other scholar chooses the second option and refuses to admit oppression or hidden structural determinations, the critical theorist has a trump card: the charge that the other scholar has been duped by the reigning ideology into ignoring the oppressive nature of the system. The very tendency of critical theory to critique alternative perspectives—to look for hidden traps and power imbalances—also creates a tendency not to look too closely at its own presumption that there are such traps and imbalances.

Is the critical theorist trapped in this unfortunate and circular mode of argument? Of course not. Numerous critical theorists—Marx the first among them—have used positive evidence in their analyses, and this makes it possible for critical analyses to be founded on evidence subject to critical tests. However, the critical scholars' underlying motivation to critique has often made them suspicious of any form of evidence gathered using positivistic or interpretivist methods on the grounds that the methods themselves have built-in distortions (see, e.g., Habermas, 1971). This presents a tall challenge to the critical social scientist who wishes to use positive evidence—not only must that evidence conform to the canons of post-positivist or interpretivist method, but these methods themselves must be critiqued and sterilized of distorting tendencies in the context of the study.

Adherents of the three perspectives might have the best of intentions, but unless they are vigilant, tendencies in each position will undermine dialogue or cross-paradigm connections. These very tendencies, though, are what have lent coherence to each of the three perspectives, a fact that Mumby clearly notes. These tendencies also make hybrid research more challenging than it is often assumed to be. Combining post-positivist assumptions with those of interpretivism counterposes the tendency to refer to reality and interrogate methods for adherence to objectivity norms with the need to get a plausible reading of the situation that seems true to some perspective of the participants, and then to supplement this with more and more layers of readings, all of which are valid within limits. These tendencies are clearly in opposition to each other. One wonders if all the scholars who claimed to be betwixt and between camps (including the first author) really could defend their claims if pressed!

Having considered possible catches in our efforts to cross perspectives, we will now turn to common patterns across the various contributions.

TRENDS AND PATTERNS IN THE ESSAYS AND RESPONSES

Strong Convictions

Many of the comments have autobiographical, even confessional, passages. Several authors and commentators recount their personal experiences related to various perspectives and the exchanges between them. These are certainly interesting and informative, but they also underscore how personally important the perspectives are to the authors. Perspective is more than just a theoretical (or methodological) convenience—it is a conviction. The authors take the choice of perspective and the problems related to crossing/combining perspectives seriously, not only because they have an important bearing on what and how we know, but also because these play an important role in the formation and maintenance of professional identities. Karl Polanyi (1959) noted the personal element in scientific knowledge, which was not as objective as the rhetoric of science presented things, but rather was informed by the scientist's tacit and often unsurfaced beliefs about what was a valid piece of knowledge.

But there may be another reason to take perspectives personally. Without personal commitment, the researcher may lack the "fire" that drives good inquiry. When the first author was in his teens (another confession), he was inspired by a movie about Louis Pasteur (played by Paul Muni), who passionately pursued dispassionate, objective scientific research for the good of all. Pasteur, a biologist and natural scientist, can make the regulative norm of objectivity his passion. But is this possible for a social investigator, whose very subject is inherently value-laden? Can we study human beings without making some commitment to a valuational frame from which to understand them? Dewey (1939) did not think so: for him problems were valuations, stances taken in response to a situation. To maintain contact with the humans we study, it may be necessary to acknowledge our own humanity by entering into inquiry with passionate adherence to a way of seeing.

But there is always a catch. Driven by our passion, our position may become, to use Kenneth Burke's (1935) apt terminology, "a trained incapacity," a way of seeing that blinds us to other possibilities by so clearly focusing our attention on one aspect that we neglect others. And we suspect that the degree of blindness is in direct proportion to the passion.

Accepting Differences

A positive glimpse of the future that this book affords may not be common ground, but separate and equal views where we talk civilly and respect differences. Many of the reviewers point to the problem of being accepting of difference politely, and of learning to live with tension, and diversity, effectively and efficiently. However, the point just raised concerning passion suggests a difficulty, because passion is not necessarily civil.

Moreover, civility may only be feasible for mature established perspectives. During the inception of a new approach, when it is being worked out as an alternative to existing approaches, it may be useful to polarize against opposing viewpoints. Polarization is useful for several reasons. Extreme statements of any position are much clearer than more nuanced, qualified ones. A clear, simple statement is more likely to be internally consistent and to yield powerful insights. It is also more likely to attract new adherents—especially those who long for innovation or are troubled with the present perspectives—than a more qualified statement. And, as students of conflict have long known, it also creates an us-versus-them mentality that adds to the motivation of adherents and spurs on their research. When the position has been established, then it is time to qualify and look for civil discourse that acknowledges no-longer-so-threatening alternative perspectives.

Educational Practices

A number of these texts call for graduate education to cultivate appreciation and respect for the diversity within the field. Barnett's essay registers an opposing concern that schools should be in the business of creating masters of methodology, not "jacks-of-all-trades." However, this does not mean that graduate students should not be asked to look long and hard at the different perspectives. A graduate student who chooses his/her path understanding the alternatives and the strengths and weaknesses that various perspectives hold will undoubtedly be happier about the direction he/she chooses.

As Scott and Lewis and as Fairhurst note, the newly minted scholar with an appreciation of multiple perspectives must still have his/her work reviewed by others who may respond with prejudice toward viewpoints other than their own. Attempts to combine or cross perspectives are likely to seem muddled to such scholars. There are two ways to look at this problem. On the one hand, we can accept and deplore the inability of people to give fair consideration to other viewpoints. This is realistic, and it suggests that young scholars should keep their "crossings" small in number and concentrate instead on cultivated well-defined fields during their pursuit of tenure. On the other hand, gaining acceptance for "unusual" work can be seen as a challenge that calls for extra ingenuity and exceptionally clear and compelling (but risky) scholarship. Rather than discouraging the young scholar, difficulties gaining acceptance for crossover work can spur them on to important insights and achievements.

Outward Orientation

Linkages with other fields of study such as management, engineering, information systems, psychology, and sociology are becoming increasingly common for organizational communication researchers. This reality is reflected in Jackson's and other contributors' comments. The increasing recognition of alternative perspectives in organizational communication facilitates the ability to form such connections in a useful way. Rather than going to other fields as disciples, looking to adopt their theories, a multiperspectival approach encourages us to view both our field and other fields as coequal partners in a potentially useful exchange of insights. Thinking about the oppositions between perspectives and possible common ground helps one see possibilities for interchange, integration, and cross-fertilization that are not so evident to scholars embedded in a single perspective. So the integrative and contrastive moves discussed in the Essays and Commentary parts can serve as useful exercises and discipline for scholars who work with other fields, regardless of whether they prefer to be rooted in a single perspective or engage in crossing.

Interpretation and Misinterpretation

Taylor and Mumby make us aware of a dangerous slippage when we attempt to bridge perspectives by using terms such as "structuration." Work at the boundaries always involves ambiguities, because the meanings of terms tend to warp as we cross perspectival bounds. For example, *interpretation* is likely to mean quite different things to an interpretivist (who is making readings to gain understanding), to a post-positivist (who is interpreting something that is really there and seeks an accurate reading in an interpretation), and to a critical scholar (who is interpreting to get a deep reading). Combining post-positivist evidence with critical readings, for example, exposes scholars to this shifting of meanings as they cross from one portion of their project to another. It is common for one meaning to have tacit privilege, but scholars are not always aware of this. Barnett, for example, advances a post-positivist reading of interpretivism.

So, too, structuration theory has been appropriated in different ways by various scholars. Each has emphasized some facets of the term and deemphasized others. One response to this is Mumby's, who (with Giddens) argues that there is an essential element of critique in structuration theory that must be honored. Another response is Taylor's, who is aware of, but accepts, different usages of structuration theory. Yet another response—also consistent with Taylor—is to argue that different emphases represent different views of the structuring process and that systems and critical approaches to structuration theory ultimately support and illuminate each other—if they are properly fit together.

In closing this comment on interpretation in the chapters and responses, it seems appropriate to note an irony: A repeated theme in comments and chapters alike is that the perspectives see themselves as misunderstood and misrepresented by scholars from other perspectives. Much energy is devoted in several of these essays to disabusing the misinterpretations and mistaken inferences. Yet in their untroubled and smooth presentations of other perspectives, there is no implication that they themselves have considered whether they might be misinterpreting and misrepresenting the others. If misinterpretation (possibly due to incommensurability?) is so endemic when others interpret us, should we not make the obvious inference that we may well be misrepresenting the other? The gap does not just loom for one side of the canyon—it holds just as much for the right as for the left bank.

On this note it is worth turning to methods and frameworks for bringing different perspectives together.

FRAMEWORKS FOR BRINGING
DIFFERENT PERSPECTIVES TOGETHER

The essays indicate two strategies for working in more than one perspective. One approach is to find a theory that cuts across perspectives.

Structuration theory has been advanced as one such approach. A second approach is to recognize the differences between perspectives and to use these to stimulate theory and research. Both are in contrast to the debunking that Conrad discusses, which sometimes becomes the prevalent mode of discourse between perspectives.

First, let's consider the strategy of finding a theory that crosses perspectives, which might be called the "transcendent strategy." A transcendent theory goes above or beyond existing perspectives by making a move on a different metalevel of analysis. This move is illustrated by Weaver and Gioia's (1994) call for integration "showing the extent to which various first-order paradigms deal with selectively bracketed aspects of organizational or social phenomena" (p. 577). Weaver and Gioia suggest that this is accomplished in Giddens's (1994) structuration theory. In line with the several authors in this volume, Weaver and Gioia suggest that "structuration provides a basis for seeing how organizational scholars can invoke different assumptions, pursue different goals, ask different questions, and use different approaches, but nonetheless be engaged in inquiry with commonalties despite such diversities" (p. 577).

It is important to remember, however, that transcendence itself is more likely a process not a state. There are problems with Giddens's notion of structuration. It has been challenged on the grounds that it takes a logical duality of system and structure and imposes it on a world that does not neatly conform to logic (see, e.g., Sztompka, 1993). In this material world, action and structure may not be a duality, but rather different moments of social system, sometimes coordinated and sometimes opposed to each other. If this duality is refuted, then the structurational bridge between perspectives collapses. So structurationist researchers are themselves engaged in a continuous process of repair whereby they show the tenability of the duality and other assumptions of structuration theory. It then becomes another perspective against which yet different perspectives may arise. So we are back to the problem of finding common ground for the scholarly Sisyphus.

The second approach accepts the differences between perspectives, and attempts to use them to stimulate productive scholarship. This is reflected in Mumby's discussion, which focuses not on how we might identify points of overlap and commonality between different approaches, but on how we can take seriously the arguments of different discourses and provide each with the space to articulate its view of human phenomena. In this sense, different discourses are seen as neither integrated nor overlapping, but as complementary. Mumby suggests that one way to enact this strategy is to focus on common problems from different perspectives. Concern with a common problem affords different perspectives opportunities for dialogue and highlights their differences in a productive manner.

Cheney gives an excellent discussion of a second method of enacting this approach, Schultz and Hatch's (1996) strategy of paradigm interplay. Shultz and Hatch concisely describe this strategy:

> The interplay strategy involved two steps: a) empirical recognition of contrast and connections and, b) examination of the implications of recognizing both contrasts and connections by moving between the two paradigms. Interplay helps researchers recognize that oppositions are always defined in terms of one another. (p. 552)

Quinn and Cameron's edited volume, *Paradox and Transformation* (1988), offers several strategies for working with diverse and seemingly opposed perspectives and ideas. Building on one of the chapters in this book, Poole and Van de Ven (1989) discuss four strategies to deal with paradoxes among theories. Two of these strategies parallel those just mentioned: (1) accept differences and learn to live with them productively and (2) make a theoretical move that cuts through the paradox and introduces a resolution of the oppositions. The other two strategies deal with paradoxes by positing a theory that situates them in different levels of the social world and specifies the relationship between levels: (3) develop a theory in which one perspective operates at one level—for example, the organizational level—and another operates at a different level—for example, the level of individual action; or (4) develop a theory in which one perspective operates or predominates during one time period and then is succeeded by the other perspective (Buckley's [1967] theory of morphogenesis, an alternative to Giddens's [1994] take on structuration, does this). Examples and techniques for developing theory using the four approaches are discussed in more detail in Poole and Van de Ven.

The two general strategies just discussed are theoretical practices. However, another perspective on common ground seems to emerge from the essays and commentaries. It is less focused on theoretical worries and more on concrete ways of practicing scholarship that would facilitate the capturing of insights from multiple perspectives. Every contributor to this volume proposes one or more such practices. An *incomplete* list includes the following:

- Barnett: Focus on the structure of concepts.
- Cheney: Search for perspective in incongruity.
- Conrad: Avoid the temptation to engage in debunking rhetoric.
- Corman: Abandon the "paradigms mentality" in favor of a search for common ground.
- Deetz: Focus more on social problems and less on theoretical debates.
- Eisenberg: Be hospitable to people who are not like you.

- Fairhurst: Be prepared for resistance to cross-paradigm research.
- Jackson: Adopt a more outward orientation.
- Krizek: Practice after-action review.
- Krone: *Really* study other perspectives.
- McPhee: Engage others' validity concerns.
- Miller: Do not essentialize and look to empirical regularities for linkages.
- Mumby: Focus on problematics that are central to the discipline.
- Scott and Lewis: Emphasize content areas over methods choices.
- Seibold and Flanagin: Think of yourself as a site for integration.
- Stohl: Practice multilingualism with respect to perspectives.
- Taylor: Focus on communication as our common object of study.
- Trethewey: Live productively with contradictions, ambiguities, and ironies.

CONCLUSION

Some readers may find it troubling that, after all the sound and fury, this volume offers no clear resolutions. We hope there is some consolation in reflecting on Karl Popper's (1962) argument that good scholarship depends not on the answers we arrive at, but on a continuous process of inquiry and criticism. For Popper, no problem or question can ever be fully settled and no theory can ever be fully established. Instead, our ability to judge the merits of a claim depends on the quality of interrogation it undergoes. That claim is best trusted that has withstood the most rigorous questioning and debate.

The many positions on finding common ground discussed in this book and the clash among them illustrates the quality of inquiry into the relationships among perspectives. While it seems unlikely that any position will win the day, the many options discussed can give us guidance in the practice of scholarship, as we are confronted with problems that indicate the need to combine, work between, or even integrate perspectives. This rich set of approaches greatly increases the possibility that the fruits of research on organizational communication will be substantial, rather than just a smile hanging in the air, with no cat at all behind it.

NOTE

1. It must be added, however, that a number of the social scientific communication researchers of the late 1960s and early 1970s contributed to this confusion by adopting the rhetoric of positivism. And there are still adherents who insist on rather narrow interpretations of what "good social science" is (see, e.g., Bostrom & Donohew, 1992).

Readings

Following is a short list of articles that the editors recommend for reading in conjunction with this text. Many of the articles were cited extensively in this volume.

POST-POSITIVIST POSITIONS

These readings cover quantitative and positive research approaches.

Cushman, D., & Pearce, W. B. (1977). Generality and necessity in three types of theory about human communication, with special attention to rules theory. *Human Communication Research, 3*, 344–353.

Deising, P. (1991). *How does social science work?: Reflections in practice*. Pittsburgh, PA: University of Pittsburgh Press.

Miller, K. (2000). Quantitative research methods in organizational communication: Practices and challenges. In F. M. Jablin & L. L. Putnam (Eds.), *Handbook of organizational communication: Advances in theory, research, and methods*. Thousand Oaks, CA: Sage.

Phillips, D. C. (1990). Postpositivistic science: Myths and realities. In E. G. Guba (Ed.), *The paradigm dialog* (pp. 31–45). Newbury Park, CA: Sage.

Poole, M. S. (1997). A turn of the wheel: The case for a renewal of systems inquiry in organizational communication research. In G. A. Barnett & L. Thayer (Eds.), *Organization<—>communication: Emerging perspectives. Vol. 5: The renaissance in systems thinking* (pp. 47–63). Norwood, NJ: Ablex.

Wilson, B. J. (1994). A challenge to communication empiricists: Let's be more forthcoming about what we do. *Western Journal of Communication, 58*, 25–31.

INTERPRETIVIST POSITIONS

Guba, E. G., & Lincoln, Y. S. (1994). Competing paradigms in qualitative research. In N. K. Denzin & Y. S. Lincoln (Eds.), *Handbook of qualitative research* (pp. 105–117). Newbury Park, CA: Sage.

Martin, J. (1992). *Cultures in organizations: Three perspectives.* New York: Oxford University Press.

Martin, J., & Frost, P. (1999). The organizational culture war games: A struggle for intellectual dominance. In S. Clegg & C. Hardy (Eds.), *Studying organization: Theory and method* (pp. 345–367). London: Sage.

Pacanowsky, M., & O'Donnell-Trujillo, N. (1982). Communication and organizational culture. *Western Journal of Speech Communication, 46,* 115–130.

Pacanowsky, M., & O'Donnell-Trujillo, N. (1983). Organizational communication as cultural performance. *Communication Monographs, 50,* 126–147.

Putnam, L. L. (1983). The interpretive perspective: An alternative to functionalism. In L. L. Putnam & M. E. Pacanowsky (Eds.), *Communication and organizations, an interpretive approach* (pp. 31–54). Beverly Hills, CA: Sage.

Taylor, C. (1985). *Philosophy and the human sciences.* New York: Cambridge University Press.

CRITICAL POSITIONS

Alvesson, M., & Deetz, S. (1996). Postmodernism and critical approaches to organizations. In S. R. Clegg, C. Hardy, & W. R. Nord (Eds.), *Handbook of organization studies* (pp. 191–217). Thousand Oaks, CA: Sage.

Deetz, S. (1992). *Democracy in the age of corporate colonization: Developments in communication and the politics of everyday life.* Albany: State University of New York Press.

Mumby, D. K. (1988). *Communication and power in organizations: Discourse, ideology, and domination.* Norwood, NJ: Ablex.

POSTMODERN POSITIONS

Mumby, D. (1997). Modernism, postmodernism, and communication studies: A rereading of an ongoing debate. *Communication Theory, 7,* 1–28.

Mumby, D. K., & Putnam, L. L. (1992). The politics of emotion: A feminist reading of bounded rationality. *Academy of Management Review, 17,* 465–486.

Spitzack, C., & Carter, K. (1988). Feminist communication: Rethinking the politics of exclusion. *Women's Studies in Communication, 11,* 32–36.

POSITIONS THAT CONTRAST TWO OR MORE OF THE ABOVE

Deetz, S. (1996). Describing differences in approaches to organization science: Rethinking Burrell and Morgan and their legacy. *Organization Science, 7,* 191–207.

Mumby, D. (1997). Modernism, postmodernism, and communication studies: A rereading of an ongoing debate. *Communication Theory, 7,* 1–28.

Putnam, L. L., Bantz, C., Deetz, S., Mumby, D., & Van Maanen, J. (1993). Ethnography versus critical theory: Debating organizational research. *Journal of Management Inquiry, 2*(3), 221–235.

Putnam, L. L., Phillips, N., & Chapman, P. (1996). Metaphors of communication and organization. In S. R. Clegg, C. Hardy, & W. R. Nord (Eds.), *Handbook of organization studies* (pp. 375–408). Thousand Oaks, CA: Sage.

POSITIONS THAT REPRESENT PARADIGM
DIALOGUE AND/OR CROSS-PARADIGM WORK

Hassard, J. (1991). Multiple paradigms and organizational analysis: A case study. *Organization Studies, 12*, 275–299.

Morgan, G. (1997). *Images of organization* (2nd ed.). Thousand Oaks, CA: Sage.

Poole, M. S., & Van de Ven, A. H. (1989). Using paradox to build management and organizational theories. *Academy of Management Review, 17*, 465–486.

Schultz, M., & Hatch, M. J. (1966). Living with multiple paradigms: The case of paradigm interplay in organizational studies. *Academy of Management Review, 21*(2), 529–557.

READINGS ON COMMENSURABILITY/
INCOMMENSURABILITY

Czarniawski, B. (1998). Who is afraid of incommensurability? *Organization, 5*, 273–275.

Gioia, D. A., & Pitre, E. (1990). Multiparadigm perspectives on theory building. *Academy of Management Review, 15*, 584–602.

Jackson, N., & Carter, P. (1991). In defense of paradigm incommensurability. *Organization Studies, 12*, 109–127.

Scherer, A. G. (1998). Pluralism and incommensurability in strategic management and organization theory: A problem in search of a solution. *Organization, 5*, 147–168.

Weaver, G. R., & Gioia, D. A. (1994). Paradigms lost: Incommensurability versus structurationist inquiry. *Organization Studies, 15*, 565–590.

Wilmot, H. (1993). Breaking the paradigm mentality. *Organization Studies, 14*, 681–719.

References

Abbott, A. (1990). Conceptions of time and events in social science methods: Causal and narrative approaches. *Historical Methods, 23*, 140–150.

Adams, D. (1979). *The hitchhiker's guide to the galaxy.* New York: Pocket Books.

Agassi, J. (1975). *Science in flux* (Boston Studies No. 28). Dordrecht, The Netherlands: Reidel.

Alexander, J. C., & Giesen, B. (1987). From reduction to linkage: The long view of the micro-macro link. In J. C. Alexander, B. Giesen, R. Munch, & N. J. Smelser (Eds.), *The micro-macro link* (pp. 1–42). Berkeley: University of California Press.

Allen, B. J. (1995). "Diversity" and organizational communication. *Journal of Applied Communication Research, 23*, 143–155.

Allen, B. J. (1996). Feminist standpoint theory: A black woman's (re)view of organizational socialization. *Communication Studies, 47*, 257–271.

Alternative theoretical bases for the study of human communication: A symposium. (1977). *Communicaion Quarterly, 25*(1), 3–73.

Althusser, L. (1971). *Lenin and philosophy.* New York: Monthly Review Press.

Altmann, G. (1999). *The ascent of Babel: An exploration of language, mind, and understanding.* Oxford, UK: Oxford University Press.

Alvesson, M., & Deetz, S. (1996). Critical theory and postmodernism approaches to organizational studies. In S. R. Clegg, C. Hardy, & W. R. Nord (Eds.), *Handbook of organization studies* (pp. 191–217). Thousand Oaks, CA: Sage.

Alvesson, M., & Deetz, S. (2000). *Doing critical management research.* London: Sage.

Alvesson, M., & Willmott, H. (Eds.). (1992). *Critical management studies.* Newbury Park, CA: Sage.

Anderson, J. (1987). *Communication research: Issues and methods.* New York: McGraw-Hill.

Anderson, R., Cissna, K. N., & Arnett, R. C. (1994). *The reach of dialogue: Confirmation, voice, and community.* Crisskill, NJ: Hampton Press.

Apel, K.-O. (1979). *Toward a transformation of philosophy* (G. Adey & D. Frisby, Trans.). London: Routledge & Kegan Paul.

Arnett, R. (1986). *Communication and community.* Carbondale: Southern Illinois University Press.

Atlan, H. (1979). *Entre le cristal et la fumée* [Between crystal and smoke]. Paris: Éditions du Seuil.

Aune, J. A. (1994). *Rhetoric and Marxism.* Boulder, CO: Westview Press.

Austin, J. L. (1970). *How to do things with words.* New York: Oxford University Press.

Axley, S. (1984). Managerial and organizational communication in terms of the conduit metaphor. *Academy of Management Review, 9,* 428–437.

Ayer, A. J. (1960). *Language, truth, and logic.* London: Gollancz.

Bakhtin, M. M. (1981). *The dialogic imagination* (M. Holquist, Ed.; M. Holquist & C. Emerson, Trans.). Austin: University of Texas Press.

Banks, S. P., & Riley, P. (1993). Structuration theory as an ontology for communication research. In S. Deetz (Ed.), *Communication yearbook 16* (pp. 167–196). Thousand Oaks, CA: Sage.

Bantz, C. R. (1993). *Understanding organizations: Interpreting organizational communication cultures.* Columbia: University of South Carolina Press.

Barbalet, J. M. (1987). Power, structural resources, and agency. *Perspectives in Social Theory, 8,* 1–24.

Barker, J. (1993). Tightening the iron cage: Concertive control in the self-managing organization. *Administrative Science Quarterly, 38,* 408–437.

Barnett, G. A. (1988). Communication and organizational culture. In G. M. Goldhaber & G. A. Barnett (Eds.), *Handbook of organizational communication* (pp. 101–130). Norwood, NJ: Ablex.

Barnett, G.A. (1997). Organizational communication systems: The traditional perspective. In G. A. Barnett & L. Thayer (Eds.), *Organization<—>communication: Emerging perspectives. Vol. 5: The renaissance in systems thinking* (pp. 1–46). Norwood, NJ: Ablex.

Barnett, G. A. (1998, March). *Challenges to speech communication in the 21st century.* Keynote address to International Conference on Speech Communication, Shih Hsin University, Taipei, Taiwan.

Barnett, G. A. (1999). The social structure of international telecommunications. In H. Sawhney & G. A. Barnett (Eds.), *Progress in communication sciences, Vol. XV: Advances in telecommunications* (pp. 151–187). Stamford, CT: Ablex.

Barnett, G. A., & Danowski, J. A. (1992). The structure of communication: A network analysis of the International Communication Association. *Human Communication Research, 19,* 264–285.

Barnett G. A., & Kincaid, D. L. (1983). Cultural convergence: A mathematical theory. In W. B. Gudykunst (Ed.), *Intercultural communication theory: Current perspectives* (pp. 171–194). Beverly Hills, CA: Sage.

Barnett, G., & Thayer, L. (Eds.). (1997). *Organization<—>communication: Emerging perspectives. Vol. 5: The renaissance in systems thinking.* Norwood, NJ: Ablex.

Basso, K. (1970). To give up on words: Silence in Western Apache culture. *Southwestern Journal of Anthropology, 26,* 213–230.

Bateson, G. (1972). *Steps to an ecology of mind.* New York: Ballantine Books.

Baudrillard, J. (1983). *In the shadow of silent majorities* (P. Foss, J. Johnston, & P. Patton, Trans.). New York: Semiotext(e).

Baxter, L. A. (1993). "Talking things through" and "putting it in writing": Two codes of communication in an academic institution. *Journal of Applied Communication Research, 21*(4), 313–326.

Baxter, L. A., & Goldsmith, D. (1990). Cultural terms for communication events among some American high school adolescents. *Western Journal of Speech Communication, 54,* 377–394.

Belk, R. W., Wallendorf, M., & Sherry, J. F. Jr. (1991). The sacred and the profane in consumer behavior: Theodicy on the odyssey. *Highways and Byways of the Association for Consumer Research*.

Berg, M. (1998). The politics of technology: On bringing social theory into technological design. *Science, Technology, and Human Values, 23*(4), 456–490.

Berger, P., & Luckmann, T. (1967). *The social construction of reality*. London: Penguin Books.

Bernstein, P. (1976). Necessary elements for effective worker participation in decision making. *Journal of Economic Issues, 10*, 490–522.

Bernstein, R. J. (1976). *The restructuring of social and political theory*. Philadelphia: University of Pennsylvania Press.

Berteotti, C. R., & Seibold, D. R. (1994). Coordination and role definition problems in health care teams: A hospice case study. In L. R. Frey (Ed.), *Communication in context: Studies of naturalistic groups* (pp. 107–131). Hillsdale, NJ: Erlbaum.

Bhaskar, R. (1979). *The possibility of naturalism: A philosophical critique of the contemporary human sciences*. Atlantic Highlands, NJ: Humanities Press.

Blair, C., Brown, J. R., & Baxter, L. A. (1994). Disciplining the feminine. *Quarterly Journal of Speech, 80*, 383–409.

Blalock, H. M. (1969). *Theory construction: From verbal to mathematical formulations*. Englewood Cliffs, NJ: Prentice-Hall.

Bochner, A. P. (1985). Perspectives on inquiry: Representation, conversation, and reflection. In M. Knapp & G. Miller (Eds.), *Handbook of interpersonal communication* (pp. 27–57). Beverly Hills, CA: Sage.

Bochner, A. P., & Eisenberg, E. M. (1985). Legitimizing speech communication: An examination of coherence and cohesion in the development of the discipline. In T. Benson (Ed.), *Speech communication in the 20th century* (pp. 299–321). Carbondale: Southern Illinois University Press.

Boden, D. (1994). *The business of talk: Organizations in action*. Cambridge, MA: Harvard University Press.

Bohm, D. (1996). *On dialogue* (L. Nichol, Ed.). London: Routledge.

Bordo, S. (1992). Postmodern subjects, postmodern bodies. *Feminist Studies, 18*, 159–175.

Bostrom, R., & Donohew, L. (1992). The case for empiricism: Clarifying fundamental issues in communication theory. *Communication Monographs, 59*, 109–129.

Bourdieu, P. (1988). *Homo academicus* (P. Collier, Trans.). Stanford, CA: Stanford University Press.

Bowers, J. W. (1968). The pre-scientific function of rhetorical criticism. In T. R. Nilsen (Ed.), *Essays on rhetorical criticism* (pp. 126–145). New York: Random House.

Brown, M. H. (1985). That reminds me of a story: Speech action in organizational socialization. *Western Journal of Speech Communication, 49*, 27–42.

Brown, M. H. (1990). Defining stories in organizations: Characteristics and functions. In J. Anderson (Ed.), *Communication yearbook 13* (pp. 162–190). Thousand Oaks, CA: Sage.

Brown, R. H. (1977). *A poetic for sociology: Toward a logic of discovery for the human sciences*. Cambridge, UK: Cambridge University Press.

Browning, L. D. (1992). Lists and stories as organizational communication. *Communication Theory, 2*(4), 281–302.

Bryant, C. G. A., & Jary, D. (Eds.). (1991). *Giddens' theory of structuration: A critical appreciation*. London: Routledge.

Buber, M. (1965a). *Between man and man*. New York: MacMillan.

Buber, M. (1965b). *The knowledge of man: A philosophy of the interhuman* (M. Friedman, Ed.). New York: Harper & Row.

Bucciarelli, L. L. (1994). *Designing engineers*. Cambridge, MA: MIT Press.

Buckley, W. (1967). *Sociology and modern systems theory*. Englewood Cliffs, NJ: Prentice-Hall.

Bullis, C. (1999). Mad or bad? A response to Kramer and Miller. *Communication Monographs, 66*, 368–373.

Bullis, C., & Bach, B. (1991). Socialization turning points: An examination of change in organizational identification. *Western Journal of Speech Communication, 53*, 273–293.

Bullis, C., & Tompkins, P. K. (1989). The forest ranger revisited: A study of control practices and identification. *Communication Monographs, 56*, 287–306.

Burawoy, M. (1979). *Manufacturing consent: Changes in the labor process under monopoly capitalism*. Chicago: University of Chicago Press.

Burke, K. (1935). *Permanence and change; an anatomy of purpose*. New York: New Republic.

Burke, K. (1945). *A grammar of motives*. New York: Prentice-Hall.

Burke, K. (1950). *A rhetoric of motives*. New York: Prentice-Hall.

Burke, K. (1959). *Attitudes toward history* (2nd ed., Rev.). Los Altos, CA: Hermes. (Original work published 1937)

Burke, K. (1962). *A grammar of motives, and A rhetoric of motives*. Cleveland, OH: World.

Burke, K. (1966). *Language as symbolic action; essays on life, literature, and method*. Berkeley: University of California Press.

Burke, K. (1969). *A grammar of motives*. Berkeley: University of California Press.

Burrell, G. (1999). Normal science, paradigms, metaphors, discourses and genealogies of analysis. In S. R. Clegg & C. Hardy (Eds.), *Studying organization: Theory and method* (pp. 388–404). London: Sage.

Burrell, G., & Morgan, G. (1979). *Sociological paradigms and organisational analysis*. London: Heinemann.

Butts, R. E. (1973). Whewell's logic of induction. In R. N. Giere & R. S. Westfall (Eds.), *Foundations of scientific method: The nineteenth century* (pp. 53–85). Bloomington: Indiana University Press.

Buzzanell, P. (1994). Gaining a voice: Feminist organizational communication theorizing. *Management Communication Quarterly, 7*, 339–383.

Calás, M. B., & Smircich, L. (1991). Voicing seduction to silence leadership. *Organization Studies, 12*, 567–602.

Calás, M. B., & Smircich, L. (1999a). From "the woman's" point of view: Feminist approaches to organizational studies. In S. R. Clegg & C. Hardy (Eds.), *Studying organization: Theory and method* (pp. 213–251). London: Sage.

Calás, M. B., & Smircich, L. (1999b). Past postmodernism? Reflections and tentative directions. *Academy of Management Review, 24*, 649–671.

Callinicos, A. (1985). Anthony Giddens: A contemporary critique. *Theory and Society, 14*, 133–166.

Cappella, J. (1990). The method of proof by example in interaction analysis. *Communication Monographs, 57*, 236–242.

Carbaugh, D. (1999). "Just listen": "Listening" and landscape among the Blackfeet. *Western Journal of Communication, 63*(3), 250–270.

Carey, A. (1995). *Taking the risk out of democracy: Propaganda in the United States and Australia.* Sydney: University of New South Wales Press.

Carley, K., & Prietula, M. J. (Eds.). (1994). *Computational organizational theory.* Hillsdale, NJ: Erlbaum.

Carlone, D., & Taylor, B. C. (1998). Organizational communication and cultural studies: A review essay. *Communication Theory, 8*(3), 337–367.

Carnap, R. (1937). *Logical syntax of language.* London: Kegan Paul.

Carroll, L. (1992). *Alice's adventures in Wonderland.* New York: Bantam-Doubleday.

Chase-Dunn, C. (1989). *Global formation: Structures of the world-economy.* London: Backwell.

Chautauqua: The case for and against critical theory. (1991). *Communication Monographs, 58*(2), 170–233.

Chautauqua: On the validity and generalizability of conversational analysis methods. (1990). *Communication Monographs, 57*(3), 231–249.

Cheney, G. (1995). Democracy in the workplace: Theory and practice from the perspective of communication. *Journal of Applied Communication Research, 23,* 167–200.

Cheney, G. (1998). "It's the economy, stupid!" A rhetorical–communicative perspective on today's market. *Australian Journal of Communication, 25,* 25–44.

Cheney, G. (1999). *Values at work: Employee participation meets market pressure at Mondragón.* Ithaca, NY: Cornell University Press.

Cheney, G., & Bullis, C. (1999, February). *Out of our heads and into the world: The enduring rationalist–symbolist bias of organizational (communication) research and the need to engage physical and biological environments within and without the organization.* Paper presented for a preconference on the "Environment and Communication Study" at the annual meeting of the Western States Communication Association, Vancouver, BC, Canada.

Cheney, G., & Frenette, G. (1993). Persuasion and organization: Values, logics, and accounts in contemporary corporate public discourse. In C. Conrad (Ed.), *The ethical nexus* (pp. 49–74). Norwood, NJ: Ablex.

Cheney, G., Straub, J., Speirs-Glebe, L., Stohl, C., DeGooyer, D., Whalen, S., Garvin-Doxas, K., & Carlone, D. (1998). Democracy, participation and communication at work: A multidisciplinary review. In M. E. Roloff (Ed.), *Communication yearbook 21* (pp. 35–91). Thousand Oaks, CA: Sage.

Cheney, G., & Wilhelmsson, M. (in press). Responsibility, rights, and privilege in organizational communication. In S. Gilmore (Ed.), *Communication in the 21st century.*

Chia, R. (1995). From modern to postmodern organizational analysis. *Organization Studies, 16*(4), 570–604.

Chiles, A. M., & Zorn, T. E. (1995). Empowerment in organizations: Employees' perceptions of the influences on empowerment. *Journal of Applied Communication Research, 23*(1), 1–25.

Chomsky, N. (1959). A review of B. F. Skinner's verbal behavior. *Language, 35*(1), 26–58.

Clair, R. P. (1993). The use of framing devices to sequester organizational narratives: Hegemony and harassment. *Communication Monographs, 60,* 113–136.

Clair, R. P. (1996). The political nature of the colloquialism, "A real job": Implications for organizational socialization. *Communication Monographs, 63,* 249–267.

Clair, R. P. (1999). Ways of seeing: A review of Kramer and Miller's manuscript. *Communication Monographs, 66,* 374–381.

Clegg, S. (1989). *Frameworks of power.* Newbury Park, CA: Sage.

Clegg, S. (1994). Weber and Foucault: Social theory for the study of organizations. *Organization, 1,* 149–178.

Cloud, D. (1994). The materiality of discourse as oxymoron: A challenge to critical rhetoric. *Western Journal of Communication, 58,* 141–163.

Cloud, D. (1996). *Fighting for words: The limits of symbolic power in the Staley lockout, 1993–1996.* Paper presented at the annual meeting of the Speech Communication Association, San Diego, CA.

Collins, H., & Pinch, T. (1993). *The golem: What everyone should know about science.* Cambridge, UK: Cambridge University Press.

Collins, P. H. (1991). *Black feminist thought: Knowledge, consciousness, and the politics of empowerment.* Boston: Unwin Hyman.

Collins, R. (1992). The confusion of the modes of sociology. In S. Seidman & D. G. Wagner (Eds.), *Postmodernism and social theory* (pp. 179–198). Cambridge, UK: Blackwell.

Collinson, D. (1988). "Engineering humor": Masculinity, joking and conflict in shop-floor relations. *Organization Studies, 9,* 181–199.

Collinson, D. (1992). *Managing the shop floor: Subjectivity, masculinity, and workplace culture.* New York: De Gruyter.

Comte, A. (1970). *Introduction to positive philosophy* (F. Ferre, Ed. & Trans.). Indianapolis, IN: Bobbs-Merrill.

Conrad, C. (Ed.). (1993). *The ethical nexus.* Norwood, NJ: Ablex.

Conrad, C. (1999, May). *Central constructs in organizational communication research and theory: 1996–1999.* Presentation at the International Communication Association Convention, San Francisco.

Conrad, C., & Haynes, J. (2000). Key constructs: Views from varying perspectives. In F. M. Jablin & L. L. Putnam (Eds.), *Handbook of organizational communication: Advances in theory, research, and methods.* Thousand Oaks, CA: Sage.

Conrad, C., & Ryan, M. (1985). Power, praxis, and self in organizational communication theory. In R. D. McPhee & P. K. Tompkins (Eds.), *Organizational communication: Traditional themes and new directions* (pp. 235–257). Thousand Oaks, CA: Sage.

Contractor, N. S. (1994). Self-organizing systems perspective in the study of organizational communication. In B. Kovacic (Ed.), *New approaches to organizational communication* (pp. 39–66). Albany: State University of New York Press.

Contractor, N. S. (1999). Self-organizing systems research in the social sciences: Reconciling the metaphors and models. *Management Communication Quarterly, 13,* 154–166.

Contractor, N. S., Eisenberg, E. M., & Monge, P. R. (1994, June). *Antecedents and outcomes of interpretive diversity in organizations.* Paper presented at the annual conference of the International Communication Association, Sydney, Australia.

Cooren, F. (1999). Applying socio-semiotics to organizational communication: A new approach. *Management Communication Quarterly, 13,* 294–304.

Cooren, F. (2000). *The organizing property of communication.* Amsterdam and Philadelphia: J. Benjamins.

Corey, F. C., & Nakayama, T. K. (1997). Sextext. *Text and Performance Quarterly,* *17,* 58–68.

Corman, S. R., & Scott, C. R. (1994). Perceived networks, activity foci, and observable communication in social collectives. *Communication Theory,* *4,* 171–191.

Courtright, J. A., Fairhurst, G. T., & Rogers, L. E. (1989). Interaction patterns in organic and mechanistic systems. *Academy of Management Journal, 32,* 773–802.

Cox, T. H., & Blake, S. (1991). Managing cultural diversity: Implications for organizational effectiveness. *Academy of Management Executive, 5,* 45–56.

Craig, R. T. (1999). Communication theory as a field. *Communication Theory, 9,* 119–161.

Crane, D. (1972). *Invisible colleges: Diffusion of knowledge in scientific communities.* Chicago: University of Chicago Press.

Cronen, V. E., Pearce, W. B., & Harris, L. M. (1979). The logic of the coordinated management of meaning: A rules-based approach to the first course in interpersonal communication. *Communication Education, 28*(1), 22–38.

Cushman, D., & Pearce, W. B. (1977). Generality and necessity in three types of theory about human communication, with special attention to rule theory. *Human Communication Research, 3,* 344–353.

Czarniawski, B. (1998). Who's afraid of incommensurability? *Organization, 5,* 273–275.

Daniels, T., Spiker, B., & Papa, M. (1998). *Perspectives on organizational communication* (4th ed.). Dubuque, IA: Brown.

Danowski, J. A. (1994). An emerging macrolevel theory of organizational communication: Organizations as virtual reality management systems. In L. Thayer (Ed.), *Organization<—>communication: Emerging perspectives. Vol. 4* (pp. 141–174). Norwood, NJ: Ablex.

Dawe, A. (1970). The two sociologies. *British Journal of Sociology, 21,* 207–218.

Dawe, A. (1978). Theories of social action. In T. Bottomore & R. Nesbit (Eds.), *A history of sociological analysis* (pp. 362–417). New York: Basic Books.

de Certeau, M. (1984). *The practice of everyday life* (S. Rendall, Trans.). Berkeley: University of California Press.

DeCock, C., & Richards, T. (1995). Of Giddens, paradigms, and philosophical garb. *Organization Studies, 16,* 699–704.

Deetz, S. (1973). An understanding of science and a hermeneutic science of understanding. *Journal of Communication, 23,* 139–159.

Deetz, S. (1990). Reclaiming the subject matter as a guide to mutual understanding: Effectiveness and ethics in interpersonal interaction. *Communication Quarterly, 38,* 226–243.

Deetz, S. (1992). *Democracy in the age of corporate colonization: Developments in communication and the politics of everyday life.* Albany: State University of New York Press.

Deetz, S. (1994). The future of the discipline: The challenges, the research, and the social contribution. In S. Deetz (Ed.), *Communication yearbook 17* (pp. 565–600). Newbury Park, CA: Sage.

Deetz, S. (1996). Describing the differences in approaches to organization science: Rethinking Burrell and Morgan and their legacy. *Organization Science, 7,* 191–207.

Deetz, S. (1998). Discursive formations, strategized subordination, and self-surveillance: An empirical case. In A. McKinlay & K. Starkey (Eds.), *Foucault, management, and organizations* (pp. 151–172). London: Sage.

Deetz, S. (in press). Putting the community into organizational science: Exploring the construction of knowledge claims. *Organization Science*.

Deetz, S., & Kersten, A. (1983). Critical models of interpretive research. In L. L. Putnam & M. E. Pacanowsky (Eds.), *Communication and organizations, an interpretive approach* (pp. 147–171). Beverly Hills, CA: Sage.

Derrida, J. (1976). *Of grammatology* (G. C. Spivak, Trans.). Baltimore: Johns Hopkins University Press.

Dervin, B., Grossberg, L., O'Keefe, B., & Wartella, E. (Eds.). (1989). *Rethinking communication. Vol. 2: Paradigm exemplars*. Newbury Park, CA: Sage.

Dewey, J. (1939). *Theory of valuation*. Chicago: University of Chicago Press.

The dialogue of evidence: A topic revisited [Special issue]. (1994). *Western Journal of Communication, 58*(1), 1–71.

Diesing, P. (1991). *How does social science work?: Reflections on practice*. Pittsburgh, PA: University of Pittsburgh Press.

DiMaggio, P. J., & Powell, W. W. (1991). Introduction. In W. W. Powell & P. J. DiMaggio (Eds.), *The new institutionalism of organizational analysis* (pp. 1–40). Chicago: University of Chicago Press.

Doerfel, M. L., & Barnett, G. A. (1999). A comparison of the semantic and affiliation networks of the International Communication Association. *Human Communication Research, 25*, 589–603.

Donaldson, L. (1988). In successful defense of organization theory: A routing of the critics. *Organization Studies, 9*, 28–32.

Donnellon, A., Gray, B., & Bougon, M. G. (1986). Communication, meaning, and organized action. *Administrative Science Quarterly, 31*, 43–55.

Douglas, M. (1986). *How institutions think*. Syracuse, NY: Syracuse University Press.

Dow, B. J. (1990). Hegemony, feminist criticism and "The Mary Tyler Moore Show." *Critical Studies in Mass Communication, 7*, 261–274.

du Gay, P. (1996). *Consumption and identity at work*. London: Sage.

Dubin, R. (1969). *Theory building*. New York: Free Press.

Dubin, R. (1978). *Theory building* (Rev. ed.). New York: Free Press.

Dutton, W. (Ed.). (1996). *Information and communication technologies: Visions and realities*. Oxford, UK: Oxford University Press.

Dutton, W. (Ed.). (1999). *Society on the line: Information politics in the digital age*. Oxford, UK: Oxford University Press.

Easton, D. (1967). *The political system: An inquiry into the state of political science*. New York: Knopf.

Ebers, M. (1985). Understanding organizations: The poetic mode. *Journal of Management, 7*(2), 51–62.

Eckberg, D. L., & Hill, L. Jr. (1980). The paradigm concept and sociology: A critical review. In G. Gutting (Ed.), *Paradigms and revolutions: Appraisals and applications of Thomas Kuhn's philosophy of science* (pp. 117–136). Notre Dame, IN: University of Notre Dame Press.

Eisenberg, E. M. (1984). Ambiguity as strategy in organizational communication. *Communication Monographs, 51*, 227–242.

Eisenberg, E. M. (1998). Flirting with meaning. *Journal of Language and Social Psychology, 17,* 97–108.

Eisenberg, E. M., Andrews, L., Laine-Timmerman, L., & Murphy, A. (1999). Transforming organizations through communication. In P. Salem (Ed.), *Organizational communication and change* (pp. 125–147). Creekskill, NJ: Hampton Press.

Eisenberg, E. M., & Goodall, H. L. Jr. (1997). *Organizational communication: Balancing creativity and constraint* (2nd ed.). New York: St. Martin's Press.

Eisenberg, E. M., & Riley, P. (1988). Organizational symbols and sense-making. In G. M. Goldhaber & G. A. Barnett (Eds.), *Handbook of organizational communication* (pp. 131–150). Norwood, NJ: Ablex.

Ellinor, L., & Gerard, G. (1998). *Dialogue: Rediscover the transforming power of conversation.* New York: Wiley.

Ellis, D. G. (1991). Poststructuralism and language: Non-sense. *Communication Monographs, 58,* 213–224.

Ellis, D. G. (1996). Editor's note. *Communication Theory, 6,* 329–330.

Engeström, Y. (1990). *Learning, working, and imagining.* Helsinki, Finland: Orienta-Konsultit Oy.

Engeström, Y., & Middleton, D. (Eds.). (1996). *Cognition and communication at work.* Cambridge, UK: Cambridge University Press.

Fairhurst, G. T. (1993). The leader–member exchange patterns of women leaders in industry: A discourse analysis. *Communication Monographs, 60,* 321–351.

Fairhurst, G. T. (1994). The leader–member exchange patterns of women leaders in industry: A discourse analysis. *Communication Monographs, 60,* 321–351.

Fairhurst, G. T. (2000). Dualisms in leadership communication research. In F. M. Jablin & L. L. Putnam (Eds.), *Handbook of organizational communication: Advances in theory, research, and methods* (pp. 379–439). Thousand Oaks, CA: Sage.

Fairhurst, G. T., Green, S. G., & Snavely, B. (1984). Face support in controlling poor performance. *Human Communication Research, 11,* 272–295.

Fairhurst, G. T., Green, S. G., & Courtright, J. A. (1995). Inertial forces and the implementation of a socio-technical systems approach: A communication study. *Organization Science, 6,* 168–185.

Fairhurst, G. T., Jordan, J. M., & Neuwirth, K. (1997). Why are we here?: Managing the meaning of an organizational mission statement. *Journal of Applied Communication Research, 25*(4), 243–263.

Fairhurst, G. T., Rogers, L. E., & Sarr, R. A. (1987). Manager-subordinate control patterns and judgments about the relationship. In M. McLaughlin (Ed.), *Communication yearbook 10* (pp. 395–415). Beverly Hills, CA: Sage.

Fasching, D. (1996). *The coming of the millennium: Good news for the whole human race.* Valley Forge, PA: Trinity Press International.

Fay, B. (1987). *Critical social science: Liberation and its limits.* Ithaca, NY: Cornell University Press.

Feagin, J. R. (1999, October 15). Soul-searching in sociology: Is the discipline in crisis? *Chronicle of Higher Education,* pp. B4–B6.

Ferguson, K. E. (1993). *The man question: Visions of subjectivity in feminist theory.* Berkeley: University of California Press.

Feyeraband, P. (1962). Explanation, reduction, and empiricism. In H. Feigl & G.

Maxwell (Eds.), *Scientific explanation, space, and time* (pp. 28–97). Minneapolis: University of Minnesota Press.

Finch, J. (1984). "It's great to have someone to talk to": The ethics and politics of interviewing women. In C. Bell & H. Roberts (Eds.), *Social researching: Politics, problems, and practice* (pp. 70–87). London: Routledge & Kegan Paul.

Fiske, J. (1986). Television: Polysemy and popularity. *Critical Studies in Mass Communication, 3,* 391–408.

Fitch, K. L. (1994). Criteria for evidence in qualitative research. *Western Journal of Communication, 58,* 32–38.

Fitzgerald, T., Fothergill, A., Gilmore, K., Irwin, L., Kunkel, C. A., Leahy, S., Nielson, J. M., Passerini, E., Virnoche, M. E., & Walden, G. (1995). What's wrong is right: A response to the state of the discipline. *Sociological Forum, 10,* 493–498.

Flick, D. L. (1998). *From debate to dialogue.* Boulder, CO: Orchid.

Folger, J. P. (1991). Interpretive and structural claims about confrontations. In J. A. Anderson (Ed.), *Communication yearbook 14* (pp. 393–402). Newbury Park, CA: Sage.

Folger, J. P., & Poole, M. S. (1984). *Working through conflict: A communication perspective.* Glenview, IL: Scott Foresman.

Foss, S. K., & Griffin, C. L. (1995). Beyond persuasion: A proposal for an invitational rhetoric. *Communication Monographs, 62,* 2–18.

Foucault, M. (1975). *The birth of the clinic: An archaeology of medical perception* (A. M. Sheridan Smith, Trans.). New York: Vintage Books.

Foucault, M. (1978). *The history of sexuality* (R. Hurley, Trans.). New York: Pantheon Books.

Foucault, M. (1979). *Discipline and punish: The birth of the prison* (A. Sheridan, Trans.). New York: Vintage Books.

Foucault, M. (1980a). *The history of sexuality, Vol. 1: An introduction* (R. Hurley, Trans.). New York: Vintage Books.

Foucault, M. (1980b). *Power/knowledge: Selected interviews and other writings, 1972–1977* (C. Gordon, Ed.; C. Gordon, L. Marshall, J. Mepham, & K. Soper, Trans.). New York: Pantheon Books.

Foucault, M. (1984). *The Foucault reader* (P. Rabinow, Ed.). New York: Pantheon Books.

Fraser, N. (1989). *Unruly practices.* Minneapolis: University of Minnesota Press.

Friedman, R. A. (1989). Interaction norms as carriers of organizational culture: A study of labor negotiations at International Harvester. *Journal of Contemporary Ethnography, 18,* 3–29.

Frost, P., Moore, L., Louis, M. R., Lunberg, C., & Martin, J. (Eds.). (1991). *Reframing organizational culture.* Newbury Park, CA: Sage.

Fulk, J., & Steinfield, C. (Eds.). (1990). *Organizations and communication technology.* Newbury Park, CA: Sage.

The future of the field: Between fragmentation and cohesion [Special issue]. (1993a). *Journal of Communication, 43*(3), 4–238.

The future of the field: Between fragmentation and cohesion [Special issue]. (1993b). *Journal of Communication, 43*(4), 4–190.

Gabriel, Y., & Lang, T. (1995). *The unmanageable consumer: Contemporary consumption and its fragmentations.* London: Sage.

Gadamer, H. G. (1975). *Truth and method* (G. Barden & J. Cumming, Trans.). London: Sheed & Ward.

Geertz, C. (1973). *The interpretation of cultures*. New York: Basic Books.

Geertz, C. (1983). *Local knowledge: Further essays in interpretive anthropology*. New York: Basic Books.

Gergen, K. J. (1991). *The saturated self*. New York: Basic Books.

Giddens, A. (1976). *New rules for sociological method: A positive critique of interpretative sociologies*. New York: Basic Books.

Giddens, A. (1979). *Central problems in social theory: Action, structure, and contradiction in social analysis*. Berkeley, CA: University of California Press.

Giddens, A. (1981). *The class structure of the advanced societies* (2nd ed.). London: Hutchinson.

Giddens, A. (1984). *The constitution of society: Outline of the theory of structuration*. Berkeley: University of California Press.

Giddens, A. (1990). *The consequences of modernity*. Stanford, CA: Stanford University Press.

Giddens, A. (1991). Structuration theory: Past, present, and future. In C. G. A. Bryant & D. Jary (Eds.), *Giddens' theory of structuration: A critical appreciation* (pp. 201–221). New York: Routledge.

Giddens, A. (1994). *Beyond left and right: The future of radical politics*. Stanford, CA: Stanford University Press.

Gillespie, R. (1991). *Manufacturing knowledge: A history of the Hawthorne experiments*. Cambridge, UK: Cambridge University Press.

Gioia, D. A., Donnellon, A., & Sims, H. P. (1989). Communication and cognition in appraisal: A tale of two paradigms. *Organization Studies, 10*, 503–530.

Gioia, D. A., & Pitre, E. (1990). Multiparadigm perspectives on theory building. *Academy of Management Review, 15*, 584–602.

Giroux, N. (1993). *Changement strategique dans une institution: Le cas Visa Desjardins*. Quebec, Canada: Gaetan Morin.

Glaser, B., & Strauss, A. (1967). *The discovery of grounded theory*. Chicago: Aldine.

Glaser, H. (1994). *Structure and struggle in egalitarian groups: Reframing the problems of time, emotion, and inequality as defining characteristics*. Unpublished doctoral dissertation, University of Illinois at Urbana–Champaign.

Goffman, E. (1956). *The presentation of self in everyday life*. Edinburgh, UK: University of Edinburgh, Social Sciences Research Centre.

Goldhaber, G. M., & Barnett, G. A. (1988). Forward. In G. M. Goldhaber & G. A. Barnett (Eds.), *Handbook of organizational communication* (pp. 1–4). Norwood, NJ: Ablex.

Goodall, L. H. (1989). *Casing a promised land*. Carbondale: Southern Illinois University Press.

Graen, G. B. (1976). Role-making processes within complex organizations. In M. D. Dunnette (Ed.), *Handbook of industrial and organizational psychology* (pp. 1201–1245). Chicago: Rand-McNally.

Graen, G. B., & Scandura, T. A. (1987). Toward a psychology of dyadic organizing. In B. Staw & L. L. Cummings (Eds.), *Research in organizational behavior* (Vol. 9, pp. 175–208). Greenwich, CT: JAI Press.

Graen, G. B., & Uhl-Bien, M. (1991). The transformation of professionals into self-managing and partially self-designing contributors: Towards a theory of leadership making. *Journal of Management Systems, 3*, 33–48.

Graham, L. (1995). *On the line at Subaru–Isuzu: The Japanese model and the American worker.* Ithaca, NY: ILR Press.

Gramsci, A. (1971). *Selections from the prison notebooks* (Q. Hoare & G. N. Smith, Trans.). New York: International Publishers.

Grenier, G. J. (1988). *Inhuman relations: Quality circles and antiunionism in American industry.* Philadelphia: Temple University Press.

Guba, E. G. (1990). The alternative paradigm dialog. In E. G. Guba (Ed.), *The paradigm dialog* (pp. 17–27). Newbury Park, CA: Sage.

Gulliver, F. (1987, March–April). Post-project appraisals pay. *Harvard Business Review,* p. 128.

Habermas, J. (1971). *Knowledge and human interests* (J. J. Shapiro, Trans.). Boston: Beacon Press.

Habermas, J. (1979). *Communication and the evolution of society* (T. McCarthy, Trans.). Boston: Beacon Press.

Habermas, J. (1981). Modernity versus postmodernity. *New German Critique, 22,* 3–14.

Habermas, J. (1984). *The theory of communicative action. Vol. 1: Reason and the rationalization of society* (T. McCarthy, Trans.). Boston: Beacon Press.

Habermas, J. (1987). *The theory of communicative action. Vol. 2: Lifeworld and system: A critique of functionalist reason* (T. McCarthy, Trans.). Boston: Beacon Press.

Habermas, J. (1988). *On the logic of the social sciences* (S. W. Nicholsen & J. A. Stark, Trans.). Cambridge, UK: Polity Press.

Hacking, I. (1982). *Language, truth, reason.* In M. Hollis & S. Lukes (Eds.), *Rationality and relativism* (pp. 48–66). Oxford, UK: Blackwell.

Hage, J. (1972). *Techniques and problems of theory construction in sociology.* New York: Wiley.

Hall, S. (1982). The rediscovery of "ideology": Return of the repressed in media studies. In M. Gurevitch, T. Bennet, J. Curran, & J. Woolacott (Eds.), *Culture, society, and the media.* New York: Methuen.

Hall, S. (1992). The West and the rest: Discourse and power. In S. Hall & B. Gieben (Eds.), *Formations of modernity* (pp. 275–331). Cambridge, UK: Polity Press.

Hanson, N. R. (1965). *Patterns of discovery.* Cambridge, UK: Cambridge University Press.

Haraway, D. (1990). A manifesto for cyborgs: Science, technology, and socialist feminism in the 1980s. In L. J. Nicholson (Ed.), *Feminism/postmodernism* (pp. 190–233). New York: Routledge.

Harding, S. (1987). The instability of the analytical categories of feminist theory. In S. Harding & J. O'Barr (Eds.), *Sex and scientific inquiry* (pp. 283–302). Chicago: University of Chicago Press.

Harris, C. C. (1980). *Fundamental concepts and the sociological enterprise.* London: Croom Helm.

Harris, W. (1999, December 3). Sociologists should use both quantitative and qualitative research to serve society. *Chronicle of Higher Education,* p. B3.

Harrison, T. (1994). Communication and interdependence in democratic organizations. In S. Deetz (Ed.), *Communication yearbook 17* (pp. 247–274). Newbury Park, CA: Sage.

Hartsock, N. C. M. (1983). The feminist standpoint: Developing the ground for a specifically feminist historical materialism. In S. Harding & M. Hintikka (Eds.), *Discovering reality: Feminist perspectives on epistemology, metaphysics, methodology, and philosophy of science* (pp. 283–311). Hingham, MA: Kluwer Boston.

Hassard, J. (1991). Multiple paradigms and organizational analysis: A case study. *Organizational Studies, 12*, 275–299.

Hassard, J. (1993). *Sociology and organization theory: Positivism, paradigms and postmodernity.* Cambridge, UK: Cambridge University Press.

Hatch, M. J. (1997). Irony and the social construction of contradiction in the humor of a management team. *Organization Science, 8*, 275–288.

Hawes, L. C. (1999). Dialogics, posthumanist theory, and self-organizing systems. *Management Communication Quarterly, 13*, 146–153.

Hayden, S. (1998). *Reversing the discourse of sexology: Margaret Higgins Sanger's "What Every Girl Should Know!"* Working paper, University of Montana–Missoula.

Heaton, L. (1998). Talking heads versus virtual workspaces: A comparison of design across cultures. *Journal of Information Technology, 13*, 259–272.

Helmer, J. (1993). Storytelling in the creation and maintenance of organizational tension and stratification. *Southern Communication Journal, 59*, 34–44.

Henderson, K. (1998). The aura of "high-tech" in a world of messy practice. *Sociological Quarterly, 39*(4), 645–672.

Heritage, P. (1984). *Garfinkel and ethnomethodology.* Cambridge, UK: Polity Press.

Heshusius, L., & Ballard, K. (Eds.). (1996). *From positivism to interpretivism and beyond: Tales of transformation in educational and social research (The mind-body connection).* New York: Teachers College Press.

Hewes, D. E., & Planalp, S. (1987). The individual's place in communication science. In C. R. Berger & S. H. Chaffee (Eds.), *Handbook of communication science* (pp. 146–183). Newbury Park, CA: Sage.

Hilmer, B. H. (1997). *Dialogue as the language of change: An examination of the discourse of organizational dialogue.* Unpublished doctoral dissertation, Department of Communication Studies, University of Kansas.

Hirsch, P., & Lounsbury, M. (1997). Ending the family quarrel. *American Behavioral Scientist, 40*, 406–418.

Hochschild, A. R. (1997a). *The second shift.* New York: Avon Books.

Hochschild, A. R. (1997b). *The time bind: When work becomes home and home becomes work.* New York: Metropolitan Books.

Hoffman, L. (1982). *Foundations of family systems theory.* New York: Basic Books.

hooks, b. (1984). *Feminist theory: From margin to center.* Boston: South End Press.

Horkheimer, M. (1982). *Critical theory: Selected essays* (M. J. O'Connell et al., Trans.). New York: Continuum.

Horkheimer, M., & Adorno, T. W. (1972). *Dialectic of enlightenment* (J. Cumming, Trans.). New York: Seabury Press.

Houston, M. (1992). The politics of difference: Race, class, and women's communication. In L. F. Rakow (Ed.), *Women making meaning: New feminist directions in communication* (pp. 45–59). New York: Routledge.

Houston, R. (1999). Self-organizing systems theory: Historical challenges to new sciences. *Management Communication Quarterly, 13*, 119–134.

Howard, L. A., & Geist, P. (1995). Ideological positioning in organizational change. *Communication Monographs, 62*, 110–131.

Hutchings, V. (1992). The woman question. *New Statesman and Society, 5*, 11.

Hutchins, E. (1995). *Cognition in the wild*. Cambridge, MA: MIT Press.

Hyatt, A., Contractor, N. S., & Jones, P. (1997, May). *Computational organizational network modeling: Strategies and an exemplar*. Paper presented at the annual meeting of the International Communication Association, Montreal, Canada.

Isaacs, W. N. (1993). Taking flight: Dialogue, collective thinking, and organizational learning. *Organizational Dynamics, 22*, 24–39.

Jablin, F. M. (1987). Organizational entry, assimilation, and exit. In F. M. Jablin, L. L. Putnam, K. Roberts, & L. Porter (Eds.), *Handbook of organizational communication: An interdisciplinary approach* (pp. 679–740). Beverly Hills, CA: Sage.

Jackson, M. (1989). *Paths toward a clearing*. Bloomington: Indiana University Press.

Jackson, N., & Carter, P. (1991). In defense of paradigm incommensurability. *Organization Studies, 12*, 109–127.

Jackson, N., & Carter, P. (1993). Paradigm wars: A response to Hugh Wilmot. *Organization Studies, 14*, 721–725.

Jacobs, S. (1986). How to make an argument from example in discourse analysis. In D. G. Ellis & W. A. Donohue (Eds.), *Contemporary issues in language and discourse processes* (pp. 149–168). Hillsdale, NJ: Erlbaum.

Jacobs, S. (1988). Evidence and inference in conversation analysis. In J. A. Anderson (Ed.), *Communication yearbook 11* (pp. 433–443). Newbury Park, CA: Sage.

Jacobs, S. (1990). On the especially nice fit between qualitative analysis and the known properties of conversation. *Communication Monographs, 57*, 243–249.

Jacques, R. (1996). *Manufacturing the employee: Management knowledge from the 19th to 21st centuries*. Thousand Oaks, CA: Sage.

Jay, M. (1984). *Adorno*. Cambridge, MA: Harvard University Press.

Jermier, J. M., Knights, D., & Nord, W. R. (Eds.). (1994). *Resistance and power in organizations*. London: Routledge.

Johnson, S. (1991). *The ship that sailed into the living room: Sex and intimacy reconsidered*. Estancia, NM: Wildfire.

Kaghan, W., & Phillips, N. (1998). Building the Tower of Babel: Communities of practice and paradigmatic pluralism in organization studies. *Organization, 5*(2), 191–215.

Kauffman, B. J. (1992). Feminist facts: Interview strategies and political subjects in ethnography. *Communication Theory, 2*, 187–206.

Kincaid, D. L., Yum, J. O., Woelfel, J., & Barnett, G. A. (1983). The cultural convergence of Korean immigrants in Hawaii: An empirical test of a mathematical theory. *Quality and Quantity, 18*, 59–78.

Koch, S., & Deetz, S. (1981). Metaphor analysis of social reality in organizations. *Journal of Applied Communication Research, 9*(1), 1–15.

Kofman, F., & Senge, P. M. (1993). Communities of commitment: The heart of learning organizations. *Organizational Dynamics, 22*, 5–23.

Kolakowski, L. (1968). *The alienation of reason*. Garden City, NY: Doubleday.

Kramer, M. (1994). Uncertainty reduction during job transitions: An exploratory study of the communication experiences of newcomers and transferees. *Management Communication Quarterly, 7*, 384–412.

Kramer, M., & Miller, V. (1999). A response to criticisms of organizational socialization research. *Communication Monographs, 66*, 358–367.

Kreps, G. L. (1989). A therapeutic model of organizational communication consultation: Application of interpretive field methods. *Southern Communication Journal, 55*(1), 1–21.

Krippendorff, K. (1999). Beyond coherence. *Management Communication Quarterly, 13,* 135–145.

Krizek, R. L. (1998). Lessons: What the hell are we teaching the next generation anyway? In A. Banks & S. P. Banks (Eds.), *Fiction and social research: By ice or fire* (pp. 89–114). Walnut Creek, CA: Altamira Press.

Krone, K. J., Chen, L., Sloan, D. K., & Gallant, L. M. (1997). Managerial emotionality in Chinese factories. *Management Communication Quarterly, 11,* 6–50.

Krone, K. J., Jablin, F. M., & Putnam, L. L. (1987). Communication theory and organizational communication: Multiple perspectives. In F. M. Jablin, L. L. Putnam, K. Roberts, & L. Porter (Eds.), *Handbook of organizational communication: An interdisciplinary perspective* (pp. 18–40). Newbury Park, CA: Sage.

Kuhn, T. S. (1962). *The structure of scientific revolutions.* Chicago: University of Chicago Press.

Kuhn, T. S. (1970). *The structure of scientific revolutions* (2nd ed.). Chicago: University of Chicago Press.

Kunda, G. (1992). *Engineering culture: Control and commitment in a high-tech corporation.* Philadelphia: Temple University Press.

Lakatos, I. (1970). Falsification and the methdology of scientific research programmes. In I. Lakatos & A. Musgrave (Eds.), *Criticism and the growth of knowledge* (pp. 91–196). Cambridge, UK: Cambridge University Press.

Lamude, K., Daniels, T., & White, K. (1987). Managing the boss: Locus of control and subordinates' selection of compliance-gaining strategies in upward communication. *Management Communication Quarterly, 1,* 232–259.

Lannamann, J. W. (1991). Interpersonal communication research as ideological practice. *Communication Theory, 1,* 179–203.

Larkey, L. K. (1996). Toward a theory of communicative interactions in culturally diverse workgroups. *Academy of Management Review, 21,* 463–491.

Latour, B. (1993). *We have never been modern.* Cambridge, MA: Harvard University Press.

Layder, D. (1985). Power, structure, and agency. *Journal for the Theory of Social Behavior, 15,* 131–149.

Layder, D. (1987). Key issues in structuration theory. *Current Perspectives in Social Theory, 8,* 25–46.

Layton, E. T. (1974). Technology as knowledge. *Technology and Culture, 15*(1), 31–41.

Leeds-Hurwitz, W. (1992). Forum introduction: Social approaches to interpersonal communication. *Communication Theory, 2,* 131–139.

Lincoln, Y. S. (Ed.). (1985). *Organizational theory and inquiry.* Beverly Hills, CA: Sage.

The Linguasphere Observatory [Online]. (2000). Available: http//www.linguasphere.com

Lueken, G. L. (1991). Incommensurability, rules of argumentation, and anticipation. In F. H. Van Eemeren et al. (Eds.), *Proceedings of the Second International Conference on Argumentation.* Amsterdam: SicSat.

Lukes, S. (1974). *Power: A radical view.* London and New York: Macmillan.

Lyotard, J.-F. (1984). *The postmodern condition: A report on knowledge* (G. Bennington & B. Massumi, Trans.). Minneapolis: University of Minnesota Press.

Markham, A. (1996). Designing discourse: A critical analysis of strategic ambiguity and workplace control. *Management Communication Quarterly, 9,* 389–421.

Marshall, A. A., & Stohl, C. (1993). Participating as participation: A network approach. *Communication Monographs, 60,* 137–157.

Martin, J. (1992). *Cultures in organizations: Three perspectives.* New York: Oxford University Press.

Martin, J., & Frost, P. (1996). The organizational culture war games: A struggle for intellectual dominance. In S. R. Clegg, C. Hardy, & W. R. Nord (Eds.), *Handbook of organization studies* (pp. 599–621). Thousand Oaks, CA: Sage.

Martin, J., & Meyerson, D. (1987). Cultural change: An integration of three different views. *Journal of Management Studies, 24*(6), 623–647.

Martin, J., & Meyerson, D. (1988). Organizational cultures and the denial, channeling, and acknowledgement of ambiguity. In L. R. Pondy, R. J. Boland Jr., & H. Thomas (Eds.), *Managing ambiguity and change* (pp. 93–125). New York: Wiley.

Martin, P. Y. (1990). Rethinking feminist organizations. *Gender and Society, 4,* 182–206.

Marx, K. (1967). *Capital* (S. Moore & E. Aveling, Trans.). New York: International Publishers.

Maturana, H. R. (1991). Science in daily life: The ontology of scientific explanations. In F. Steier (Ed.), *Research and reflexivity: Self-reflexivity as social process* (pp. 30–52). Newbury Park, CA: Sage.

Mayo, E. (1929–1930). Changing methods in industry. *Personnel Journal, 8,* 326–332.

McKelvey, B. (1997). Quasi-natural organization science. *Organization Science, 8,* 352–380.

McPhee, R. D. (1985). Formal structure and organizational communication. In R. D. McPhee & P. K. Tompkins (Eds.), *Organizational communication: Traditional themes and new directions* (pp. 149–177). Beverly Hills, CA: Sage.

McPhee, R. D. (1998). *Traditional, interpretive, critical, and postmodern discourses in communication studies: Another telling of the paradigm debates story.* Paper Presented at the International Communication Association convention, Jerusalem.

Merleau-Ponty, M. (1962). *Phenomenology of perception* (C. Smith, Trans.). New York: Humanities Press.

Merton, R. (1973). *The sociology of science.* Chicago: University of Chicago Press.

Meyer, J. W., & Rowan, B. (1977). Institutionalized organizations: Formal structure as myth and ceremony. *American Journal of Sociology, 83,* 340–363.

Meyers, R. A., & Garrett, D. E. (1993). Contradictions, values, and organizational argument. In C. Conrad (Ed.), *The ethical nexus* (pp. 131–144). Newbury Park, CA: Sage.

Mies, M. (1979). *Towards a methodology of women's studies.* The Hague, Netherlands: Institute of Social Studies.

Miller, D. W. (1999, September 3). Sociologists debate how to broaden scholarship in their flagship journal. *Chronicle of Higher Education,* p. A24.

Miller, K. (1998). The evolution of professional identity: The case of osteopathic medicine. *Social Science and Medicine, 47,* 1739–1748.

Miller, K. (1999). *Organizational communication: Approaches and processes* (2nd ed.). Belmont, CA: Wadsworth.

Miller, K. (2000). Quantitative research methods in organizational communication: Practices and challenges. In F. M. Jablin & L. L. Putnam (Eds.), *Handbook of organizational communication: Advances in theory, research, and methods*. Thousand Oaks, CA: Sage.

Miller, K. (forthcoming). *Communication theories*. Mountain View, CA: Mayfield.

Miller, V. D., & Kramer, M. W. (1999). A reply to Bullis, Turner, and Clair. *Communication Monographs, 66*, 390–392.

Mintzberg, H. (1968). *The manager at work: Determining his activities, roles, and programs by structured observation*. Unpublished master's thesis, Massachusetts Institute of Technology.

Mohr, L. (1982). *Explaining organizational behavior*. San Francisco: Jossey-Bass.

Mokros, H., & Deetz, S. (1996). What counts as real? A constitutive view of communication and the disenfranchised in the context of health. In E. B. Ray (Ed.), *Communication and the disenfranchised: Social health issues and implications* (pp. 29–44). Hillsdale, NJ: Erlbaum.

Monge, P. R., Fulk, J., Kalman, M., Flanagin, A. J., Parnassa, C., & Rumsey, S. (1998). Production of collective action in alliance-based interorganizational communication and information systems. *Organization Science, 9*, 411–433.

Morgan, G. (1986). *Images of organization*. Beverly Hills, CA: Sage.

Morgan, G. (1997). *Images of organization* (2nd ed.). Thousand Oaks, CA: Sage.

Morley, D., & Chen, K. H. (Eds.). (1996). *Stuart Hall: Critical dialogues in cultural studies*. London: Routledge.

Mouffe, C. (1992). Feminism, citizenship, and radical democratic politics. In J. Butler & J. W. Scott (Eds.), *Feminists theorize the political* (pp. 369–384). London: Routledge.

Mumby, D. K. (1987). The political function of narrative in organizations. *Communication Monographs, 54*, 113–127.

Mumby, D. K. (1988). *Communication and power in organizations: Discourse, ideology, and domination*. Norwood, NJ: Ablex.

Mumby, D. K. (1989). Ideology and the social construction of meaning: A communication perspective. *Communication Quarterly, 37*, 291–304.

Mumby, D. K. (1997a). Modernism, postmodernism, and communication studies: A rereading of an ongoing debate. *Communication Theory, 7*, 1–28.

Mumby, D. K. (1997b). The problem of hegemony: Rereading Gramsci for organizational studies. *Western Journal of Communication, 61*, 343–375.

Mumby, D. K. (2000). Power, politics, and organizational communication. In F. M. Jablin & L. L. Putnam (Eds.), *Handbook of organizational communication: Advances in theory, research, and methods*. Thousand Oaks, CA: Sage.

Mumby, D. K., & Putnam, L. L. (1992). The politics of emotion: A feminist reading of bounded rationality. *Academy of Management Review, 17*, 465–486.

Mumby, D. K., & Stohl, C. (1996). Disciplining organizational communication studies. *Management Communication Quarterly, 10*(1), 50–72.

Nietzsche, F. W. (1997). *Daybreak* (M. Clark & B. Leiter, Eds.; R. J. Hollingdale, Trans.). Cambridge, UK: Cambridge University Press.

Oakley, A. (1981). Interviewing women: A contradiction in terms. In H. Roberts (Ed.), *Doing feminist research* (pp. 30–61). London: Routledge & Kegan Paul.

O'Keefe, B. (1993). Against theory. *Journal of Communication, 43*(3), 75–82.

Orr, C. J. (1978). How shall we say "Reality is socially constructed through communication?" *Central States Speech Journal, 29*(4), 263–274.

Ortner, S. (1984). Theory in anthropology since the sixties. *Comparative Studies in Society and History, 26*, 126–167.

Oxford Universal Dictionary. (1955). Oxford, UK: Clarendon Press.

Pacanowsky, M. (1989). Creating and narrating organizational realities. In B. Dervin, L. Grossberg, B. J. O'Keefe, & E. Wartella (Eds.), *Rethinking communication, 2: Paradigm exemplars* (pp. 250–257). Newbury Park, CA: Sage.

Pacanowsky, M., & O'Donnell-Trujillo, N. (1982). Communication and organizational culture. *Western Journal of Speech Communication, 46*, 115–130.

Pacanowsky, M., & Putnam, L. L. (Eds.). (1982, Spring). Interpretive approaches to the study of organizational communication. *Western Journal of Speech Communication, 46*, 114–207.

Pace, R. W., & Faules, D. F. (1994). *Organizational communication* (3rd ed.). Englewood Cliffs, NJ: Prentice-Hall.

Palmer, P. J. (1998). *The courage to teach: Exploring the inner landscape of a teacher's life.* San Francisco: Jossey-Bass.

Papa, M. J., Auwal, M. A., & Singhal, A. (1995). Dialectic of control and emancipation in organizing for social change: A multi-theoretical study of the Grameen Bank in Bangladesh. *Communication Theory, 5*, 189–223.

Papa, M. J., Auwal, M. A., & Singhal, A. (1997). Organizing for social change within concertive control systems: Member identification, empowerment, and the masking of discipline. *Communication Monographs, 64*, 219–249.

Pearce, W. B., & Littlejohn, S. (1997). *Moral conflict: When social worlds collide.* Thousand Oaks, CA: Sage

Peirce, C. S. (1955). *Philosophical writings of Peirce* (J. Bochler, Ed.). New York: Dover.

Perrow, C. (1986). *Complex organizations: A critical essay* (3rd ed.). New York: Random House.

Pfeffer, J. (1993). Barriers to the advance of organizational science: Paradigm development as a dependent variable. *Academy of Management Review, 18*, 599–620.

Pfeffer, J. (1995). Mortality, reproducibility, and the persistence of styles of theory. *Organization Science, 6*, 681–686.

Philipsen, G. (1975). Speaking "like a man" in Teamsterville: Cultural patterns of role enactment in an urban neighborhood. *Communication Monographs, 48*, 301–317.

Phillips, D. C. (1987). *Philosophy, science, and social inquiry.* Oxford, UK: Pergamon Press.

Phillips, D. C. (1990). Postpositivistic science: Myths and realities. In E. G. Guba (Ed.), *The paradigm dialog* (pp. 31–45). Newbury Park, CA: Sage.

Phillips, D. C. (1992). *The social scientist's bestiary: A guide to fabled threats and defences of naturalistic social science.* Oxford: Pergamon Press.

Polanyi, K. (1959). *Tacit knowledge.* New York: Harper.

Polkinghorne, D. (1983). *Methodology for the human sciences: Systems of inquiry.* Albany: State University of New York Press.

Poole, M. S. (1997). A turn of the wheel: The case for a renewal of systems inquiry in organizational communication research. In G. A. Barnett & L. Thayer (Eds.),

Organization<—>communication: Emerging perspectives. Vol. 5: The renaissance in systems thinking (pp. 47–63). Norwood, NJ: Ablex.

Poole, M. S. (1998). The small group should be the fundamental unit of communication research. In J. S. Trent (Ed.), *Communication: Views from the helm for the 21st century* (pp. 94–97). Needham Heights, MA: Allyn & Bacon.

Poole, M. S., & DeSanctis, G. (1990). Understanding the use of group decision support systems: The theory of adaptive structuration. In J. Fulk & C. Steinfeld (Eds.), *Organizations and communication technology* (pp. 173–193). Newbury Park, CA: Sage.

Poole, M. S., & DeSanctis, G. (1992). Microlevel structuration in computer-supported group decision making. *Human Communication Research, 19,* 5–49.

Poole, M. S., Putnam, L. L., & Seibold, D. R. (1997). Organizational communication in the 21st century. *Management Communication Quarterly, 11,* 127–138.

Poole, M. S., Seibold, D. R., & McPhee, R. D. (1985). Group decision-making as a structurational process. *Quarterly Journal of Speech, 71,* 74–102.

Poole, M. S., Seibold, D. R., & McPhee, R. D. (1986). A structurational approach to theory-building in group decision-making research. In R. Y. Hirokawa & M. S. Poole (Eds.), *Communication and group decision-making* (pp. 237–264). Beverly Hills, CA: Sage.

Poole, M. S., Seibold, D. R., & McPhee, R. D. (1996). The structuration of group decisions. In R. Y. Hirokawa & M. S. Poole (Eds.), *Communication and group decision making* (2nd ed., pp. 114–146). Thousand Oaks, CA: Sage.

Poole, M. S., & Van de Ven, A. H. (1989). Using paradox to build management and organizational theories. *Academy of Management Review, 17,* 465–486.

Poole, M. S., Van de Ven, A. H., Dooley, K., & Holmes, M. (2000). *Organizational change and innovation processes: Theory and methods for research.* New York: Oxford University Press.

Popper, K. R. (1959). *The logic of scientific discovery.* New York: Basic Books.

Popper, K. R. (1962). *Conjectures and refutations: The growth of scientific knowledge.* New York: Basic Books.

Popper, K. R. (1972). *Objective knowledge: An evolutionary approach.* Oxford, UK: Clarendon Press.

Putnam, H. (1981). *Reason, truth, and history.* Cambridge, UK: Cambridge University Press.

Putnam, L. L. (1982, Spring). Paradigms for organizational communication research: A synthesis. *Western Journal of Speech Communication, 46*(2), 192–206.

Putnam, L. L. (1983). The interpretive perspective: An alternative to functionalism. In L. L. Putnam & M. E. Pacanowsky (Eds.), *Communication in organizations, an interpretive approach* (pp. 31–54). Beverly Hills, CA: Sage.

Putnam, L. L., Bantz, C., Deetz, S., Mumby, D., & Van Maanen, J. (1993). Ethnography versus critical theory: Debating organizational research. *Journal of Management Inquiry, 2*(3), 221–235.

Putnam, L. L., & Cheney, G. (1983). A critical review of research traditions in organizational communication. In M. S. Mander (Ed.), *Communication in transition* (pp. 206–224). New York: Praeger.

Putnam, L. L., & Cheney, G. (1985). Organizational communication: Historical developments and future directions. In T. W. Benson (Ed.), *Speech communication in the 20th century* (pp. 130–159). Carbondale: Southern Illinois University Press.

Putnam, L. L., & Fairhurst, G. T. (2000). Discourse and interaction analysis in organizations. In F. M. Jablin & L. L. Putnam (Eds.), *Handbook of organizational communication: Advances in theory, research, and methods* (pp. 78–136). Thousand Oaks, CA: Sage.

Putnam, L. L., & Pacanowsky, M. E. (Eds.). (1983). *Communication in organizations: An interpretive approach.* Beverly Hills, CA: Sage.

Putnam, L. L., Phillips, N., & Chapman, P. (1996). Metaphors of communication and organization. In S. R. Clegg, C. Hardy, & W. R. Nord (Eds.), *Handbook of organization studies* (pp. 375–408). Thousand Oaks, CA: Sage.

Putnam, L. L., & Stohl, C. (1990). Bona fide groups: A reconceptualization of groups in context. *Communication Studies, 41,* 248–265.

Quinn, R., & Cameron, K. (Eds.). (1988). *Paradox and transformation.* Cambridge, MA: Ballinger.

Redding, W. C. (1985). Stumbling toward identity: The emergence of organizational communication as a field of study. In R. D. McPhee & P. K. Tompkins (Eds.), *Organizational communication: Traditional themes and new directions* (pp. 15–54). Beverly Hills, CA: Sage.

Redding, W. C., & Tompkins, P. K. (1988). Organizational communication—past and present tenses. In G. M. Goldhaber & G. A. Barnett (Eds.), *Handbook of organizational communication* (pp. 5–33). Norwood, NJ: Ablex.

Reed, M. (1988). The problem of agency in organizational analysis. *Organization Studies, 9,* 33–46.

Reed, M. (1999). Organizational theorizing: A historically contested terrain. In S. R. Clegg & C. Hardy (Eds.), *Studying organization: Theory and method* (pp. 25–50). London: Sage.

Reich, D. (1986). *Language development.* New York: Prentice Hall.

Rice, R. E. (1993). Using network concepts to clarify sources and mechanisms of social influence. In W. D. Richards & G. A. Barnett (Eds.), *Progress in communication sciences* (Vol. 12, pp. 43–67). Norwood, NJ: Ablex.

Ricoeur, P. (1993). *The rule of metaphor: Multi-disciplinary studies of the creation of meaning in language* (R. Czerny, Trans.). Toronto: University of Toronto Press.

Riley, P. (1983). A structurationist account of political culture. *Administrative Science Quarterly, 28,* 414–437.

Roethlisberger, F. J., & Dickson, W. J. (1939). *Management and the worker: An account of a research program conducted by the Western Electric Company, Hawthorne Works, Chicago.* Cambridge, MA: Harvard University Press.

Rogers, E. M., & Kincaid, D. L. (1981). *Communication networks: Toward a new paradigm for research.* New York: Free Press.

Romaine, S. (1995). *Bilingualism* (2nd ed.). Oxford, UK: Blackwell

Rorty, R. (1982). *The consequences of pragmatism.* Minneapolis: University of Minnesota Press.

Rose, N. (1990). *Governing the soul: The shaping of the private self.* London: Routledge.

Rosenau, P. M. (1992). *Post-modernism and the social sciences.* Princeton, NJ: Princeton University Press.

Rosengren, K. (1989). Paradigms lost and regained. In B. Dervin, L. Grossberg, B.

O'Keefe, & E. Wartella (Eds.), *Rethinking communication, 2: Paradigm exemplars* (pp. 21–39). Beverly Hills, CA: Sage.

Rousseau, D. M., & House, R. J. (1994). Meso organizational behavior: Avoiding three fundamental biases. In C. L. Cooper & D. E. M. Rousseau (Eds.), *Trends in organizational behavior* (Vol. 1, pp. 13–30). New York: Wiley.

Rozeboom, W. (1962). The factual content of theoretical concepts. In H. Feigl & G. Maxwell (Eds.), *Minnesota studies in the philosophy of science* (Vol. 3, pp. 273–357). Minneapolis: University of Minnesota Press.

Said, E. W. (1994). *Representations of the intellectual.* New York: Pantheon Books.

Salmon, W. (1989). *Four decades of scientific explanation.* Minneapolis: University of Minnesota Press.

Sathe, V. (1983). Implications of corporate culture: A manager's guide to action. *Organizational Dynamics, 12*(3), 5–23.

Saussure, F. de (1959). *Course in general linguistics* (C. Bally & A. Reidlinger, Eds.; W. Baskin, Trans.). New York: Philosophical Library.

Scarf, M. (1987). *Intimate partners.* New York: Random House.

Scherer, A. G. (1998). Pluralism and incommensurability in strategic management and organization theory: A problem in search of a solution. *Organization, 5,* 147–168.

Scherer, A. G., & Dowling, M. (1995). Toward a reconciliation of theory-pluralism in strategic management: Incommensurability and the constructive approach of the Erlangen School. *Advances in Strategic Management, 12A,* 195–247.

Schultz, M., & Hatch, M. J. (1996). Living with multiple paradigms: The case of paradigm interplay in organizational cultural studies. *Academy of Management Review, 21*(2), 529–557.

Schutz, A. (1967). *The phenomenology of the social world.* Evanston, IL: Northwestern University Press.

Schwartz, H. S. (1993). Deconstructing my car at the Detroit airport. *Organization Studies, 14,* 279–281.

Schwartzman, H. (1989). *The meeting.* New York: Plenum Press.

Scott, C. R., Corman, S. R., & Cheney, G. (1998). Development of a structurational model of identification in the organization. *Communication Theory, 8,* 298–336.

Scott, J. C. (1990). *Domination and the arts of resistance: Hidden transcripts.* New Haven, CT: Yale University Press.

Searle, J. R. (1970). *Speech acts: An essay in the philosophy of language.* Cambridge, UK: Cambridge University Press.

Searle, J. R. (1995). *The construction of social reality.* New York: Free Press.

Seibold, D. R. (1998). Groups and organizations: Premises and perspectives. In J. S. Trent (Ed.), *Communication: Views from the helm for the 21st century* (pp. 162–168). Needham Heights, MA: Allyn & Bacon.

Seibold, D. R., Rossi, S. M., Berteotti, C. R., Soprych, S. L., & McQuillan, L. P. (1987). Volunteer involvement in a hospice care program. *American Journal of Hospice Care, 4,* 43–55.

Seibold, D. R., & Shea, B. C. (2000). Participation and decision making. In F. M. Jablin & L. L. Putnam (Eds.), *Handbook of organizational communication: Advances in theory, research, and methods* (pp. 664–703). Thousand Oaks, CA: Sage.

Seidman, S. (1992). Postmordem social theory as narrative with a moral intent. In S.

Seidman & D. G. Wagner (Eds.), *Postmordemism and social theory: The debate over general theory* (pp. 47–81). Cambridge, MA: Blackwell.

Senge, P. (1990). *The fifth discipline*. New York: Doubleday.

Shepherd, G. (1993). Building a discipline of communication. *Journal of Communication, 43*, 83–91.

Shields, S. (1975). Functionalism, Darwinism and the psychology of women: A study in social myth. *American Psychologist, 30*, 739–754.

Shotter, J. (1993). *Conversational realities: Constructing life through language*. London: Sage.

Sias, P., & Jablin, F. M. (1995). Differential superior–subordinate relations, perceptions of fairness, and co-worker communication. *Human Communication Research, 22*, 5–38.

Sigman, S. J. (1987). *A perspective on social communication*. Lexington, MA: Lexington Books.

Skinner, B. F. (1957). *Verbal behavior*. New York: Appleton-Century-Crofts.

Slack, J. D., & Semati, M. M. (1997). Intellectual and political hygiene: The "Sokal Affair." *Critical Studies in Mass Communication, 14*, 201–27.

Smircich, L., & Calás, M. (1987). Organizational culture: A critical assessment. In F. M. Jablin, L. L. Putnam, K. Roberts & L. Porter (Eds.), *Handbook of organizational communication: An interdisciplinary perspective* (pp. 228–263). Newbury Park, CA: Sage.

Smith, J. K. (1990). Goodness criteria: Alternative research paradigms and the problem of criteria. In E. G. Guba (Ed.), *The paradigm dialog* (pp. 167–187). Newbury Park, CA: Sage.

Smith, L. (1994, September 19). New ideas from the Army (really). *Fortune*, pp. 203–209.

Smith, R. C. (1993, May). *Images of organizational communication: Root-metaphors of the organization–communication relation*. Paper presented at the annual meeting of the International Communication Association, Washington, DC.

Smith, R. C., & Eisenberg, E. (1987). Conflict at Disneyland: A root-metaphor analysis. *Communication Monographs, 54*(4), 367–380.

Smith, R. C., & Turner, P. (1995). A social constructionist reconfiguration of metaphor analysis: An application of "SCMA" to organizational socialization. *Communication Monographs, 62*, 152–180.

Sokal, A. (1996a). Transgressing the boundaries: Towards a transformative hermeneutics of quantum gravity. *Social Text, 46*, 217–252.

Sokal, A. (1996b, May–June). A physicist experiments with cultural studies. *Lingua Franca*, pp. 62–64.

Spitzack, C., & Carter, K. (1988). Feminist communication: Rethinking the politics of exclusion. *Women's Studies in Communication, 11*, 32–36.

Sridhar, K. K. (1996). Societal multilingualism. In S. L. McKay & N. H. Hornberger (Eds.), *Sociolinguistics and language teaching* (pp. 47–70). Cambridge, UK: Cambridge University Press.

Stacey, J. (1988). Can there be a feminist ethnography? *Women's Studies International Forum, 11*, 21–27.

Stanley, L. (Ed.). (1997). *Knowing feminisms: On academic borders, territories, and tribes*. London: Sage.

Starhawk. (1987). *Truth or dare: Encounters with power, authority, and mystery*. San Francisco: Harper and Row.

Steier, F. (Ed.). (1991). *Research and reflexivity: Self-reflexivity as social process.* Newbury Park, CA: Sage.

Stewart, J. (1991). A postmodern look at traditional communication postulates. *Western Journal of Speech Communication, 55,* 354–379.

Stohl, C. (1995). *Organizational communication: Connectedness in action.* Newbury Park, CA: Sage.

Strine, M. S., & Pacanowsky, M. E. (1985). How to read interpretive accounts of organizational life: Narrative bases of textual authority. *Southern Communication Journal, 50*(3), 283–297.

Suppe, F. (1977). The search for philosophic understanding of scientific theories. In F. Suppe (Ed.), *The structure of scientific theories* (pp. 3–232). Urbana, IL: University of Illinois Press.

Symposium: What criteria should be used to judge the admissability of evidence to support theoretical propositions in communication research? (1977). *Western Journal of Communication, 41*(1), 3–65.

Sztompka, P. (1993). *The sociology of social change.* Oxford: Blackwell.

Tannen, D. (1998). *The argument culture.* New York: Random House.

Taylor, B. (1997). Revis(it)ing nuclear history: Narrative conflict at the Bradbury Science Museum. *Studies in Cultures, Organizations, and Societies, 3,* 119–145.

Taylor, C. (1979). Interpretations and the sciences of man. In P. Rabinow & W. M. Sullivan (Eds.), *Interpretive social science: A reader* (pp. 25–72). Berkeley: University of California Press.

Taylor, C. (1985). *Philosophy and the human sciences.* New York: Cambridge University Press.

Taylor, J. R. (1999). The other side of rationality: Socially distributed cognition. *Management Communication Quarterly, 13,* 317–326.

Taylor, J. R., Cooren, F., Giroux, N., & Robichaud, D. (1996). The communicational basis of organization: Between the conversation and the text. *Communication Theory, 6,* 1–39.

Taylor, J. R., Flanagin, A. J., Cheney, G., & Seibold, D. R. (2000). Organizational communication research: Key moments, central concerns, and future challenges. In W. B. Gudykunst (Ed.), *Communication yearbook 24* (pp. 99–137). Thousand Oaks, CA: Sage.

Taylor, J. R., & Van Every, E. J. (2000*). The emergent organization: Communication as its site and surface.* Mahwah, NJ: Erlbaum.

Taylor, R., & Gurd, G. (1996). Contrasting perspectives on nonpositivist communication research. In L. Thayer (Ed.), *Organization<—>communication: Emerging perspectives. Vol. 4* (pp. 38–79). Norwood, NJ: Ablex.

Therborn, G. (1980). *The ideology of power and the power of ideology.* London: Verso.

Tompkins, P. K. (1993). *Organizational communication imperatives: Lessons of the space program.* Los Angeles, CA: Roxbury.

Tompkins, P. K. (1994). Principles of rigor for assessing evidence in "qualitative" communication research. *Western Journal of Communication, 58,* 44–50.

Tompkins, P. K. (1997). How to think and talk about organizational communication. In P. Y. Byers (Ed.), *Organizational communication: Theory and behavior* (pp. 361–373). Boston: Allyn & Bacon.

Tompkins, P. K., & Cheney, G. (1985). Communication and unobtrusive control in contemporary organizations. In R. D. McPhee & P. K. Tompkins (Eds.), *Organizational communication: Traditional themes and new directions* (pp. 179–210). Thousand Oaks, CA: Sage.

Tong, R. (1989). *Feminist thought: A comprehensive introduction.* Boulder, CO: Westview Press.

Toulmin, S. (1953). *The philosophy of science: An introduction.* New York: Hutchinson's University Library.

Trethewey, A. (1997). Resistance, identity, and empowerment: A postmodern feminist analysis of clients in a human service organization. *Communication Monographs, 64,* 281–301.

Trethewey, A. (1999a). Isn't it ironic: Using irony to explore the contradictions of organizational life. *Western Journal of Communication, 63,* 140–167.

Trethewey, A. (1999b). Disciplined bodies: Women's embodied identities at work. *Organization Studies, 20,* 423–450.

Trigg, R. (1985). *Understanding social science.* Oxford, UK: Blackwell.

Trujillo, N. (1985). Organizational communication as cultural performance. *Southern Speech Communication Journal, 50,* 210–244.

Trujillo, N. (1992). Interpreting the work and talk of baseball: Perspectives on ballpark culture. *Western Journal of Communication, 56,* 350–371.

Turner, B. (1992). The symbolic understanding of organizations. In M. Reed & M. Hughes (Eds.), *Rethinking organization: New directions in organization theory and analysis* (pp. 46–66). London: Sage.

Turner, P. K. (1999). What if you don't?: A response to Kramer and Miller. *Communication Monographs, 66,* 382–389.

Turner, V. W. (1981). Social drama and stories about them. In W. J. Mitchell (Ed.), *On narrative* (pp. 137–164). Chicago: University of Chicago Press.

Van Maanen, J. (1988). *Tales of the field: On writing ethnography.* Chicago: University of Chicago Press.

Van Maanen, J. (1995a). Fear and loathing in organization studies. *Organization Science, 6,* 687–692.

Van Maanen, J. (1995b). Style as theory. *Organization Science, 6,* 133–143.

Victor, D. (1992). *International business communication.* New York: HarperCollins.

Vincenti, W. G. (1990). *What engineers know and how they know it.* Baltimore: Johns Hopkins University Press.

Vincenti, W. G. (1997). Engineering theory in the making: aerodynamic calculation "breaks the sound barrier." *Technology and Culture, 38*(4), 819–851.

von Wright, G. (1971). *Explanation and understanding.* Ithaca, NY: Cornell University Press.

Waldeck, J. H., & Seibold, D. R. (1998). *Organizational socialization processes and outcomes: A meso-level approach.* Unpublished manuscript, Department of Communication, University of California–Santa Barbara.

Wallerstein, I. (1976). *The modern world system.* New York: Academic Press.

Watts, A. (1972). *The book: On the taboo against knowing who you really are.* New York: Vintage Books.

Weaver, G. R., & Gioia, D. A. (1994). Paradigms lost: Incommensurability versus structurationist inquiry. *Organization Studies, 15,* 565–590.

Weaver, G. R., & Gioia, D. A. (1995). Paradigms lost and paradigms found. *Organization Studies, 16,* 704–705.

Weber, M. (1968). *Economy and society; an outline of interpretive sociology* (3 vols.) (G. Roth & C. Wittich, Eds.; E. Fischoff, Trans.). New York: Bedminster Press.

Weick, K. E. (1979). *The social psychology of organizing* (2nd ed.). Reading, MA: Addison-Wesley.

Weick, K. E. (1987). Theorizing about organizational communication. In F. M. Jablin, L. L. Putnam, K. Roberts, & L. Porter (Eds.), *Handbook of organizational communication: An interdisciplinary perspective* (pp. 97–122). Newbury Park, CA: Sage.

Weick, K. E. (1995). *Sense-making in organizations*. Thousand Oaks, CA: Sage.

Weick, K. E. (1999). Theory construction as disciplined reflexivity: Tradeoffs in the 90s. *Academy of Management Review, 24*, 797–807.

Weick, K. E., & Roberts, K. H. (1993). Collective mind in organizations: Heedful interrelating on flight decks. *Administrative Science Quarterly, 38*, 357–381.

Weinberg, S. (1998, October 8). The revolution that didn't happen. *New York Review of Books*, pp. 1–10.

Wheatley, E. E. (1994). How can we engender ethnography with a feminist imagination?: A rejoinder to Judith Stacey. *Women's Studies International Forum, 17*, 403–416.

Whyte, M. K. (1999, December 3). To the editor. *Chronicle of Higher Education*, p. B3.

Wilkins, A. (1983). The culture audit: A tool for understanding organizations. *Organizational Dynamics, 12*(3), 24–38.

Willis, P. (1977). *Learning to labor: How working-class kids get working-class jobs*. New York: Columbia University Press.

Wilmot, H. (1993). Breaking the paradigm mentality. *Organization Studies, 14*, 681–719.

Wilson, B. J. (1994). A challenge to communication empiricists: Let's be more forthcoming about what we do. *Western Journal of Communication, 58*, 25–31.

Winch, P. (1958). *The idea of social science and its relations to philosophy*. London: Routledge & Kegan Paul.

Wiseman, R., & Shuter, R. (Eds.). (1994). *Communicating in multinational organizations*. Thousand Oaks, CA: Sage.

Wittgenstein, L. (1953). *Philosophical investigations* (G. E. M. Anscombe, Trans.). New York: Macmillan.

Young, E. (1989). On the naming of the rose: Interests and multiple meanings as elements of organizational culture. *Organization Studies, 10*(2), 187–206.

Zorn, T. E., Page, D. J., & Cheney, G. (2000). Nuts about change: Multiple perspectives on change-oriented communication in a public-sector organization. *Management Communication Quarterly, 13*, 515–566.

Zucker, L. G. (1988). Where do institutional patterns come from? In L. G. Zucker (Ed.), *Institutional patterns and organizations* (pp. 23–49). Cambridge, MA: Ballinger.

Index

About the Editors

Steven R. Corman (PhD, University of Illinois at Urbana–Champaign, 1988) is Associate Professor in the Hugh Downs School of Human Communication at Arizona State University. He serves on the editorial boards of *Human Communication Research* and *Management Communication Quarterly*. His publications on communication networks, interaction processes, and computer models of communication have appeared in that outlet, and in others such as *Communication Theory, Communication Research, Management Communication Quarterly, Social Networks*, and *Technology Studies*.

Marshall Scott Poole (PhD, University of Wisconsin, 1980) is Professor of Speech Communication at Texas A&M University. He has conducted research and published extensively on the topics of group and organizational communication, computer-mediated communication systems, conflict management, and organizational innovation. He has coauthored or edited four books, including *Communication and Group Decision-Making, Working through Conflict*, and *Research on the Management of Innovation*. He has published in a number of journals, including *Management Science, MIS Quarterly, Human Communication Research, Academy of Management Journal*, and *Communication Monographs*. He is currently a Senior Editor of *Information Systems Research* and *Organization Science*.

Contributors

George A. Barnett (PhD, Michigan State University, 1976) is Professor of Communication at the State University of New York–Buffalo. He edited *Handbook of Organizational Communication* (Ablex, 1988) and is editor of the *Progress in Communication Sciences* and the *Organization<—>Communication: Emerging Perspectives* series for Ablex. His research examines network models of organizational communication and international information flows.

George Cheney (PhD, Purdue University, 1985) is Professor and Director of Graduate Studies in the Department of Communication Studies at the University of Montana–Missoula. Also, he is Adjunct Professor in Management Communication at the University of Waikato, Hamilton, New Zealand. Recognized for both teaching and research, Cheney has published two books and over fifty journal articles, book chapters, and reviews. He has lectured widely in the United States, Western Europe, Latin America, and Australia, and has consulted with organizations in a variety of sectors.

Charles Conrad (PhD, Kansas, 1980) is Professor of Speech Communication at Texas A&M University. His primary research has examined the interrelationships among power, powerlessness, and the communicative strategies adopted by members of formal organizations and informal social collectives. He currently is involved in a group of projects that examine the role that organizational discourse has played in the development of public policies regarding health and health care–sex education policy at the state and local levels, HMO regulation and the formation of physicians' associations at state and national levels, and tobacco policy at the federal level.

Steven R. Corman. See "About the Editors."

Stanley Deetz (PhD, Ohio University, 1973) is Professor of Communication at the University of Colorado–Boulder, where he teaches courses in organizational theory, organizational communication, and communication theory. He is author of *Transforming Communication, Transforming Business: Building Responsive and Responsible Workplaces* (Hampton, 1995), and *Democracy in an Age of Corporate Colonization: Developments in Communication and the Politics of Everyday*

Life (State University of New York Press, 1992); and has served as coauthor or editor of numerous other books. He has lectured widely in the United States and Europe, and is a Fellow of the International Communication Association and served as its President from 1996 to 1997. His scholarly interests include stakeholder representation, decision making, culture, and communication in corporate organizations.

Eric M. Eisenberg (PhD, Michigan State University, 1982) is Professor and Chair of the Department of Communication at the University of South Florida. The recipient of numerous awards for research and pedagogy, he is an internationally recognized scholar, consultant, and teacher. His main area of expertise is organizational communication, focusing specifically on how organizations use communication to create and sustain positive change.

Gail T. Fairhurst (PhD, University of Oregon, 1978) is Professor of Communication at the University of Cincinnati. Her research interests include organizational leadership, language analysis, and downsizing. Her articles have appeared in *Human Communication Research, Communication Monographs, Academy of Management Journal, Organization Science,* and *Academy of Management Review,* among others. She recently coauthored *The Art of Framing: Managing the Language of Leadership* (Jossey-Bass, 1996).

Andrew J. Flanagin (PhD, University of Southern California, 1996) is Assistant Professor in the Department of Communication, University of California–Santa Barbara. His research focuses on the social impact of advanced communication and information technologies, particularly inter- and intraorganizational patterns of communication and information sharing supported by technological systems. Toward this end, he explores the Internet, intranets, and other means of computer-supported collaborative work within and outside of organizations.

Michele H. Jackson (PhD, University of Minnesota, 1994) is on the faculties of the Department of Communication and the Interdisciplinary Telecommunications Program, University of Colorado–Boulder. Her teaching and research focuses on the intersections of communication and technology in small groups and organizations. Information on current activities can be found at http://stripe.colorado.edu/~jackson.

Robert L. Krizek (PhD, Arizona State University, 1995) is Director of Graduate Studies for the Department of Communication at Saint Louis University. He teaches in the areas of organizational communication, narrative, and ethnographic methodologies. In addition to his research into storytelling and socialization/narrativization in organizational contexts, he studies communication in third places and the personal impact of nonroutine public events, both from an ethnographic perspective.

Kathleen J. Krone (PhD, University of Texas–Austin, 1985) is Associate Professor in the Communication Studies Department at the University of Nebraska–Lincoln. Her current research interests are in the areas of organizational emotional labor, alternative approaches to community dispute resolution, and interest representation in high energy physics.

Laurie K. Lewis (PhD, University of California–Santa Barbara, 1994) is Assistant Professor in the Department of Communication Studies at the University of Texas–Austin. She has research interests in the areas of organizational planned change, communication in nonprofit organizations, feedback and appraisal in organizations, and interorganizational communication. Her publications have appeared in *Academy of Management Review, Communication Monographs, Journal of Applied Communication Research, and Management Communication Quarterly.*

Owen Hanley Lynch is a PhD candidate at Texas A&M University in the Department of Speech Communication. He received his M.A. from Texas A&M University, Department of Speech Communication, in 1998. He has taught in the department of Speech Communication at Texas A&M University since 1996. His current research interests are humor within organizations, change and transformation, and health communication. Lynch also holds a B.A. (1995) in communication from the University of North Carolina–Chapel Hill.

Robert D. McPhee (PhD, Michigan State University, 1978) is Herberger Professor in the Hugh Downs School of Human Communication at Arizona State University. Specializing in organizational communication and communication theory, he has served as Chair of the Organizational Communication Division of NCA and as Associate Editor for Organizational Communication of *Human Communication Research.* His special interests are formal/hierarchical communication and structuration theory.

Katherine I. Miller (PhD, University of Southern California, 1985) is Professor of Speech Communication at Texas A&M University. Her current research focuses on the role of emotion in human service work and the impact of organizational changes such as managed care on the work lives of health care professionals. Her work has been published in outlets including *Journal of Applied Communication Research, Human Communication Research, Management Communication Quarterly, Communication Monographs,* and *Health Communication.* She is the author of *Organizational Communication: Approaches and Processes* (1st ed., Wadsworth, 1995; 2nd ed., Wadsworth, 1999).

Dennis K. Mumby (PhD, Southern Illinois University at Carbondale, 1985) is Professor of Communication at Purdue University. He has published in journals such as *Communication Monographs, Communication Theory, Academy of Management Review,* and *Management Communication Quarterly.* He is author of *Communication and Power in Organizations* (Ablex, 1988), and editor of *Narrative and Social Control* (Sage, 1993). He is interested in the relationships among communication, identity, power, and processes of domination and resistance in organizations. He is currently working on a book titled, *Organizing Gender: Feminism, Postmodernism, and Organization Studies.*

Marshall Scott Poole. See "About the Editors."

Craig R. Scott (PhD, Arizona State University, 1994) is Assistant Professor in the Department of Communication Studies at the University of Texas–Austin. His primary research in organizational communication focuses on users of communication technologies in the workplace and communicative aspects of identifications in organizational members. His *Communication Theory* article with Steven R. Corman and George Cheney won the 1999 "top paper" award from the Organizational Communication Division of the National Communication Association.

David R. Seibold (PhD, Michigan State University, 1975) is Professor and Chair, Department of Communication, University of California–Santa Barbara. Author of nearly 100 publications on organizational communication, group processes, and interpersonal influence, he has received numerous research and teaching awards. He is past Editor of the *Journal of Applied Communication Research* and serves on the boards of many other journals. He has served as Chair of the Interpersonal and Small Group Interaction Division of the National Communication Association, and is the current Chair of the Organizational Communication Division of the International Communication Association. He also works closely with many business, government, and health organizations.

Cynthia Stohl (PhD, Purdue University, 1982) is the Margaret Church Distinguished Professor of Communication and Head of the Department of Communication at Purdue University. She teaches courses in organizational and group communication and has published widely in these areas. She has received several awards for her research and teaching, including the Organizational Communication Division's National Communication Association Award for "best book" (1995) and "best article" (1998).

James R. Taylor (PhD, University of Pennsylvania, 1978) is Emeritus Professor of Communication at the University of Montreal. He has written extensively on the theory of organizational communication. He is a coauthor of two recently published books: *The Emergent Organization: Communication as Its Site and Surface* (Erlbaum, 2000, with Elizabeth Van Every) and *The Computerization of Work: A Communicational Perspective* (Sage, 2000, with Carole Groleau, Lorna Heaton, Elizabeth Van Every).

Angela Trethewey (PhD, Purdue University, 1994) is Assistant Professor in the Hugh Downs School of Human Communication at Arizona State University, where she teaches organizational communication and qualitative research methods. Her research interests center on the relationships among organizational discourse, power, and identity. Her work has been published in *Communication Monographs*, *Western Journal of Communication*, *Organization Studies*, and *Text and Performance Quarterly*.